Technical English

Basics

4. Auflage

VERLAG EUROPA-LEHRMITTEL • Nourney, Vollmer GmbH & Co. KG
Düsselberger Straße 23 • 42781 Haan-Gruiten
Europa-Nr.: 71918

Autoren

Bernhard Busch	Hamburg
Uwe Dzeia	Gleichen
Birgit Haberl	Regensburg
Jürgen Köhler	Northeim

Lektorat

Dr. Astrid Grote-Wolff

4. Auflage 2010

Druck 5 4 3 2

Alle Drucke derselben Auflage sind parallel einsetzbar, da sie bis auf die Behebung von Druckfehlern untereinander unverändert sind.

ISBN 978-3-8085-7194-1

http://www.europa-lehrmittel.de
Umschlaggestaltung: tiff.any GmbH, Berlin
Layout und Satz: tiff.any GmbH, 10999 Berlin
Druck: Media-Print Informationstechnologie, 33100 Paderborn

Vorwort

„Technical English – Basics“ wendet sich an Auszubildende in gewerblich-technischen Berufen. Darüber hinaus eignet es sich zum Einsatz in der Fachschule Technik, für Schulungen, in denen englisches Fachvokabular vermittelt oder reaktiviert wird, sowie zum Selbststudium.

In der vorliegenden **4. Auflage** wurden wiederum Verbesserungen und Anpassungen vorgenommen, die u. a. auf den konstruktiven Anregungen der Leser beruhen.

Basierend auf den Englischkenntnissen, die an allgemeinbildenden Schulen vermittelt werden, ermöglicht das Lehrbuch die Erarbeitung berufsfeldübergreifender sowie berufsspezifischer Inhalte. Dabei werden in den Bereichen Metall-, Kfz-, Elektro-, Computer-, und Umwelttechnik besondere Schwerpunkte gesetzt.

Berufsbezogene Sachtexte und Dialoge bilden in Verbindung mit zahlreichen „Activities“ eine wertvolle Grundlage für den handlungsorientierten Unterricht. Ein wichtiger Schwerpunkt ist die Schulung des **Leseverständnisses**, das für Auszubildende in gewerblich-technischen Berufen von zentraler Bedeutung ist. Die Schüler werden darüber hinaus dazu angeregt, sich über technische Zusammenhänge und Probleme auszutauschen und somit ihre mündliche und schriftliche **Kommunikationsfähigkeit** in der englischen Sprache zu verbessern.

Umfangreiche Vokabellisten sowie anschauliche Abbildungen bilden eine wesentliche Basis für das Verständnis auch komplizierter technischer Zusammenhänge.

Die englische Grammatik nimmt im Buch nur einen geringen Raum ein. Auf die Wiederholung von Grammatikstrukturen wurde verzichtet, um den Lehrenden dadurch nicht auf bestimmte Kapitel festzulegen. Statt dessen wurde in Ergänzung zum Lehrbuch ein Informations- und Arbeitsbuch zur englischen Grammatik entwickelt: **Technical English – Grammar** (Europa-Nr. 71880) vermittelt grundlegende Grammatikstrukturen, die mithilfe zahlreicher Aufgaben eingeübt und vertieft werden können.

Aufgrund seines konsequent verfolgten Konzeptes, nach dem praxisnahe Texte immer mithilfe mehrerer „Activities“ erarbeitet werden, ist Technical English – Basics auch zum Selbststudium und zur Vorbereitung auf Zertifizierungsprüfungen geeignet. Die Gesamtvokabellisten im Anhang (Englisch – Deutsch sowie Deutsch – Englisch) ermöglichen ein zügiges Nachschlagen der gesuchten Fachbegriffe.

Den Lernenden wünschen wir viel Freude und Erfolg bei der Aktivierung und Optimierung ihrer Englischkenntnisse. Wir bitten unsere Leser auch weiterhin um konstruktive Kritik und Anregungen, die zur Verbesserung des Lehrbuches beitragen.

Autoren und Verlag
Sommer 2010

Inhaltsverzeichnis – Contents

1 Visiting people abroad

In this unit you will learn something about a European exchange programme and you will get some information about Bristol. Furthermore, you will learn how to introduce yourself and how to describe the way.

An exchange visit

"Travelling broadens the mind." This sentence is certainly true. That is why the European Union offers a programme called LEONARDO which is designed to support exchange visits of trainees to other countries of the EU to help them to improve their foreign language skills and to get to know people from other countries.

A number of students from a vocational school in Hanover are on a trip to Bristol, their twin town in England.

The English hosts are waiting for their guests at Bristol Airport. John Granger and his parents are waiting for Frank Bartels, John's exchange partner. After having collected his luggage Frank meets his hosts and they can drive home to the Grangers' home in a suburb of Bristol.

The young Germans are all apprentices with a big car manufacturer and are learning in different jobs in mechanical engineering. They receive their theory training at a vocational college once a week. This is called "vocational training in the dual system".

The young English people are also trainees. They get their practical training at different firms in and around Bristol and attend day release classes at City of Bristol College.

Activity 1 Comprehension

Answer the following questions in complete sentences.

1. What is LEONARDO and what is it designed for?
2. What relationship do Bristol and Hanover have?
3. Where do Frank's hosts live?
4. What jobs are the German apprentices training for?
5. What is a vocational training in the dual system?
6. Where do the English students get their practical training?
7. Where do the English trainees get their theory training?

Information about Bristol

Bristol is situated in the south west of England in the county of Avon, about 8 miles from the Severn Estuary, where the rivers Frome and Avon flow together.

In its long history the city of Bristol has been a shipping and trading centre. It was trading with Spain, Portugal, Iceland and ships from Bristol also supported the colonies in the New World. In 1497, John Cabot was financed by Bristol merchants to find a passage to the spice islands. He actually discovered Newfoundland.

Today Bristol has about 500,000 inhabitants and is an important industrial city. Bristol is also a lively city, with a very interesting and rich history. In and around Bristol there are a number of modern industries, including sugar refining, tobacco processing, cocoa and chocolate making, wine bottling and the making of fine glass, porcelain and pottery.

Many big names have chosen the city as their headquarters. British Aerospace e.g., a major aero-space and engineering group, and one of the world's leading air-craft builders design and construct their planes, including the wings of the Airbus A 380 airliner, in Filton, a suburb of Bristol. The famous British-French super-sonic Concorde was also built there.

Bristol has many beautiful buildings and landmarks that document of its former glory.

Among them are the beautiful Gothic cathedral St. Mary Redcliffe, built in the 13th century, and the famous Clifton Suspension Bridge, which spans the Avon Gorge at a height of 245 feet above the high water mark (see picture above). It is a beautiful example of the engineering skills of the famous engineer Isambard Kingdom Brunel (see picture on the left) who also constructed the first steel steam ship in the world.

Bristol is a multicultural city. All year round there are numerous activities and festivals e.g. of balloons and kites. Architecture and park land, business and new technology, theatres and museums, artists and animators, music and film are always worthwhile a visit. Bristol has been officially designated a 'Centre of Culture' and a 'Science City' by the Government.

Activity 2 Finding information in a text

a) Look at the text above and write down some information about Bristol.
Start like this:

Bristol is situated in south-west England. ...

The following words and expressions may help you:

It is situated in ... it is a(n) ... city ... town ... it is twinned with ... it lies on ... it has ...

b) Give some information about your home town or village.

You may use the expressions from activity 2 a) to help you.
Start like this:
I live in a village / town about ... km north / south of ..... Its name is ...

Activity 3 Vocabulary

Find words in the text about Bristol that fit these definitions.

1. the wide part of a river where it goes into the sea
2. the people who live in a town or village
3. the main place from which a company controls its activities
4. very large or important
5. plane or other vehicle that can fly
6. faster than the speed of sound
7. an area outside the town centre
8. ability to do something well
9. a bridge that is hung from strong steel ropes fixed to a tower
10. someone who designs bridges, machines etc.
11. a deep narrow valley with steep sides
12. you get this when water boils

Activity 4 Translation

Translate the following sentences into English.

1. Bristol ist eine sehr lebendige Industriestadt im Südwesten von England.
2. Bristol hat eine lange Geschichte, die eng mit der Seefahrt verbunden ist.
3. Von hier wurden die Kolonien in Amerika unterstützt.
4. Heute hat Bristol eine halbe Million Einwohner und ist eine wichtige Industriestadt.
5. Ein bedeutendes Bauwerk ist die Clifton-Hängebrücke, die in einer Höhe von 245 Fuß den Fluss Avon überspannt.

Welcome to City of Bristol College

Introducing the situation

After the first night at his hosts' home in Filton Frank Bartels and the other German trainees meet their English partners at the City of Bristol College canteen and are welcomed by Mrs. Honeywell, the principal of the college.

Good morning. As the principal of City of Bristol College I'd like to welcome you here at Bedminster Centre. At the beginning I want to give you some information about our college. City of Bristol College is the third largest college in the UK. It was formed by the merger of "Brunel College" with "South Bristol College" and later with "Soundwell College". We provide an excellent education over a wide range of subjects. As well as full time courses, there are numerous part time courses, ranging from plumbing to computer programming. There are also flexible study courses where students can choose the day and time to study, work at their own pace and have the support of the college tutors. Our students enjoy the lively adult learning environment and our student service provides support. Our College Green Centre contains excellent facilities and resources to support a wide range of courses and includes modern equipment, laboratories, and computers. In our Learning Resource Centre nearly 50,000 books, a lot of magazines, journals, CD-ROMs, videos and PCs with full internet access are available. Our accomodation officer can help you to find suitable lodgings. Alternatively we are able to offer 70 friendly, affordable study bedroom units, only a five-minutes walk from our College Green Centre.

I hope you will enjoy your stay at our college and learn a lot while you work together with your partners. Furthermore I'm sure you will get to know each other well and have a good time together. And now you are all invited for a snack. As you can see, students from our home economics department have prepared a set buffet for you.
We'll meet again in room 305 at 12 o'clock to discuss the programme for the week. Please enjoy your meal. Thank you.

Activity 5 Answering questions

Look at the following questions on the text above and answer them in complete sentences.

1. Who is Mrs Honeywell?
2. How was City of Bristol College formed?
3. What facilities does the Learning Resource Centre of the college offer?
4. How does the college help students to find accommodation?
5. Who prepared the buffet for the trainees?
6. What do the trainees do after they have been welcomed?

Getting to know each other

Introducing the situation

After the principal, Mrs. Honeywell, had welcomed the students they go to the college canteen to have lunch. Frank sees an empty seat next to Eileen and asks her if he may sit down there.

FRANK Hello. May I sit down here?
EILEEN Yes, certainly. Wherever you like,
FRANK My name is Frank. I'm one of the German trainees. Nice to meet you.
EILEEN I'm Eileen. Nice to meet you. Where are you from, Frank?
FRANK I'm from Hildesheim in northern Germany, about 15 miles south of Hanover.
EILEEN I see. And what do you do in Hildesheim?
FRANK I'm a trainee industrial mechanic at VW in Hanover. I'm in the third year of my apprenticeship. And what do you do?

EILEEN I'm doing an NVQ course as a toolmaker. I work with a firm called "Click-Clock".
FRANK That's a funny name. What do they produce?
EILEEN They produce cardboard packaging machines.
FRANK That's interesting. You must tell me more about it later. Do you live here in Bristol?
EILEEN No, I live a few miles north of Bristol at a village called Easter Comptom. Who are you staying with?
FRANK I'm staying with John Granger. He lives in Filton and works with British Aerospace.
EILEEN Yes, I know. He is in my course.
FRANK Oh, it's almost 12 o'clock. I think we have to go to our room now. Can we meet again somewhere this afternoon?
EILEEN Sure.

Activity 6 Answering questions

Look at the following questions on the dialogue above and answer them in complete sentences.

1. Where does Eileen come from?
2. What does Eileen do?
3. What does the firm produce which Eileen works with?
4. Where does John Granger work?
5. Why do they have to go back to their room?

Activity 7 Introducing oneself

After having had a snack the trainees come together again and introduce themselves to each other. Imagine you are one of the students and introduce yourself.

Tell the others your name, where you live, how old you are, what you do in your free time, etc.

The following words and expressions may help you:

My name is ....; I'm ... years old ; I live in ...; I'm training as a ...; I work at ...; I attend ...; I'm staying with ...; my hobbies are ...; I'm interested in ...; I want to become ... .

Activity 8 Completing a dialogue

Frank and Eileen have made an appointment for the afternoon. They continue their conversation at a café in town.

Fill in the missing parts in this dialogue

FRANK Hi there. Nice to see you again.
EILEEN Hi Frank. Did you enjoy the first day at college?
FRANK Well, not really, it was a bit boring. What ...1 ?
EILEEN I'll have a cup of tea, please.
FRANK ... 2.
EILEEN No, thanks. I'm not hungry. Now, Frank, have you ever been in England before?
FRANK Yes, ...3 , but I have never been to Bristol. And you? Have you ever been to Germany?
EILEEN No, ...4 . But, I'm thinking of travelling to Germany next year.
FRANK Really? Then you must come and see me and my parents.
EILEEN Well, I'd like to.
FRANK You told me you live at Easter Compton. ...5?
EILEEN No, I live with my parents.
FRANK ...6?
EILEEN My Dad is an engineer at British Aerospace and my Mum is a doctor's receptionist.
FRANK I see, and ...7?
EILEEN Yes, I have got a brother and a sister. ...8?
FRANK We own a detached house in a suburb of Hildesheim called "Himmelsthür" that's "heaven's door" in English.
EILEEN That's a funny name. ...9?
FRANK Yes, I have got a brother. Have you already got any idea about what you are going to do after your apprenticeship?

EILEEN Well, I'm not sure yet, but I would like to go to university and study mechanical engineering. ...10?

FRANK I want to study mechanical engineering, too. ...11 ?

EILEEN Well, I think I'll stay here in Bristol, because the university is very good and I can live at home. ...12?

FRANK I think I'll go to the Fachhochschule in Hildesheim.

EILEEN Fachhochschule? ...13

FRANK I think it is a technical college of higher education in English.

EILEEN .....

Activity 9 Writing a dialogue

Now work with a partner and take the roles of Frank and Eileen and continue their dialogue.

You may talk about

age, details of the job, place of work, town, job training, travelling, programme of the week, going to the pub together, etc.

Present your dialogue to the class.

Activity 10 Writing a report

Write a report about the dialogue between Frank and Eileen in which you tell your friend about the two young people.

You may start like this:

Frank is a German trainee. He ...

Describing the way

Introducing the situation

Before Frank went to Bristol he had received a letter from his friends in Gloucester. They invite him to visit them while he is in England. In the letter they describe the way from Bristol to their new home in Gloucester.

June 20th, 20..

Dear Frank,

We were very pleased to hear that you are going to spend three weeks in Bristol. We would like to invite you to come and see us in Gloucester. We hope you'll find some time to visit us in our new house. To make it easier for you to find us, We'll explain the route to you in some detail. I suppose you'll be able to find your way through Bristol to the motorway leading to the North.

First, take the M32 and drive towards the M32/ M4 interchange. Then change to the M4 westbound. After about 5 miles you'll reach the M4/ M5 interchange. Take the M5 towards the North and the Midlands. Leave the M5 at junction 12. You are now about three miles away from us. The slip road leads onto a country road. You can only go in one direction. At the roundabout after about 1/4 of a mile take the A38 towards Gloucester. After about another 1/2 a mile take the B4008 to Quedgeley. At the first roundabout that follows drive straight on. At the next roundabout stay on the B4008. Then turn left at the next traffic light.

You'll then come to a roundabout where you have to go straight ahead. And at a mini roundabout that follows after 200 m turn right into Elmore Lane. The next side road to the right is Peregrine Close. Turn right again. You're almost there. Our house is the last one on the right hand side.

We hope to see you on one of the Sundays while you are in Bristol.

Best regards
Harry and Joanne

Activity 11 Answering questions

Answer the following questions in complete sentences.

1. Why did Frank's friends send him a letter?
2. Which general direction does Frank have to go from Bristol to his friends' home?
3. Where does Frank have to leave the motorway?
4. How far is his friends' home from the motorway?
5. Where exactly do Frank's friends live?

Activity 12 Translation

When we describe the way from one point to another we often use imperatives to give instructions for directions and distances.

Translate the following German sentences into English.

1. Nimm die Autobahn in Richtung Norden.
2. Fahre bei der Auffahrt Nr. 14 nach Westen.
3. Biege an der dritten Ampel nach rechts ab.
4. Nach 2 km siehst du den Kreisverkehr vor dir.
5. Fahre in den Kreisverkehr und biege bei der zweiten Ausfahrt nach Cheltenham ab.
6. Folge dieser Straße ungefähr eine halbe Meile.
7. Fahre dann an der nächsten Ampel geradeaus weiter.
8. Biege bei der nächsten Ampel nach links ab.
9. Biege nach 200 m rechts in die Gloucester Road ein.
10. Sieh nach links und du wirst unser Haus sehen.

Preparing the trip to the North

Introducing the situation

Frank tells John that he has got an invitation to visit his friends in Gloucester. He asks him for help to get there.

FRANK — I have got an invitation to my friends' house in Gloucester. They sold their old house in Stroud last year and bought a new one a few months ago.

JOHN — Oh, that's nice. When are they expecting you?

FRANK — It should be on a Sunday, because they work during the week.

JOHN — I see. Maybe we can arrange something for Sunday next week. Our family has got an invitation to my uncle's birthday party in Swindon. We'll go there in my father's car. So you may have my car and drive to Gloucester that day. What do you think about that?

FRANK — Oh, thank you, that would be great. Can you also show me on the map how I get to the motorway?

JOHN — Sure, no problem. Just a moment, I'll get a map to show you. …
Well, let's see. This is Filton. We live here in Mayville Avenue and over there is the motorway.

FRANK — What do you think, how long does it take to get to Gloucester?

JOHN — About an hour, I would say. At the weekend there won't be much traffic on the motorway.

Activity 13 Describing the way

a) Look at the map clipping below and take John's part to describe the way from the Grangers' home to junction 1 on the M32. Remember, in England cars drive on the left hand side of the road.

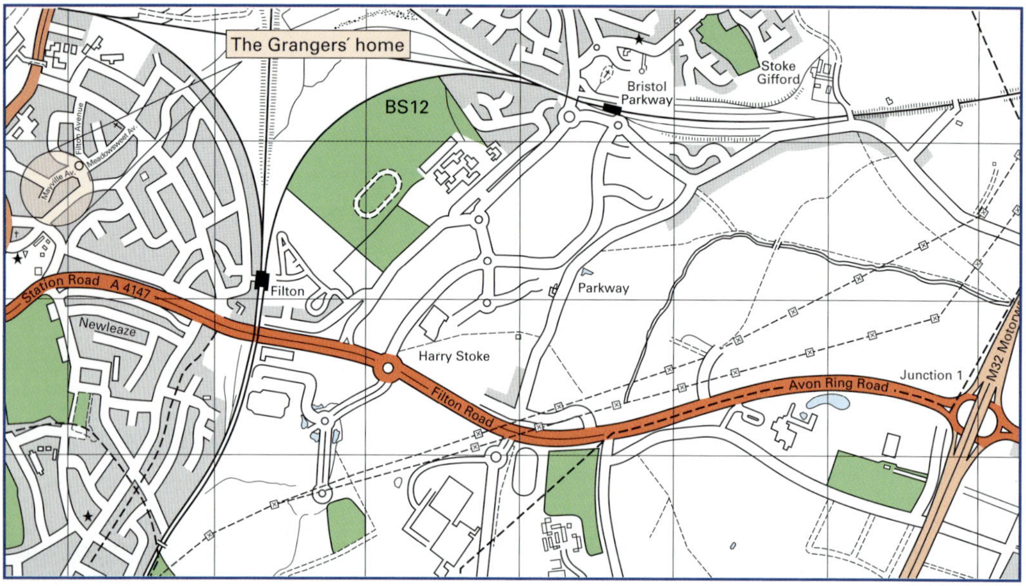

b) Read the following instructions and find out where you arrive. You are driving on the M32 northbound.

1. Leave the M32 at junction 1.
2. Turn left into Avon Ring Road.
3. Drive straight on to Filton Road until you come to a roundabout.
4. Leave the roundabout at the third exit on the left.
5. Follow this road until you come to another roundabout.
6. At this roundabout go straight ahead.
7. Drive straight on until you see another roundabout in front of you.
8. Take the first exit on the left and you'll see the building on your right.

c) Describe the way from the M32 to Filton Station

Vocabulary Unit 1

ability	Fähigkeit
above [ə'bʌv]	oberhalb
access	Zugang
accommodation	Unterkunft
actually	eigentlich
aerospace	Luftfahrt
affordable	leistbar
ahead	voraus
aircraft	Flugzeug
almost	beinahe, fast
among [ə'mʌŋ]	unter, bei
apprentice	Lehrling
area	Gebiet, Gegend
to attend	besuchen
available	verfügbar
base	Basis
be situated	liegen an/in
be twinned with	Partnerschaft haben mit
to boil	kochen
to broaden	erweitern
cardboard	Pappe
century	Jahrhundert
certainly	gewiss, sicherlich
to collect	einsammeln
to construct	bauen
to contain	enthalten
to control	steuern
county	Grafschaft
crowded	überfüllt
daily routine	Tagesablauf
day release class	Teilzeitklasse
department	Abteilung
to describe	beschreiben
to design	entwerfen
different	verschieden
direction	Richtung
due to	wegen, infolge
during	während
easy	leicht
enjoy	genießen
environment	Umgebung
estuary ['estʃʊərɪ]	Mündung
exchange programme	Austauschproramm
to explain	erklären
expression	Ausdruck
facility	Einrichtung
famous	berühmt
finally	endlich
to finance	finanzieren
fixed to	befestigt an
flight controllers	Fluglotsen
flow [fləʊ]	fließen
foreign language	Fremdsprache
former	früher
furthermore	darüber hinaus
generous	großzügig
glory	Glanz
goods	Güter, Waren
gorge [gɔːdʒ]	Schlucht
guest	Gast
head office	Hauptsitz
height	Höhe
high water mark	Hochwassermarke
history	Geschichte
home economics	Hauswirtschaft
host	Gastgeber
to imagine	sich etwas vorstellen
important	wichtig
to improve	verbessern
including	einschließlich
inhabitant	Einwohner
interchange	Autobahnkreuz
introduce	einführen, vorstellen
introduction	Einführung
to invite	einladen
junction	Anschluss
kind	freundlich
landmark	Wahrzeichen
lively	lebendig, quirlig
luggage	Gepäck
major ['meɪdʒə(r)]	Haupt-
main	hauptsächlich
manufacturer	Hersteller
map	Landkarte
maybe	vielleicht
mechanical engineering	Maschinenbau
merger	Zusammenschluss
narrow	eng, schmal
news	Nachrichten
numerous	zahlreich
NVQ	National Vocational Qualification
to offer	anbieten
the offer	Angebot
pace	Schritt
packaging	Verpackung
to pay attention	aufpassen
plane	Flugzeug

Vocabulary Unit 1

pleased	**erfreut**
pleasure	**Vergnügen**
plumbing	**Klempnern**
porcelain ['pɔːsəlɪn]	**Porzellan**
pottery	**Töpferwaren**
practical	**praktisch**
to prepare	**vorbereiten**
principal	**Direktor(in)**
to produce	**herstellen**
to provide	**bereitstellen, bieten**
purpose	**Zweck**
range	**Bereich**
relationship	**Verhältnis**
relatives	**Verwandte**
to remind	**erinnern**
resource	**Quelle**
rope	**Seil**
roundabout	**Kreisverkehr**
set buffet	**kaltes Buffet**
sight seeing trip	**Stadtrundfahrt**
skill	**Können, Geschick**
slip road	**Autobahnzubringer**
sound	**Schall**
to span	**überspannen**
speed of sound	**Schallgeschwindigkeit**
to spend	**verbringen**
to stay	**bleiben, wohnen**
steamship	**Dampfschiff**
steel	**Stahl**
steep	**steil**
straight on	**geradeaus**
subject	**Unterrichtsfach**
suburb ['sʌbɜːb]	**Vorort**
sugar refining	**Zuckerherstellung**
to suggest	**vorschlagen**
supersonic	**Überschall-**
to support	**unterstützen**
to suppose	**vermuten**
surprised	**überracht**
theoretical training	**theoretische Ausbildung**
tired	**müde**
tobacco processing	**Tabakverarbeitung**
toolmaker	**Werkzeugmacher**
towards [tə'wɔːdz]	**nach**
trading centre	**Handelszentrum**
traffic light	**Ampel**
trainee	**Auszubildender**
training	**Ausbildung**
translation	**Übersetzung**
trip	**Reise**
twin town	**Partnerstadt**
unsual [ʌn'juːʒl]	**ungewöhnlich**
vehicle ['viːɪkl]	**Fahrzeug**
village	**Dorf**
to visit	**besuchen**
vocational school	**Berufsschule**
to welcome	**willkommen heißen**
wherever	**wo auch immer**
westbound	**nach Westen**

2 Cars and Tools

In this unit you will learn something about cars and many English expressions for parts of the car. You will also learn how various tools are named in English.

Parts of the car

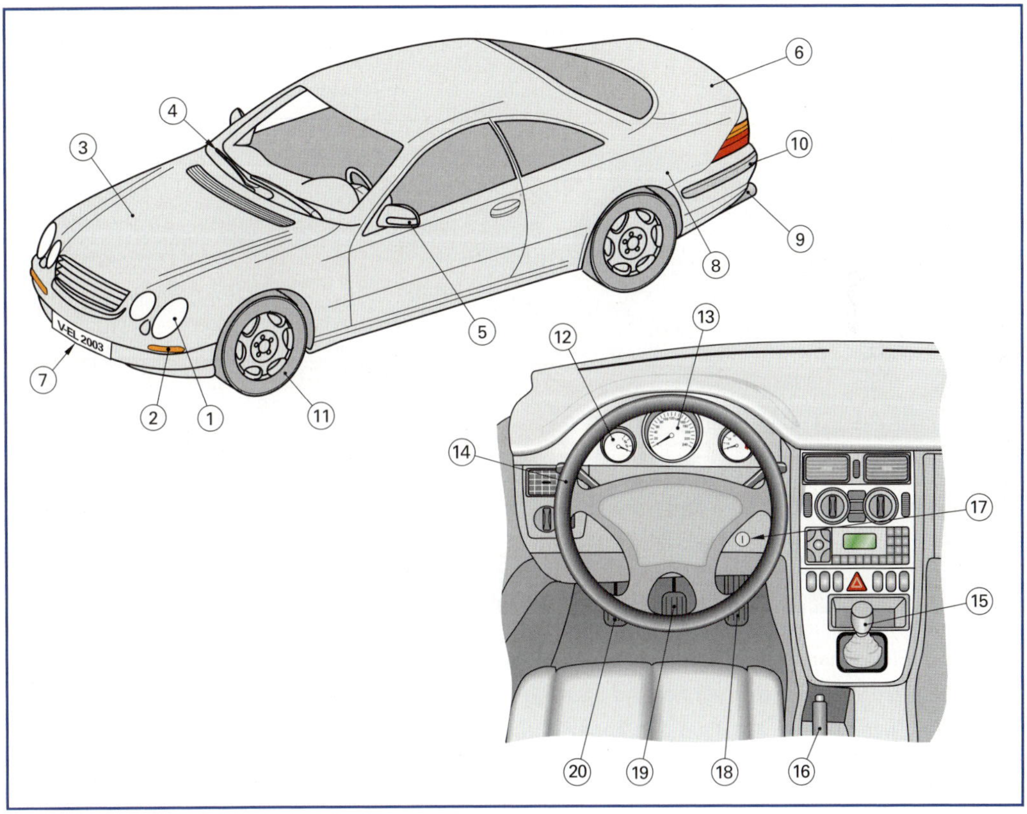

Activity 1 Which car parts do you know?

Match the following car parts to the numbers given in the picture. Translate the words into German.

Here are the English words:

tyre ... bonnet ... windscreen wiper ... boot ... number plate ... indicator ... bumper ... headlight ... exhaust pipe ... wing ... wing mirror ... handbrake ... gear stick ... speedometer ... fuel gauge ... steering wheel ... ignition switch ... clutch ... brake pedal ... accelerator

Is it the alternator?

Introducing the situation

Keith Graham is in the second year of his apprenticeship as a car mechanic at Drake's Garage in Torbay. One day, after having finished his regular work, he is trying to mend his own car which has got a flat battery. Keith's friend Frank is helping him.

KEITH Please hand over the 11/16 inch ring spanner. I first have to loosen the fan belt.

FRANK Are you sure that it's not the battery? ... Here you are.

KEITH Thank you ... Yes, I am. I've changed the battery twice. This is a brand new one but it's flat again. So it must be the alternator.

FRANK There could also be a short circuit in the electric system.

KEITH I don't think so. If there were a short circuit, a fuse would blow ... I need the ratchet and a 1/2" socket.

FRANK Here you are. But have you checked all the relays? As far as I know defective relays can also unload the battery.

KEITH I've checked them all. I'm sure, it's the alternator. When the battery was flat for the first time two weeks ago, my neighbour Mr Flint helped me with a jump start. It worked, but if you don't do it correctly it can damage your alternator. I'm afraid this has happened with mine ... Please give me a Phillips screwdriver.

FRANK A new alternator is quite expensive, isn't it?

KEITH Yes, it is. But first we will just check the regulator, you know, it's a part of the alternator. If we are lucky, we just have to change that. Otherwise, I will try to get a used alternator somewhere from a scrap yard.

Activity 2 Understanding the text

a) True or false? Correct the statements that are wrong.

1. They are repairing the car at Frank's place.
2. Frank has got trouble with his engine.
3. The battery of Keith's car is brand new.
4. The two friends have replaced fuses twice.
5. Keith has checked all the relays.
6. Frank believes that the alternator does not work.
7. A new alternator is quite expensive.

b) Match the following sentences.

1. Keith is sure	a) a fuse would blow.
2. If there were a short circuit	b) for a jump start.
3. You need a ring spanner	c) can unload the battery.
4. Defective relays	d) to tighten or loosen hexagonal nuts.
5. Jump leads are used	e) are quite expensive.
6. New alternators	f) it's not the battery.

c) Name the tools that Frank may need to remove the alternator.

Activity 3 Vocabulary

Find words in the text that fit these definitions.

1. safety device in an electric circuit
2. machine that produces electricity
3. tool to loosen or tighten a nut
4. device that stores electricity
5. device that switches high currents by low currents
6. place where old and damaged cars are kept
7. two times

Activity 4 Translation

Translate the following sentences into English.

1. Ich brauche keinen Maulschlüssel. Bitte reiche mir einen Ringschlüssel herüber.
2. Ich habe die Batterie schon zweimal ausgewechselt.
3. Wo hast du die Batterien gekauft?
4. Ein neuer Generator ist ziemlich teuer, nicht wahr?
5. Die neue Batterie ist schon wieder leer.
6. Überspannungen (overvoltage) können die Lichtmaschine beschädigen.
7. Zwei Relais funktionieren nicht.

Tools

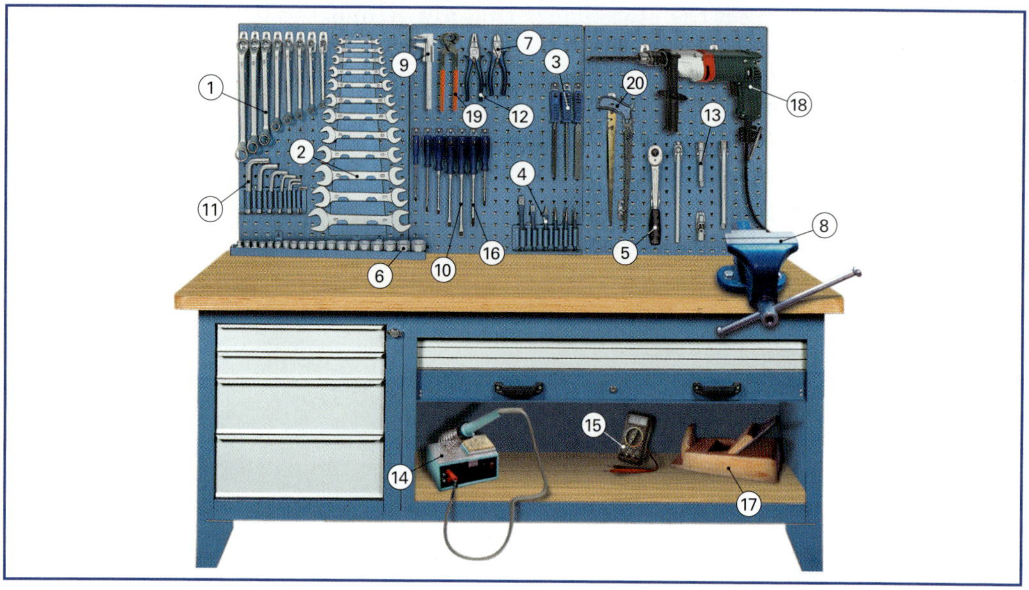

Activity 5 Working with tools

a) Look at the tools in the picture and find the German expressions for the following tools.

1. ring spanner
2. open-ended spanner
3. file
4. chisel
5. ratchet
6. socket
7. side cutter
8. vice
9. vernier calliper
10. screwdriver
11. Allen keys
12. (a pair of) pliers
13. socket wrench
14. soldering iron
15. multimeter
16. Phillips screwdriver
17. plane
18. electric drill
19. (a pair of) pincers
20. saw

b) What tools do you need to do the following?

1. changing the battery of a car
2. changing a tyre of a car
3. changing the sparking plugs of a car
4. repairing a TV set
5. installing a new wall socket
6. building a garden shed

c) What can you do with the following tools?

1. ring spanner
2. screwdriver
3. soldering iron
4. side cutter
5. multimeter
6. hammer
7. saw
8. (a pair of) pincers
9. electric drill

The following words will help you:

to cut ... to tighten ... to loosen ... to saw ... to solder ... to screw ... to measure ... to nail ... to drill ... hexagonal nut ... screw ... wire ... voltage ... electric current ... electric parts ... wooden board ... nail

Activity 6 How to exchange an alternator

Put the following actions into the correct order. Name the tool you need to do each single step.

1. Put in fan belt and tighten it.
2. Loosen and remove fan belt.
3. Unscrew alternator and remove it.
4. Clamp ground from battery.
5. Insert all plugs.
6. Connect ground to negative pole of battery.
7. Remove all plugs and wires from the back of the alternator.
8. Put in new alternator and fasten screws with torque key.

Activity 7 How to give a jump start correctly

Copy the following text into your exercise book and complete it with words from the box below.

1. Make sure that both ●●●[1] have the same ●●●[2].
2. Connect the red end of one of the ●●●[3] with the positive pole of the battery that is ●●●[4]. Then ●●●[5] the other end to the positive pole of the donator battery (PLUS TO PLUS).
3. Connect the black cable with the negative pole of the donator battery to a ●●●[6] of the other car. Do not connect it to the ●●●[7] of the defective battery (MINUS TO GROUND)!
4. Start the engine of the donator vehicle. If you ●●●[8] the headlight or something else that needs a lot of energy, you can be sure not to ●●●[9] electronic components when you remove the jump-leads.
5. Start the ●●●[10] car.
6. ●●●[11] the jump-leads. Start with the black cable that combines minus and ground. Then disconnect the positive poles.

Starthilfe

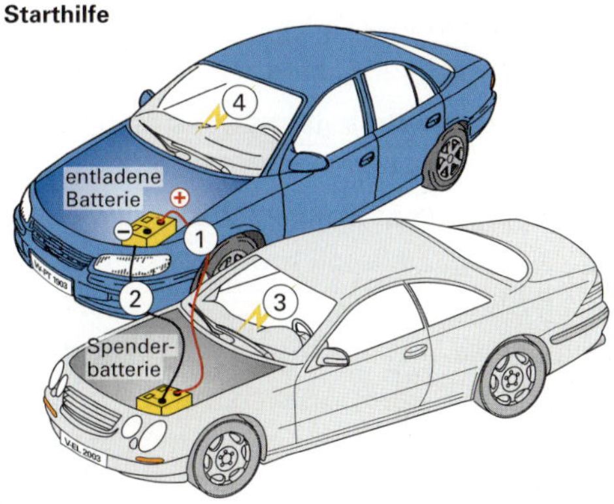

(1) Pluspole verbinden

(2) Minuspol der Spenderbatterie mit Fahrzeugmasse am Empfängerfahrzeug verbinden

(3) Motor des Spenderfahrzeuges starten

(4) Motor des Empfängerfahrzeuges starten

Use these words:

metal part ... remove ... voltage ... negative pole ... jump-leads ... defective ... damage ... unloaded ... batteries ... connect ... switch on

Car quiz

How much do you know about car parts? You can find that out by answering the following questions. Write your answers in a list. Then take certain letters from the answers to make up the name of the man shown in the picture. He began his career with a horse-drawn carriage company in America. Later he founded the company which still is one of the biggest car manufacturers in the USA: General Motors.

1. The glass front window of a car that the driver looks through.
2. Keyhole in the dashboard in which you put the key to start the engine.
3. A part of a car that disconnects the power of the engine from the wheels when you change gears.
4. Instrument in the dashboard that shows the amount of petrol that is still in the tank.
5. Lights at the front and back of a car that show the others if you want to turn left or right.
6. The pedal that you press with your foot in order to make the vehicle go faster.
7. Bars that are fixed at the front and the back of a car to protect it from damage when it collides with another car or crashes into something else.
8. The American word for the metal part of the car that covers the engine.
9. A pipe that carries the gas out of the engine of a motor vehicle.
10. A long piece of metal with a rubber edge that you switch on when it is raining.
11. Device for slowing or stopping a car.
12. Part of a car that is above a wheel.
13. A thick ring of rubber which is fitted round each wheel of a vehicle and which is usually filled with air.

1. = first letter
2. = fourth letter
3. = second letter
4. = fourth letter
5. = fourth letter
6. = first letter
7. = third letter
8. = fourth letter
9. = fifth letter
10. = last letter
11. = third letter
12. = third letter
13. = first letter

Vocabulary Unit 2

accelerator (pedal) [ak'seləreɪtə(r)]	**Gaspedal**
Allen keys	**Inbusschlüssel**
alternator	**Generator**
apprenticeship	**Lehre**
bar	**Stange, Stab**
to blow	***hier:* auslösen**
bolt	**(Schrauben-)Bolzen**
bonnet	**Motorhaube**
boot	**Kofferraum**
brake	**Bremse**
brake pedal	**Bremspedal**
bumper	**Stoßfänger**
carriage	**Kutsche, Wagen**
to change gears	**einen Gang umschalten**
chisel ['tʃɪzl]	**Meißel**
clutch	**Kupplung**
to connect	**anschließen, verbinden**
dashboard	**Armaturenbrett**
defective	**defekt**
device	**Gerät**
to disconnect	**trennen**
donator	**Spender, Geber**
to drill	**bohren**
edge	**Kante**
electric current	**elektrischer Strom**
electric drill	**elektrische Bohrmaschine**
electronic component	**elektronisches Bauteil**
engine	**Motor**
to exchange	**(aus)wechseln**
exhaust pipe	**Auspuff**
expression	**Ausdruck**
fanbelt	**Keilriemen**
file	**Feile**
to fit	**anbringen, montieren**
flat	***hier:* leer; entladen**
to found	**gründen**
fuel gauge [fju:əl geɪdʒ]	**Tankuhr**
fuse	**Sicherung**
garden shed	**Gartenhäuschen**
gear stick	**Schalthebel**
ground	**Masse**
handbrake	**Handbremse**
headlight	**Scheinwerfer**
hexagon	**Sechseck**
hexagonal	**sechseckig**
ignition switch	**Zündschloss**

indicator	**Blinklicht**
jump leads [dʒʌmp li:dz]	**Starthilfekabel**
jump-start	**Starthilfe**
to loosen	**lösen**
manufacturer	**Hersteller**
to measure	**messen**
to mend	**reparieren**
multimeter	**Vielfachmessgerät**
nail	**Nagel**
to nail	**(an)nageln**
negative pole	**Minuspol**
number plate	**Nummernschild**
nut	**Mutter (techn.)**
open-ended spanner	**Maulschlüssel**
otherwise	**ansonsten**
overvoltage	**Überspannung**
Phillips screwdriver	**Kreuzschlitz-schraubendreher**
pincers (a pair of)	**Kneifzange**
pipe	**Rohr**
plane	**Hobel**
pliers (a pair of)	**Zange**
plug	**Stecker**
positive pole	**Pluspol**
to protect	**schützen**
ratchet	**Knarre, Ratsche**
regulator	**Regler**
relay [ri:leɪ]	**Relais**
to remove	**entfernen**
to replace	**ersetzen**
ring spanner	**Ringschlüssel**
rubber	**Gummi**
saw [sɔ:]	**Säge**
to saw	**sägen**
scrap yard	**Schrottplatz**
screw	**Schraube**
to screw	**(an)schrauben**
screwdriver	**Schraubendreher**
shelf	**Regal(-brett)**
short circuit	**Kurzschluss**
side cutter	**Seitenschneider**
side mirror	**Seitenspiegel**
socket	**Nuss (für Ratsche)**
socket wrench	**Steckschlüssel**
to solder	**löten**
soldering iron	**Lötkolben**
sparking plug	**Zündkerze**
speedometer	**Tachometer**
steering wheel	**Lenkrad**

Vocabulary Unit 2

to store	speichern	vernier calliper [vɜːnjə kælɪpəz]	Messschieber
to tighten	festziehen, anziehen	vice [vaɪs]	Schraubstock
tool	Werkzeug	voltage	Spannung
torque key	Drehmomentenschlüssel	wall socket	Steckdose
tyre	Reifen	windscreen wiper	Scheibenwischer
to unload	entladen	wing	Kotflügel
to unscrew	ab-/aufschrauben	wing mirror	Seitenspiegel
various	verschiedene	wire	Draht
vehicle	Fahrzeug	wooden	aus Holz; hölzern

Additional Vocabulary: Tools

Abisolierzange	wire strippers	Kombizange	combination pliers
Blechschere	metal cutting shears	Maßlehre	feeler gauge
Drahtbürste	wire brush	Pinzette	pair of tweezers
Drehmomentschlüssel	torque wrench	Rundfeile	round file
		Rundzange	round-nosed pliers
Flachzange	flat-nose pliers	Schere	(a pair of) scissors
Gabelschlüssel	open-ended spanner	Schweißbrenner	welding torch [tɔːtʃ]
Gewinde	thread [θred]	Spachtel	spatula ['spætjʊlə]
Kettensäge	chain saw	Wasserwaage	spirit level

Additional Vocabulary: Car parts

Anlasser	starter motor	Sonnenschiebedach	sunroof
Kilometerzähler	mileometer	Tankverschluss	petrol cap
Kraftstoffpumpe	fuel pump	Türgriff	door handle
Kühler	radiator	Ventilator	fan
Luftfilter	air filter	Vergaser	carburettor
Nebelscheinwerfer	fog light	Zündspule	ignition coil [ɪg'nɪʃn kɔɪl]
Ölmessstab	dipstick	Zündverteiler	distributor [dɪ'strɪbjʊtə(r)]
Parkleuchte	side light		
Rücklicht	rear light		

British English vs American English

accelerator	gas pedal	number plate	licence plate
bonnet	hood	petrol cap	gas cap
boot	trunk	rear light	tail light
carburettor	carburetor	reversing light	back-up light
fuel pump	gasoline pump	sidelight	parking light
gear stick	gear shift	tyre	tire
handbrake	emergency brake	windscreen	windshield
indicator	turn signal	wing	fender
mileometer	odometer	wing mirror	side mirror

3 Measuring

The following unit deals with measurements, introduces commonly known measuring instruments and shows how these instruments can be used.

Exact measuring units

Introducing the situation

One day Tobias, a German exchange student, talks to an English trainee in the workshop about metric and imperial measures.

TOBIAS Now, here they talk about inches. Yesterday in the weather forecast the lady also talked about six inches of rain. At school I heard about the differences between the metric system used in Germany and the imperial system you still use over here. But to be honest I didn't pay much attention. Can you tell me what exactly the differences are?

SARAH Sure, one inch is about 25.4 mm.

TOBIAS Do you still use these imperial units a lot?

SARAH Oh, yes, in everyday life everybody talks about inches, feet, pints, and Fahrenheit. If you talk about the height of a person, you say he is six feet two. In a pub you'll get a pint of beer and our temperature today is 66.2 degrees Fahrenheit. I can copy the most important imperial measures for you.

TOBIAS Thanks. That would be nice.

Activity 1 Understanding the text

Answer the following questions.

1. What did the lady in the weather forecast talk about?
2. What was Tobias reminded of?
3. What does Sarah say about measures in Great Britain in everyday life?
4. Which examples of imperial measures does Sarah mention?
5. Which other imperial units do you know? Use a dictionary to look them up if necessary.

Activity 2 Imperial versus metric measures

a) Find the metric equivalents of the measures mentioned in the text. To get some exercise in dealing with mathematical operations, write down the complete equations in words.

This information may help you:

1 inch = 25.4 mm, in words: one inch equals twenty-five point four millimetres
1 foot = 30.5 cm, in words: one foot equals thirty point five centimetres
1 pint = 0.57 l, in words: one pint equals zero point five seven litres

°C = (°F – 32) · 5/9	**°F = 32 + °C · 9/5**
degrees Celsius equals (open) round bracket degrees Fahrenheit minus thirty-two (close) round bracket times five ninths	degrees Fahrenheit equals thirty-two plus degrees Celsius times nine fifths

Additional information

Symbol	example	In words
= | +	2=1+1	two **equals** one **plus** one
-	2-2	two **minus** two
: | /	2:2 | $\frac{2}{2}$	two **divided by** two / two **over** two
· | x	2·2 | 2x2	two **multiplied** by two / two **times** two
( )	(2+2)	(open) **round bracket** two plus two (close) **round bracket**
%	2%	two **per cent**
.	2.2	two **point** two

fractions	In words
$^1/_2$	one half / a half
$^1/_3$	one third / a third
$^1/_4$	one or a forth / one or a quarter
$^3/_5$	three fifths

b) Convert the metric values into imperial values.

1. At home your best friend lives next door which is only 50 m away.
2. Your sister is 163 cm tall.
3. The average temperature in your hometown in the summer is about 20 °C.
4. In winter the thermometer sometimes shows –15 °C.
5. In Bavaria you order one “Maß” which is one litre of beer.

Unit 3

c) Find words in the text that fit these definitions. Pick the letters referred to in brackets and you will find a word for a long straight mark on a surface, for example, on paper.

1. system based on inches, feet and Fahrenheit (4th letter)
2. measure for beer in Great Britain (3rd letter)
3. a Swede who invented a temperature scale at the beginning of the 18th century (5th letter)
4. opposite of minus (2th letter)

Basic units

For many centuries a lot of different measuring systems have been used over the world. In Germany we use the metric system which has become standard in almost every country.
A common measuring system is necessary for the industry and business world because people must know whether their manufactured goods have achieved certain qualities. The system of units used worldwide is the International System of Units (SI-units) which has developed from the metric system. Take length, which is an important physical quantity, as an example. Measuring length is nothing else but a comparison with a defined unit. Scientists first used a special bar as the defined unit for a meter. Years later they found a more precise way to define length. One meter is the distance which light moves in a vacuum in $^{1}/_{299\ 792\ 458}$ of a second. There are similar examples looking at mass and time. The basic units are shown in the table.

Basic units (SI-units)

Basic quantity	Unit	Symbol
length	meter	m
mass	kilogram	kg
time	second	s
current	ampere	A
thermodynamic temperature	kelvin	K
luminous intensity	candela	cd
amount of substance	mole	mol

Unit 3

Activity 3 Comprehension

a) Replace the words in bold type with expressions from the text.

1. Worldwide **the same** measuring system is used.
2. Goods, which have been **produced with the help of machines**.
3. To check if two things are **equal**.
4. They found a **more exact** way to define length.

b) Answer the following questions on the text.

1. Which system of measurement is used worldwide?
2. Why is a common measuring system necessary throughout the world?
3. What standard was length based on first?
4. What standard is length based on now?

Activity 4 Translation

Translate the following sentences into English.

1. Viele Jahrhunderte wurden weltweit verschiedene Maßeinheiten verwendet, was nie Probleme verursachte.
2. Das metrische System ist für die moderne Industrie und die internationalen Wirtschaftsbeziehungen am besten geeignet.
3. Alle Maßeinheiten basieren auf nur wenigen Grundeinheiten.
4. Geschwindigkeit, zum Beispiel, wird definiert über Länge und Zeit.

Measuring distances

There are different types of instruments for measuring distances. If your task is to make a technical drawing at school, you use a ruler to draw a line with the exact length of, for example, 12 millimetres. If you want to know how long a straight line is, you can read the millimetres or centimetres off the ruler's scale. With a geometric triangle you can draw an angle of any degree and of course you can also measure the degree of a drawn angle.

At work you may need 40 centimetres of a metal rod for your workpiece. You can use a folding rule to mark where to cut off the metal.

Metal workers use more precise instruments like vernier callipers or micrometers. They are available in different sizes and there are analogue as well as digital ones. With commonly used analogue vernier callipers you can measure up to an accuracy of 1/10 of a millimetre. With analogue micrometers the accuracy is even up to 1/100 of a milimetre.

Activity 5 Instruments for measuring distances

a) Look at the picture below. Find the appropriate word for each measuring instrument in the text.

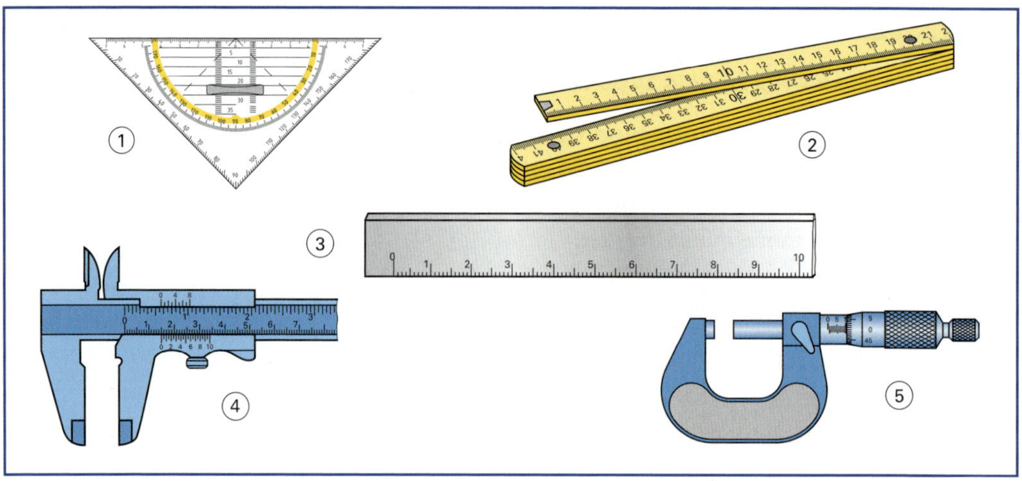

b) Complete the sentences with words from the text above.

1. The ... is divided into millimetres.
2. For drawing a ... ... you normally use a ruler.
3. With a folding rule you can measure the ... and the width of a room.
4. Micrometers and vernier callipers are available as ... as well as ... ones.
5. With a ... you can measure and draw angles.
6. Vernier callipers are mainly used by ... .
7. One meter can be divided into one thousand ... .
8. Vernier callipers are ... in different sizes.
9. With a micrometer you can measure very small ... .
10. For constructing a ... ... at school you can use a ruler or a geometric triangle.

Activity 6 Vernier callipers

a) Match the German words to the numbers 1 to 10 in the picture. Find the English term for each German word.

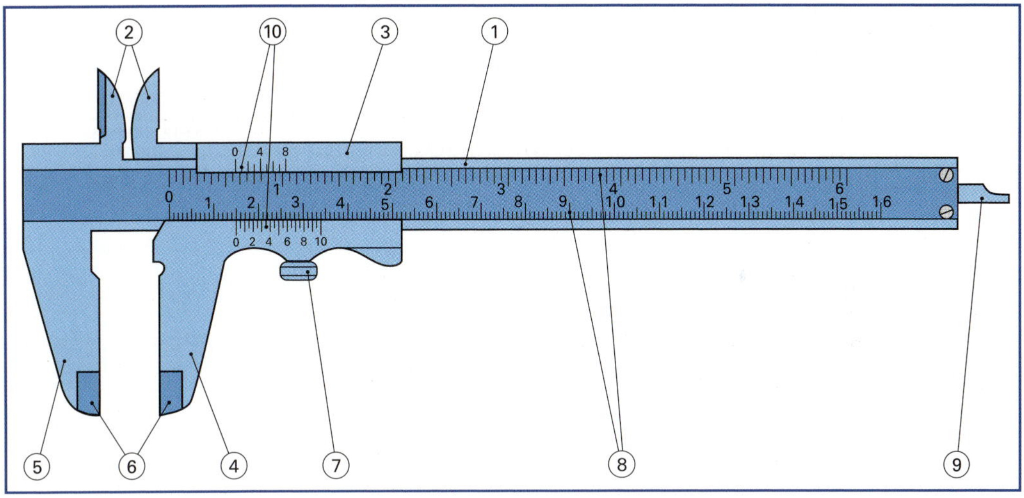

Here are the German words:

Feststellschraube ... Tiefenmessgerät ... Messschenkel für Innenmessung ... Messschenkel für Außenmessung ... fester Messschenkel ... beweglicher Messschenkel ... Nonien ... Schieber ... Schiene ... Skala

Here are the English words:

fixed jaw ... movable jaw ... outside jaws ... inside jaws ... depth bar ... clamp screw ... vernier scale ... slider ... main beam (bar) ... scale

Activity 7 — What vernier callipers can be used for

Copy the following texts into your exercise book and fill in one of the words from the box.

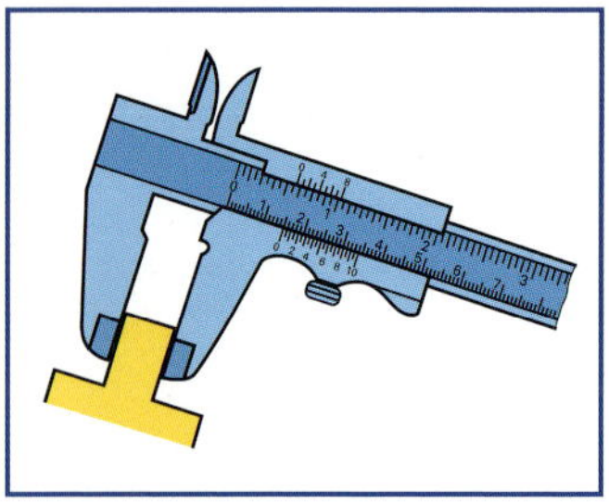

This picture shows an example how a vernier calliper is used. You can see the outside •••[1] of a vernier calliper and the •••[2] of a workpiece. What you want to measure is the •••[3] dimension. In order to get an •••[4] answer, you must firmly hold the workpiece against the •••[5] jaw and carefully push the •••[6] jaw against it.

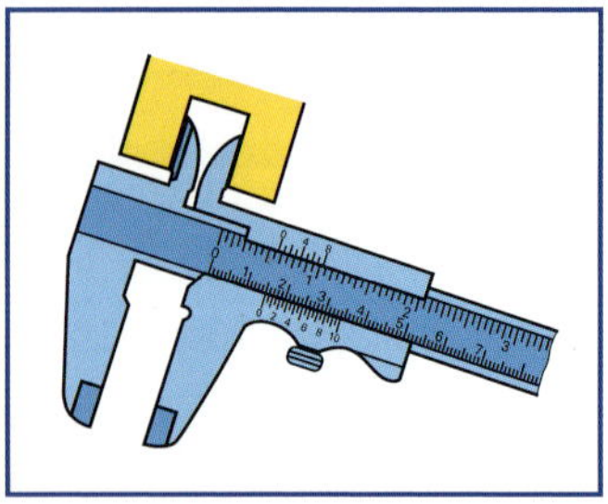

In this picture you can see again a part of a vernier calliper and a workpiece. This time you want to know the inside •••[7] of a workpiece. You use the inside jaws for finding the •••[8] dimension. You must press the fixed jaw against the •••[9]. Now move the other jaw to the opposite •••[10].

Use these words:

internal ... jaws ... workpiece ... movable ... exact ... side ... fixed ... dimension ... external ... part

Activity 8 — Vocabulary

a) Find the correct words for the following definitions.

1. something that cannot be moved
2. device for fastening something
3. marked at regular distances
4. to be at the other end or side of something
5. something that illustrates what a person talks about

b) Find definitions for the following words.

1. workpiece
2. internal
3. skill
4. device
5. to move

Measuring weight

Introducing the situation

Tom comes home from school and joins his mother, who is making a cake, in the kitchen.

TOM Hi, mom.

MOM Hi. How was school today?

TOM All right. Got an A in my maths test. Physics was quite interesting. We talked about mass, weight, and force.

MOM Oh. Can you give me a hand? I need half a kilo of flour for my cake.

TOM Sure. Do you know that you cannot measure weight? You actually measure force. Your scale should show Newton.

MOM Newton?

TOM Yes. Newton. He was an English scientist. Sir Isaac Newton.

MOM What's he got to do with my cake?

TOM He developed some famous laws. Mass is the amount of material of an object. The unit of mass is the kilogram, which is a standard measure.

MOM Quite interesting. But what is one kilo?

TOM To define one kilo an international prototype is used. It is a cylinder with 39 mm in diameter and 39 mm in height. It's made of a special material.

MOM Really? I need 150 grams of powdered sugar.

TOM Here you are.

MOM What about weight?

TOM Weight is the force of gravity. The downward force of a falling object is called acceleration because of gravity. The unit of force is Newton. At the surface of the earth a one kilogram body weighs about 9.81 N. Further away from the earth's surface there is less gravitational force, therfore, a one kilogram object weighs less.The mass of the one kilogram object, however, is still the same.

MOM How did he find out?

TOM One day he was sitting under an apple tree, when all of a sudden an apple fell down on his head. This was the beginning of everything.

MOM Nice story. Let's put the cake into the oven so that our young scientist gets some food.

Unit 3

Activity 9 Understanding the text

Answer the following questions.

1. What is said about Tom's day at school?
2. What does Tom's mother ask him to do?
3. Who was Newton?
4. What is the standard measure of mass?
5. How is the standard measure of mass defined?
6. How did Newton discover his law?

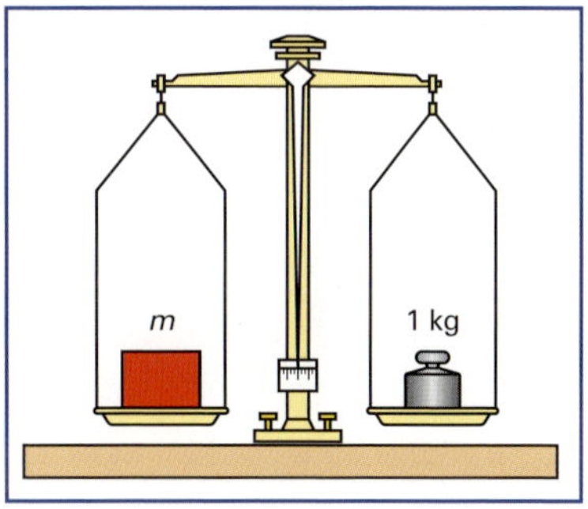

Activity 10 Newton's law

Fill in the gaps using the words from the box below.

$F_G\,[N] = m\,[kg] \cdot g\,[\frac{m}{s^2}]$

1. F_G stands for •••[1].
2. N stands for •••[2] and is the unit of F_G which is a combination of SI-units. It combines •••[3], •••[4] and •••[5].
3. m stands for •••[6].
4. kg stands for •••[7] and is the unit of m.
5. g stands for •••[8].
6. $\frac{m}{s^2}$ stands for •••[9] and is the unit of g.

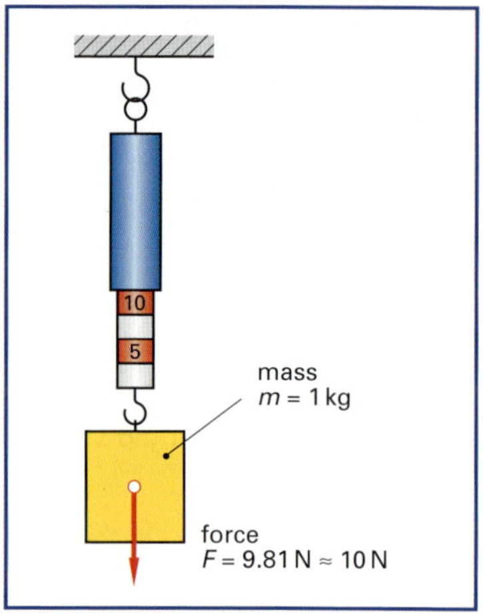

Use these words:

meter ... meter per second squared ... kilogram (2x) ... Newton ... gravitational force ... second ... acceleration because of gravity ... mass

Measuring temperature

If you have a room temperature of 18 degrees Celsius, some people will surely feel cold while others feel comfortable. Temperature is felt subjectively and this does not cause any problems in daily life. You simply turn the thermostat of the radiator in your room up or down. If you need to define temperature correctly, however, you have to use a special instrument with an accurate scale.

If you use the Celsius scale, you measure in °C (degrees Celsius). In this system the freezing point of water is 0 °C (zero degrees Celsius). The boiling point of water is 100 °C (a hundred degrees Celsius). The Fahrenheit scale shows the freezing point of water at 32 °F and the boiling point at 212 °F.

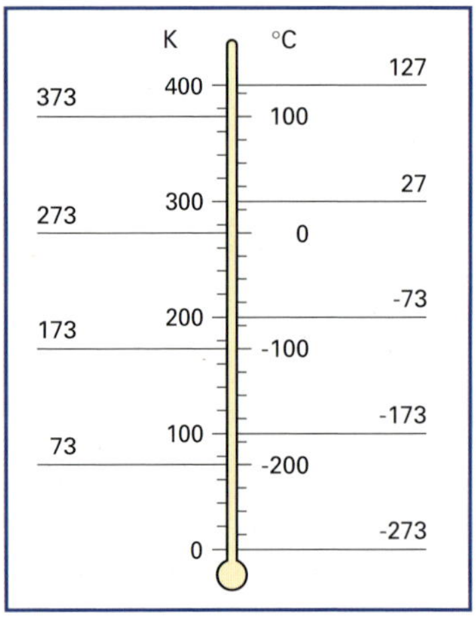

To measure a temperature difference a scale is needed which shows a change in the state of matter of a substance. Water which occurs in all three states of matter as a solid, a liquid, and a gas is used to get the two fixed points on the Celsius scale. Between the freezing and the boiling point the Celsius scale is divided into one hundred equal parts.
The lowest temperature that is possible is –273 °C. This point is defined as absolute zero.

The Kelvin scale begins at the absolute zero point. Kelvin is one of the basic units. Differences in temperature can be given either in Kelvin or in degrees Celsius.

Activity 11 Talking about Kelvin

Translate the following text into English.

Weißt Du eigentlich etwas über Kelvin?

Ja. Kelvin hieß eigentlich William Thomson. Er wurde 1824 in Irland geboren. Sein Vater unterrichtete ihn und seinen Bruder zuhause. Mit zehn Jahren begann er an der Universität von Glasgow zu studieren. Das kommt uns heute vielleicht seltsam vor, aber damals war das für intelligente junge Leute durchaus nicht ungewöhnlich. Bereits fünf Jahre später erhielt er seinen ersten Preis. 1892 wurde er in den Adelsstand erhoben und deshalb kennen wir ihn heute als Lord Kelvin. Er liebte seine Arbeit und wurde mit Ehrungen überhäuft. Mit 75 Jahren beschloss er Jüngeren das Feld zu überlassen. Er starb 1907 und liegt in Westminster Abbey in London begraben.

Activity 12 Instruments for measuring temperature

Look at the pictures and complete the texts with one of the words in the box.

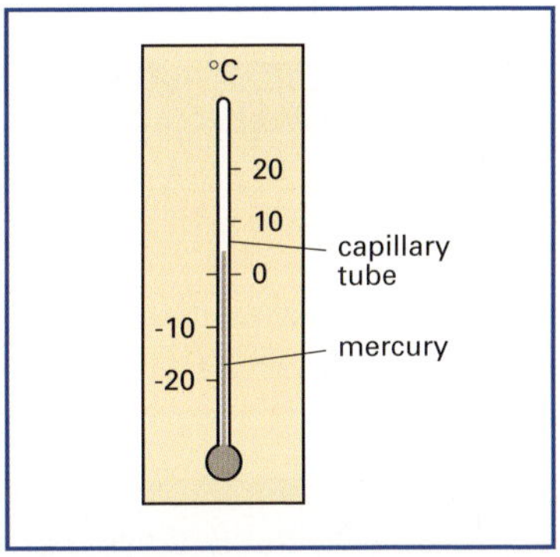

Liquid thermometer

In every household, in every company and in laboratories you can find a measuring •••[1] like the one in the picture on the left. Before you leave for work in the morning, you can have a look at it and then decide •••[2] to take a warm coat or not for today's •••[3]. A •••[4] normally contains mercury. It is in a •••[5] and changes its volume if the •••[6] changes. If you heat mercury, it •••[7]. If the temperature •••[8], it contracts.

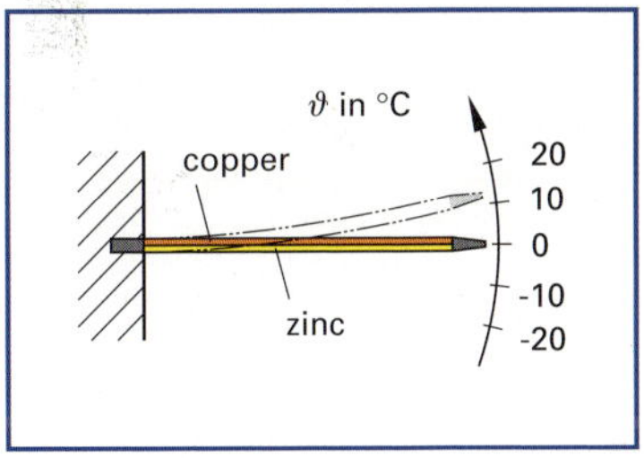

Bimetallic thermometer

You can use the instrument on the left for •••[9] temperature, too. In a •••[10] you have two metals with different rates of •••[11].
If the temperature changes, the metal bends and the temperature can be read off a •••[12] by an indicator.

Use these words:

scale ... falls ... liquid thermometer ... measuring ... expansion ... bimetallic thermometer ... capillary tube ... expands ... temperature ... instrument ... whether ... weather

Unit 3

Activity 13 Fundamental laws of science

Form statements that are always true.

Here is an example:

If you use the Celsius scale, the freezing point of water is 0 °C.

Form similar sentences with the following phrases.

1. heat water	a) streets become white
2. snows	b) steam condenses
3. put water into the freezer	c) get green
4. mix blue and yellow	d) turns into steam
5. temperature falls	e) becomes ice
6. reach zero degrees Kelvin	f) turns into water
7. temperature rises	g) refers to lowest temperature possible
8. melt ice	h) boiling point of water is 100°C.
9. use the Celsius scale	i) materials are solid
10. someone mentions absolute zero	j) mercury in capillary tube expands

Unit 3

Measuring electricity

Introducing the situation

Kathy is in the first year of her apprenticeship. She and David are in the workshop together. David, who is an apprentice in his third year, is showing Kathy how to work with a multimeter.

DAVID Have you ever worked with a multimeter before?

KATHY No, not really.

DAVID Okay, let's have a look at the multimeter first. You have a display, a range selector and two leads with a probe tip each. If you want to measure electric current, you must break the circuit. The multimeter has to be connected in series with the consumer, because the electric current must flow through it.
Make sure that you start with the highest range. Then you switch to a suitable range. On the display you can read the amps.

KATHY What about voltage?

DAVID If you want to measure voltage, you have to connect the multimeter in parallel. Make sure again that you start with the highest range. On the display you can read the volts.

KATHY Okay, I got that. Could we do some practising?

DAVID Sure, come on.

Activity 14 Understanding the text

Answer the following questions.

1. Who are Kathy and David?
2. Where are Kathy and David at the moment?
3. What are they doing?
4. Which parts of a multimeter does David mention?
5. Name the unit and symbol of
   a) electric current
   b) voltage
6. Why must you break the circuit if you want to measure electric current?
7. How must the multimeter be connected if you want to measure voltage?

Activity 15 Measuring electric current

Look at the circuit diagram and complete the description.

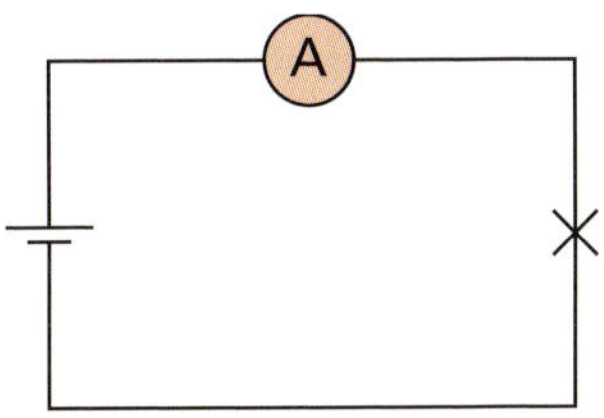

Circuit diagram

For ●●●[1] electric current you use a multimeter as an ammeter. The symbol for an ●●●[2] in a circuit diagram is a ●●●[3] with an A in the centre. In ●●●[4] to measure ●●●[5], the ammeter must be connected ●●●[6].

Use these words:

electric current ... in series ... ammeter ... circle ... measuring ... order

Activity 16 Measuring voltage

Look at the circuit diagram and complete the description.

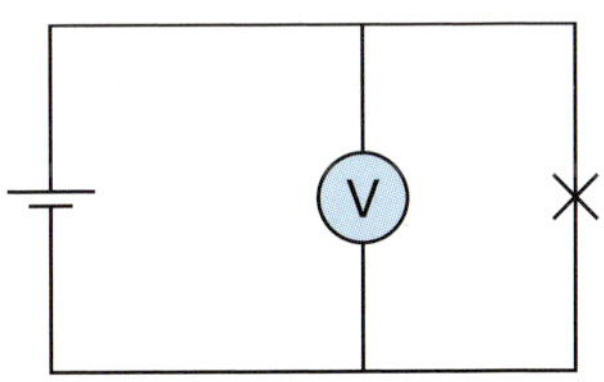

Circuit diagram

For measuring voltage you use the multimeter as a voltmeter. The ●●●[1] for voltmeter in a ●●●[2] is a circle with a V in the ●●●[3]. In order to ●●●[4] voltage, the voltmeter must be connected ●●●[5].

Use these words:

circuit diagram ... centre ... measure ... in parallel ... symbol

Vocabulary Unit 3

ability	Fähigkeit
to accelerate	beschleunigen
acceleration	Beschleunigung
accurate	genau
to achieve	erreichen
actually	genau genommen, eigentlich
additional	zusätzlich
all of a sudden	ganz plötzlich
almost	fast
a lot of	viele
ammeter	Amperemeter
amount	Menge
amp/ampere	Ampere
angle	Winkel
apprenticeship	Ausbildung
average ['ævərɪdʒ]	Durchschnitt, durchschnittlich
avoid	vermeiden
balance	Waage
bar	Stab, Stange
to be based on	sich stützen auf, basieren
to become	werden
to bend	biegen
bimetallic thermometer	Bimetallthermometer
boiling point	Siedepunkt
bracket	Klammer
to break the circuit	den Stromkreis unterbrechen
capillary tube	Kapillargefäß
circuit	(Strom-)Kreis
circuit diagram	Schaltplan
clamp	Klemme
clamp screw	Feststellschraube
comparison	Vergleich
column ['kɒləm]	Säule, Spalte
commonly	allgemein
to condense	kondensieren
conductor	elektrischer Leiter
to connect in parallel	parallel schalten
to connect in series	in Reihe schalten
consumer	Verbraucher
to contain	beinhalten
to contract	zusammenziehen
copper	Kupfer
current	Stromfluss
cylinder	Zylinder
to deal with	handeln von, behandeln
to decide	entscheiden
to define	bestimmen
degree	Grad
to depend on	abhängen von
depth	Tiefe
depth bar	Tiefenmessgerät
derived from	abgeleitet von
to describe	beschreiben
to develop	entwickeln
device	Vorrichtung, Gerät
diameter	Durchmesser
difference	Unterschied
dimension	Maß, Abmessung
distance	Entfernung
to distinguish [dɪ'stɪŋgwiʃ]	unterscheiden
to divide	teilen
downward	nach unten
electric current	elektrischer Strom
equal ['ɪkwəl]	gleich
equation [ɪ'kweɪʒn]	Gleichung
error	Irrtum, Fehler
exchange student	Austauschschüler
to expand	ausdehnen
external	Außen-
external diameter	Außendurchmesser
to fasten	befestigen
fault	Fehler, Defekt
feature	Merkmal
firmly	fest
to fix	befestigen
fixed jaw	fester Messschenkel
flour	Mehl
folding rule	Zollstock
force	Kraft
fraction	Bruch
freezer	Gefrierschrank
freezing point	Gefrierpunkt
further	weiter
gauge [geɪdʒ]	Lehre
geometric triangle	Geodreieck
goods (pl)	Waren
gravitation	Schwerkraft
gravitational pull	Anziehungskraft
gravity	Schwerkraft
height [haɪt]	Höhe
honest	ehrlich

Unit 3

Vocabulary Unit 3

hook	Haken
however	jedoch
imperial	imperial
inaccurate [ɪn'ækjərət]	ungenau
indicator	Anzeiger
inside	innerhalb
inside jaw	Messschenkel für Innenmessung
to insulate	isolieren (elektr.)
internal	Innen-
internal diameter	Innendurchmesser
to invent	erfinden
laboratory	Labor
law	Gesetz
lead	Leitung (elektr.)
length	Länge
less (than)	weniger (als)
liquid	flüssig, Flüssigkeit
liquid thermometer	Flüssigkeitsthermo-meter
to manufacture [mænjʊ'fæktʃə(r)]	herstellen, fertigen
mark	Markierung
to mark	kennzeichnen, markieren
mass	Masse
means (pl)	Mittel
measure	Maßeinheit
to measure	messen
measurement	Messung
to mention	erwähnen
mercury	Quecksilber
metric	metrisch
micrometer	Messschraube
movable (*also:* moveable)	beweglich
movable jaw	beweglicher Messschenkel
over	geteilt (math)
per cent (AmE percent)	Prozent
power source	Stromquelle
precise [prɪ'sais]	genau
precision	Genauigkeit
prototype	Muster, Prototyp
to push	schieben
quite	ziemlich
radiator	Heizkörper
range	*hier:* Messbereich
range selector	Messbereichswähler
rate of expansion	Ausdehnungs-geschwindigkeit
to refer to	Bezug nehmen auf
regular	regelmäßig
to reject	zurückweisen
to remind of	sich erinnern an
resistance	Widerstand (elektr.)
to rise	(an-)steigen
round bracket	runde Klammer (math)
scale	Skala, Gradeinteilung
science	Wissenschaft
scientist ['saɪəntɪst]	Wissenschaftler
to select	auswählen
shape	Form
similar	ähnlich
skill	Fähigkeit, Geschick
slider	Schieber
solid	fest
spring balance	Federwaage
still	noch
steam	Dampf
straight	gerade
strength	Kraft, Stärke
suitable	geeignet
surface	Oberfläche
switch	Schalter
to switch on/off	ein-/ausschalten
table	Tabelle
times	mal (math)
trainee	Auszubildender
to transfer	übertragen
unit	Einheit
value	Wert
vapour (AmE vapor)	Dunst, Dampf, Nebel
to verify	überprüfen
vernier	Nonius
vernier calliper (AmE vernier caliper)	Messschieber
versus	gegen
voltage	Spannung
volume	Volumen
weather forecast	Wetterbericht
to weigh	wiegen
weight [weɪt]	Gewicht
whether	ob
width [wɪdθ]	Weite, Breite
workshop	Werkstatt
zinc	Zink

4 Health and Safety at Work

In this unit you will learn something about First-Aid, how to avoid accidents and how to protect yourself and others.

A stupid accident

Introducing the situation

Ann and Mike are friends and they are in the same class at vocational school. Ann gives Mike a call. She is a bit worried because Mike did not show up for today's lesson.

ANN Hi Mike, this is Ann. What is wrong with you? Why didn't you come to school today?

MIKE Hi Ann, good to hear from you. I don't feel very well.
You won't believe what happened yesterday. I had almost finished with work and I only wanted to sharpen my knife on the bench grinder. I was in a hurry so I didn't want to waste time looking for some protective goggles. As soon as the knife touched the grinding disc a splinter hit my eye.

ANN Ouch, that really hurts. But how can you be so silly not to wear protective goggles. Didn't you know what could happen?

MIKE Sure I knew what could happen. I even saw the safety sign on the machine but I thought this time nothing would happen.

ANN What a coincidence. Today at school we were talking about health and safety at work.
A Health and Safety Inspector was invited to the lesson who told us about his work and the importance of using safety equipment. He also showed some pictures to us of typical accidents and injuries which can happen in the workplace. Guess what one of the pictures was about.

MIKE I guess it was about a splinter in an eye.

ANN Yes. Did you go to see the doctor?

MIKE Yes, he had to take the splinter out, but it still feels like there is sand in my eye.
In future I will always wear protective goggles even if I am only sharpening a pencil.

(Ann and Mike are both laughing)

ANN Sure Mike, I think you should.
I will come to see you later if that's all right?

MIKE Oh yeah, that's nice. So, see you later.

ANN Yeah, see you later.

Activity 1 | Understanding the text

a) Answer the questions in full sentences and with your own words.

1. How do Ann and Mike know each other?
2. Why is Ann worried about Mike?
3. When did the accident happen to Mike?
4. Why did the accident happen to Mike?
5. What did the doctor do?
6. How does Mike's eye feel now?
7. What are Ann and Mike laughing about?
8. When does Ann want to visit Mike?

b) Think about an accident that happened to you or to somebody you know. Tell your story to the class.

Personal protective equipment

In the picture above you can see protective equipment which is necessary for your own safety and the safety of others at work.

Personal protective equipment is your first line of defence against accidents. Keep your workplace clean and tools, machines and all safety equipment in good condition. Always be aware that accidents happen "accidentally".

Some dangers are not visible or they can be odourless. But they are there! Bright light, dust, loud noise, toxic liquid or gas, electricity, etc. are also very dangerous.

Therefore it is very important to be aware of what you are doing. For example never bridge a fuse or put a toxic liquid in a mineral water bottle.

Activity 2 Working with words

a) Complete the following sentences with the words from the box below.

1. On construction sites helmets are necessary to reduce the possibility of getting injured when things are •••[1].
2. By using a dust mask you are less likely to contract a •••[2].
3. In case you step on a nail, or something •••[3] onto your foot you are much safer when wearing a pair of safety shoes.
4. Protective goggles prevent a splinter getting into the eyes while •••[4].
5. When grinding or working in noisy areas you should use ear plugs to prevent •••[5].

Use these words:
falling down ... grinding ... lung disease ... hearing damage ... falls

b) Translate the following sentences into English.

1. Arbeitssicherheit ist zum Schutze aller.
2. Schutzeinrichtungen sind zum Schutze aller notwendig.
3. Ein Verbandkasten ist auch im privaten Haushalt wichtig.
4. Einige giftige Gase sind geruchlos.
5. Lärm ist sehr schädlich für das Gehör.
6. Ein sauberer Arbeitsplatz ist ein wichtiger Unfallschutz.
7. Unfallschutz geht alle an.

Activity 3 Talking about safety

a) Answer the questions in full sentences.

1. From where you are at the moment where can you find the nearest first aid box?
2. Describe the way to the nearest first aid box.
3. Why is it important to wear protective equipment?
4. Why should you not fill toxic liquids into a water bottle?
5. Why should safety become a habit?

b) Name further personal protective equipment. Describe where and why you have to use it.

Safety Signs

Safety signs are intended to enhance safety at work. Standardised sign formats identify instructions, prohibitions, warnings and first aid information.

Instruction signs are round and coloured in blue and white. Symbols indicate that the required safety measures are strict mandatory procedures.

Additional information may be used to support the instructions and to clarify the situation. An example is the use of a high visible vest.

Remember: Blue signs indicate mandatory instruction.

Prohibition signs are round signs with a red periphery with a diagonal red bar on a white background. The prohibited action is represented in black.

Additional information may be used to support prohibition. An appropriate prohibition sign must be displayed at a prominent location in the room.

Remember: Red signs indicate a prohibition.

Warning signs are triangular notices featuring black symbols and a black periphery against a yellow background. They should always be placed in highly visible locations. They warn against specific hazards that may be encountered within an individual area.

Additional information may be used to support the warning.

Remember: Yellow signs indicate a hazard or danger.

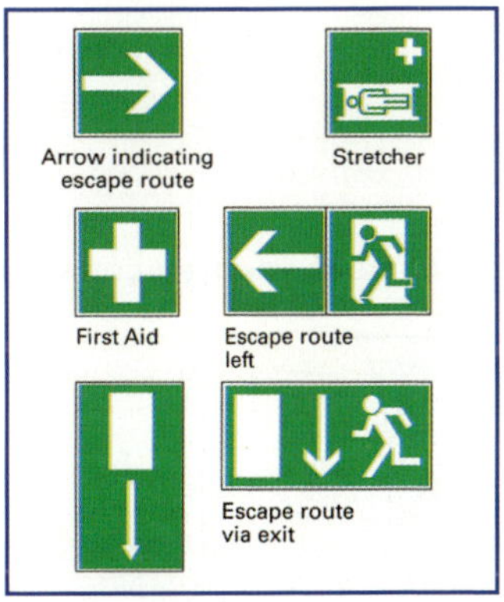

First aid and emergency exit signs are rectangular signs bearing white symbols on a green background. Arrows indicate the directions in which first aid and lifesaving equipment such as stretchers are located. They also identify exits and mark directions for a fast and secure escape from hazardous areas.

Additional symbols next to the arrows may be found. For example, escape by using the door or other exits.

Escape routes must remain clear and unobstructed at all times.

Remember: Green signs indicate a safe condition.

Activity 4 Questions

Answer the questions in full sentences and with your own words.

1. What do warning signs look like? Describe them.
2. What is the difference between prohibition signs and warning signs?
3. What do first aid and emergency signs identify?
4. Where are warning signs located and why?
5. How do you know which specific hazard they warn against?

First aid

This part is not meant to provide people with comprehensive or professional advice on how to treat casualties.

First aid is one of those things that you hope you will never need, but is a good thing to know in case such a situation arises. Therefore it is recommended to visit a first aid course. Local first aid organisations offer these courses regularly. During the courses you will learn how to treat wounds, what to do in case of unconsciousness, how to place somebody in the recovery position and much more.

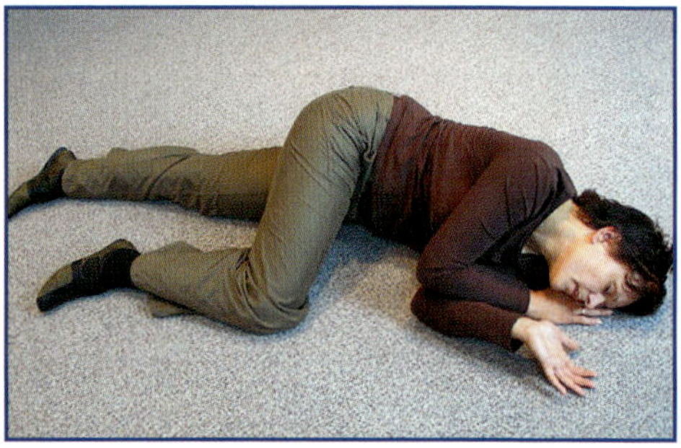

Recovery position

The first rule in first aid is safety. When assisting someone else do not become the second casualty. For instance, do not enter a burning building to rescue someone. And if you are not a good swimmer do not enter deep water to rescue someone who is drowning. Make sure that you are not doing more harm than good.

First aid is defined as:
– treatment for preserving life
– treatment for minimizing the consequence of injury
– treatment of minor injuries

In case you find yourself with the need to give first aid to somebody you have to pay attention to some important steps to take:

1. Ensure rescuer safety.
2. Remove victim from danger.
3. Give first aid.
4. Call for help.

Unit 4

Inside the first aid kit

Do you know where to find the next first aid kit? And would you know how to use it?

The employer should provide materials and facilities needed to ensure that first aid is available at all times. The minimum level of first aid equipment is a suitably stocked and identified first aid container.

Here you can find some examples of contents of a first aid kit:

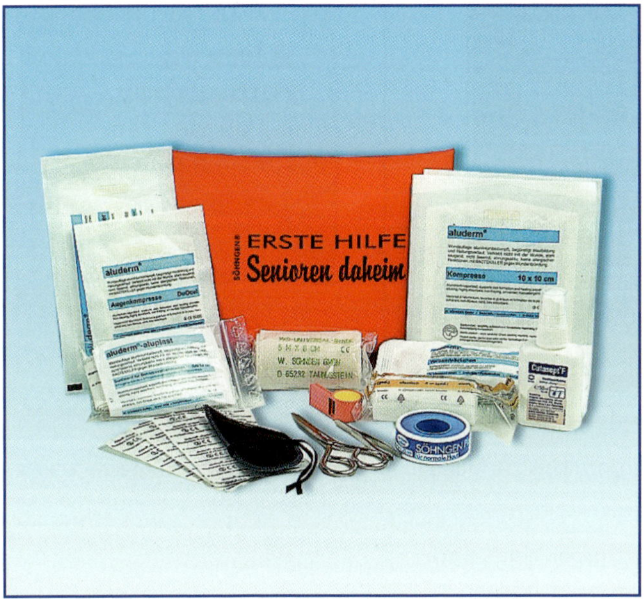

1. sterile gauze swab
2. tweezers
3. scissors
4. cold pack
5. adhesive tape
6. adhesive bandage
7. cotton wool wad
8. safety pins
9. povidon-iodine pads
10. latex gloves
11. space blanket
12. gauze bandage

Remember, the sterile items of the first aid kit expire after some time. So, to be on the safe side, you better check its expiry date from time to time.

Activity 5 Understanding the text

Complete the sentences and copy them in your exercise book.

1. In first aid courses you will learn how to treat . . . .
2. The employer should provide materials and facilities. . . .
3. The sterile items of the first aid kit do . . . . . .
4. Many injuries could be prevented if people were . . . .
5. Ensure rescuer . . .
6. Remove victim . . . .
7. Give first aid and then call . . . . .

The fire extinguisher

In case of fire, would you know what to do? Are you sure where to find the next fire extinguisher and would you know how to use it?

Before using the fire extinguisher, be sure to read the instructions before it's too late. Although there are many different types of fire extinguisher, all of them operate in a similar manner.

Always remember:

1. Pull ring pin.
2. Aim nozzle at base of flame.
3. Squeeze trigger.

Here are the classifications of a fire extinguisher as found in Germany. Classification means which type of fire you can use it for.

Class A = ordinary combustibles: wood, paper, cloth, trash
Class B = flammable liquids: oil, gasoline, paint, lacquer
Class C = gases: ethane, natural gas, hydrogen
Caution: when used on electrical equipment.
1000 Volts maximum; Distance 1 meter minimum.

Activity 6 Working with words

Complete the following text with the words from the box below.

A typical fire extinguisher contains 10 •••1 of extinguishing power. This could be less if it has already been partially •••2. Always read the •••3 that come with the fire extinguisher beforehand and get •••4 with its parts. It is recommended by fire prevention experts that you get •••5 training before operating a fire extinguisher. Most local fire departments offer this service. Once the fire is out, don't •••6 away! Watch the area for a few minutes in case it reignites. •••7 or replace the extinguisher immediately after use.

Use these words:

discharged ... hands-on ... walk ... instructions ... familiarized ... refill ... seconds

Activity 7 How to use a fire extinguisher

Match the words from the box to the corresponding pictures.

Use these words:

a) do not waste extinguishing powder by trying;

b) do not return used cylinders to its place;

c) discharge with the wind, start from the bottom of the fire;

d) do not fight large fires with a single cylinder;

e) fight burning liquids from top with a wide stream of powder;

f) replace used cylinders to service immediately;

g) do not discharge against the wind;

h) do not discharge at once, keep some powder in reserve;

i) fight large fires with assistance;

j) do not fight burning liquids with a single stream

Activity 8 Questions

Answer the following questions.

1. What do you have to be sure of before using a fire extinguisher?
2. What is the minimum distance reguired when a fire extinguisher is used on electrical equipment?
3. What do you have to pay attention to when fighting burning liquids?
4. For how many seconds does the fire extinguisher contain extinguishing powder?
5. What do you have to pay attention to after using a fire extinguisher?

Activity 9 Fill a form

a) Fill in an accident or incident report by copying the following form into your exercise book.

b) Tell your neighbour or class about the accident or incident.

		ACCIDENT/INCIDENT REPORT	Safety Office **494-2495**
PERSONAL	**Surname:**	**First name:**	**Date:**
	Home Address:		
	Department:	**Phone:**	
INCIDENT	**Date, Time and Location of Incident:**	**Name and Phone of Witnesses:**	
	Describe the incident in detail:		
	When and to whom was the incident reported?	**Did the incident result in an early departure from work?** ☐ Yes ☐ No	
INJURY	**Describe Injuries:**		
	Briefly describe medical treatment, if needed:		
	Will the injury result in time away from work beyond the day of the incident? ☐ Yes ☐ No	**Will further treatment be necessary?** ☐ Yes ☐ No	
Date:	**Person involved in Incident:**		

Activity 10 Comprehension

True or false? Correct the statements that are wrong.

1. Once the fire is out you can walk away.
2. In case of fire you better get out, stay out and call 112.
3. Aim at the base of fire, not at the flames.
4. Watch the area for a few minutes in case of reignition.
5. There is no need to read the instructions on a fire extinguisher.
6. It is recommended to get hand on training before operating a fire extinguisher.

Vocabulary Unit 4

absent-minded	geistesabwesend, selbstvergessen
accident source	Unfallursache
act of god	höhere Gewalt
adhesive bandage	Wundpflaster
adhesive tape	Haftklebeband
to aim	anvisieren
appropriate	entsprechend
assessment	Abschätzung, Bewertung
beforehand	im Voraus, vorher
bench grinder	Schleifbock
breakage	Bruch
to bridge a fuse	eine Sicherung überbrücken
casualty	verunglückte Person
caustic	ätzend
cold pack	Kühlbeutel
combustibles	feuergefährliche Güter
cotton wool wad	Wattebausch
to discharge	entladen
distinctive features	ausgeprägte Charakterzüge
electrical installation	elektrische Schaltungen
emergency blanket	Rettungsdecke
emergency exit	Fluchtweg
ethyne	Azetylen
extinguishing powder	Löschpulver, Löschmittel
eye pad	Augenklappe
fatigue	Ermattung, Ermüdung
fire extinguisher	Feuerlöscher
fire prevention expert	Feuerexperte
first aid dressing	Wundschnellverband
first aid guide	Erste-Hilfe-Broschüre
first aid kit	Erste-Hilfe-Kasten
to foster	fördern, pflegen
gauze bandage	Mullbinde
grinder	Schleifmaschine
grinding disc	Schleifscheibe
guard screen	Schutzschild
hand-on training	Praktikum
hazard	Gefährdung, Risiko
human error	menschlicher Fehler
hydrogen	Wasserstoff
immediately	sofort, unverzüglich
incident	Begebenheit, Ereignis
injury	Verletzung, Beschädigung
instructions	Anleitung, Anweisung
iodine pad	Jodtupfer
laquer	Lack
latex gloves	Latexschutzhandschuhe
mandatory	zwingend, vorgeschrieben
natural gas	Erdgas
negligence	Fahrlässigkeit
nozzle	Strahlrohr, Spritzdüse
paint	Farben
periphery	Umfeld, Rand
professional advice	fachlicher Rat
prohibition	Verbot
protective equipment	Schutzausrüstung
protective goggles	Schutzbrille
to recharge	wiederaufladen, wiederbefüllen
recovery position	stabile Seitenlage
to reignite	wieder anzünden
rescuer	Retter, Retterin
resealable plastic bag	wiederverschließbare Plastiktüte
ring pin	Sicherungsstift mit Ring
safety pin	Sicherheitsnadel
safety sign	Sicherheitsschild
safety switches	Notausschalter
secure escape	Fluchtweg, Notausgang
sissors (a pair of)	Schere
splinter	Splitter
standard dressing	Verbandpäckchen
sterile gauze swab	Mulltupfer
sterility	Keimfreiheit, Sterilität
stretcher	Krankentrage
sulphuric acid	Schwefelsäure
toxic substance	Giftstoff
triangular bandage	Dreiecktuch
trigger	Abzugshahn
unconsciousness	Bewusstlosigkeit
unforeseeable	unerwartet
unpredictable	unvorhersehbar, unberechenbar
vinyl gloves	Schutzhandschuhe

5 Computer Hardware

In this unit you will learn something about computer hardware and what you may do in case your sound does not work correctly.

Components of a personal computer system

Activity 1 Parts of a computer system

a) Find the English expressions for the PC components shown in the picture on page 50 and assign them to the numbers 1 to 10.

b) For which of these expressions is there also a German word?

c) Find as much technical data as possible for the following components of a PC system: a) computer, b) monitor, c) printer, d) USB stick. Do you know the most recent figures?

Activity 2 Abbreviations

When talking about computers we often use abbreviations. What do the following abbreviations stand for?

1. RAM
2. CD-ROM
3. Mbps
4. CPU
5. GB
6. DVD
7. BIOS
8. PC
9. SATA
10. ISDN
11. MPEG
12. GHz
13. USB
14. W-LAN

CPU with cooling fan

Activity 3 Working with words

Find words that fit the following definitions.

1. Device that provides hardcopies.
2. Part of the computer that can store many gigabytes of information.
3. The "heart" of a computer.
4. Something you need to play certain games on a computer with (e.g. car races).
5. The part of a computer that looks like a television and that shows information.
6. Computer equipment that can copy texts or images from paper onto the monitor screen.
7. Small portable device that you can store huge amounts of data on.
8. Electronic device that links different networks or parts of a network.
9. Circuit board in a computer that you connect your microphone, headphone or loudspeakers to.
10. A small device that you move by hand in order to change the position of the cursor on the screen.

Inside a computer

Have you ever opened the casing of a computer? The photography shows a computer from the inside with its most important parts: the motherboard, the power supply and the disk drives.

The motherboard is the main circuit board inside the computer. It contains the CPU (central processing unit), the memory, the system bus, the controllers and the expansion slots which hold network cards or graphic cards, for example.

The Central Processing Unit (CPU), also called the microprocessor, is the 'brain' of the computer. This integrated circuit contains millions of transistors on a small piece of silicon and is responsible for all the logic operations that a computer performs. The unit consists of three main parts namely the control unit, the arithmetic logic unit (ALU) and the registers. Microprocessors handle a wide range of different tasks.

A small block of ROM (Read Only Memory), which is separate from the main system memory, is a very important part on the motherboard. It contains the computer's BIOS (Basic Input / Output System) and is needed at start-up. The BIOS first checks if the most important components function properly and then searches for an operating system (OS) and loads it into the main memory.

The main memory of a PC system is a block of chips called RAM (random access memory). While the microprocessor is working, it can read data from and write data to any storage position of this memory at any time. In other words RAM can be accessed randomly, and therefore it is very fast. However, RAM is a temporary memory and that means its information is lost when the computer is switched off. The more RAM a system contains, the more information can be handled and the more programs can be run at one time.

A bus in a computer can be considered as a highway on which data travel. Buses inside a computer connect its internal components to the processor and the main memory. They are either made of a collection of parallel wires put together in a cable or simply a number of parallel conductor lines on the main board.

Bus systems in computers have three components: the address bus, the data bus and the control bus. The data bus is the pathway where the actual data travels, whereas the address bus carries information which tells the data where to go. The control bus is needed by the system to coordinate how data and address signals travel across the bus.

The amount of data that a bus can transfer at one time is measured in bits and called the data bus width. A 32-bit bus, for example, is able to transfer 32 bits of a data at one time, a 64-bit bus can do the same with 64 bits of an information and so on. The bus width has nothing to do with the speed at which the data travel. The speed of the data in a computer is measured in Hertz (MHz, GHz) and refers to the number of operations that the CPU is able to carry out per second.

Activity 4 Comprehension

Do the following tasks using your own words as far as possible.

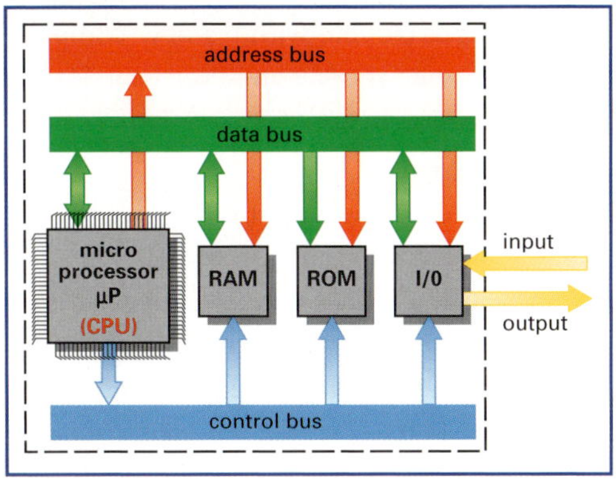

1. Which important components of a computer are on the motherboard?
2. Why is the CPU also called the brain of a computer?
3. What is a microprocessor made of?
4. What does a computer need the BIOS for?
5. Explain the difference between RAM and ROM.
6. What is the function of a bus in a computer system?
7. What is meant by data bus width?
8. What does a bus in a computer look like?
9. How do we measure the speed of a computer?
10. Only the data bus in a computer is a so called bi-directional bus. With the help of the drawing explain the difference between a uni-directional and a bi-directional bus.

Activity 5 Working with words

Find words in the text that match the following explanations.

1. board with electronic components which are connected by thin lines of metal
2. the information that are processed by a computer
3. used in a computer system to store information
4. set of programs that control the basic functions of a computer

Activity 6 Modems

Copy the following text about modems into your exercise book and complete it with words from the box below.

Modem is formed from the words modulator and •••1. It lets a computer transmit and •••2 information over telephone lines. Modems •••3 analogue data into digital data so that computers can read them. They also convert •••4 into analogue data so that it can be •••5 over telephone lines. Computer users need a modem whenever they want their computers to be connected to outside •••6 such as the Internet or online •••7. Modems can transmit data at different •••8, but faster modems are always able to •••9 with slower modems at the •••10 shared speed.

communicate ... networks ... highest ... transmitted ... demodulator ... speeds ... services ... receive ... digital data ... convert

Unit 5

Trouble with the sound card

Introducing the situation

Bert has got trouble with his new computer. Therefore he is calling his friend Alan who has been an experienced computer user for many years.

ALAN Hello.

BERT Hi Alan. This is Bert calling.

ALAN Hi Bert, how are you doing?

BERT I'm fine, thanks. But my computer is not.

ALAN Ah, you've got trouble with your computer. What's the problem?

BERT You know, I bought this used computer four weeks ago and it works quite well, besides the sound. Sometimes it's okay but then I simply hear nothing or it sounds like "Mickey Mouse".

ALAN I see. Have you ever tried to use your DVD drive simply as a CD player?

BERT Yes, I have. That always works. The fault occurs when I use my encyclopaedia DVD and start a video clip or a sound clip. It can also happen when I simply open a wavesound file.

ALAN Okay. I think I should drop in at your place and have a look at it.

2 hours later Alan arrives at Bert's place.

Are you experienced with computers? What would you suggest to do?

BERT Hello Alan. Thanks a lot that you have come so quickly.

ALAN Never mind. You know, I always like to help a good friend. … Let's see what we can do. First, we have to start the computer and then we should check if the driver for your sound card has been installed correctly.

BERT I've checked that already. I have also reinstalled the driver but nothing has changed.

ALAN All right. Then I suggest changing the sound card. I've brought a new one with me.

BERT That means that we have to open the computer. So, what tools do we need?

ALAN Just a Phillips screwdriver.

A few minutes later the two men have removed the old sound card.

ALAN Please hand over the new sound card. … Okay it's mounted. Now, let's close the casing and try if it works.

BERT Right. Now we have to reinsert all plugs and cables, don't we?

ALAN Yes, and then, after booting the computer, the driver for the new sound card must be installed. It's on the CD-ROM which you'll find somewhere in the box that contained the new sound card…

Activity 7 Comprehension

The following statements are all wrong. Correct them.

1. Alan has just started to work with computers.
2. Bert has bought a brand new computer.
3. Bert has got trouble with his DVD drive.
4. Bert takes his computer to Alan.
5. At first Alan suggests installing a new driver for the sound card.
6. Bert has already installed a new driver.
7. The two friends need a ring spanner to open the casing of the computer.
8. They can use the old driver for the new sound card.

Changing a sound card

User's Manual

Hardware Installation

CAUTION

Static electricity can severely damage electronic parts. **Take these precautions:**

- Before touching any electronic parts, drain the static electricity from your body. You can do this by touching the internal metal frame of your computer while it's unplugged.
- Don't remove a card from the anti-static container it is shipped in until you're ready to install it. When you remove a card from your computer, place it back in its container.
- Don't let your clothes touch any electronic parts.
- When handling a card, hold it by its edges, and avoid touching its circuitry.

Before you begin

Before installing the sound card and the software that goes with it, make sure your computer meets the system requirements.

Prepare your computer for installation

Before working on your computer, make sure the power of the computer and any connected equipment is turned off.

Select a vacant expansion slot

Insert your sound card

Remove the cover for the slot you intend to use and save the screw for the mounting bracket. Then, pick up the sound card and position it over the expansion slot you have chosen. Push the card firmly in until it's fully seated in the slot. Replace the screw to secure the bracket of the sound card to the computer chassis.

Activity 8 Changing a sound card

Describe in your own words what the two friends have to do in order to change the sound card.

Start like this:

First, they have to check if the computer meets the system requirements. Then ...

Activity 9 Translation

Translate the following sentences into English.

1. Alan hat viel Erfahrung mit Computern.
2. Bert hat den gebrauchten Computer vor vier Wochen gekauft.
3. Bert hat Probleme mit dem Sound seines Computers.
4. Der Fehler tritt nur auf, wenn er eine Datei auf einer DVD öffnet.
5. Wir müssen zuerst prüfen, ob der Treiber für die Soundkarte richtig installiert ist.
6. Alan schlägt vor, die Soundkarte zu wechseln.
7. Wir benötigen nur einen Kreuzschlitzschraubendreher, um das Gehäuse zu öffnen.
8. Wo finde ich den Treiber für die neue Soundkarte?
9. Hast du alle Stecker und Kabel wieder angeschlossen?
10. Das System hat die neue Hardware entdeckt.

Activity 10 Mounting a second hard disk drive (HDD)

The following text describes the single steps to install a second HDD in your computer in case you need more storage space. The description, however, is not in the correct order and all the full stops are missing. Write down the instruction correctly.

Boot the computer and if necessary install the new driver slide the new drive into the drive slot and secure the drive in place with screws remove the cover from your computer make sure that you have set the jumpers at the new HDD correctly the second HDD must be connected as slave connect the 40-pin EIDE cable to the back of the new drive turn your computer off and unplug it from the mains make sure that the red edge of the IDE cable is connected to Pin 1 on the new hard disk drive unplug all peripheral devices attached to the computer push the power supply cable connector firmly into the power in connector remove the cover plate from the drive slot

Vocabulary Unit 5

abbreviation	**Abkürzung**
access	**Zugriff**
address bus	**Adressbus**
amount	**Menge**
arithmetic logic unit [ə'rɪθmatɪk]	**Rechenwerk**
to assign	**zuweisen, zuordnen**
to attach	**an-, beiheften**
to avoid	**vermeiden**
besides	**außer, abgesehen von**
bi-directional	**bidirektional, in zwei Richtungen gehend**
bracket	**Klammer**
brain	**Gehirn**
bus width [wɪdθ]	**Busbreite**
casing	**Gehäuse**
central processing unit	**Zentraleinheit**
chassis	**Chassis, Montagerahmen**
to check	**überprüfen**
circuit board	**Leiterplatte**
circuitry ['sɜːkɪtri]	**Schaltkreise, Schaltung**
collection	**(An)Sammlung**
component	**Baustein, Baugruppe**
conductor	**Leiter**
conductor line	**Leiterbahn**
to connect	**verbinden**
connector	**Steckverbindung**
to consider (as)	**betrachten (als)**
to consist of	**bestehen aus**
to contain	**beinhalten**
container	**Behälter, Behältnis**
control bus	**Steuerbus**
control unit	**Steuereinheit**
controller	**Steuerbaustein**
to convert	**umwandeln**
cooling fan	**Ventilator**
to coordinate	**koordinieren**
cover	**Abdeckung**
cover plate	**Abdeckplatte**
to damage	**beschädigen**
data [dertə]	**Daten**
decision	**Entscheidung**
description	**Beschreibung**
device	**Gerät**
to drain	***hier:* ableiten**
drawing	**Zeichnung**
drive (n)	**Laufwerk**
drive slot	**Laufwerksschacht**
driver	**Treiber**
to drop in	**vorbeikommen**
edge	**Kante, Rand**
electronic part	**elektronisches Bauteil**
to enable	**ermöglichen**
to enclose	**beifügen**
encyclopaedia [ɪnsəɪklə'piːdiə]	**Lexikon, Enzyklopädie**
equipment	**Ausrüstung**
expansion slot	**Steckplatz für Steckkarte**
experienced	**erfahren**
explanation	**Erklärung**
expression	**Ausdruck**
file	**Datei**
firmly	**fest**
to function	**funktionieren**
graphic card	**Graphikkarte**
to handle	**handhaben, bearbeiten**
hardcopy	**(Papier-) Ausdruck**
headphone	**Kopfhörer**
image	**Bild**
to install	**installieren**
instruction	**Anweisung**
integrated circuit	**integrierter Schaltkreis**
to intend	**beabsichtigen**
internal	**innere(n)**
to link	**verbinden**
mains	**(Strom)netz**
to measure	**messen**
memory	**Speicher**
metal frame	**Metallrahmen**
microphone	**Mikrofon**
to modify	**erneuern**
motherboard	**Hauptplatine**
to mount	**montieren**
mounting bracket	**Befestigungsklammer**
namely	**nämlich**
operation system	**Betriebssystem**
pathway	**Weg, Pfad**
to perform	**durchführen, leisten**
peripheral device [pə'rɪfərəl]	**Peripheriegerät**
plug	**Stecker**
power supply	**Stromversorgung**

Vocabulary Unit 5

power supply cable	**Verbindung für die Stromversorgung**
precautions	**Vorsichtsmaßnahmen**
to prepare	**vorbereiten**
properly	**richtig**
to provide	**liefern, bereitstellen**
random access memory	**Speicher mit wahlfreiem Zugriff**
randomly	**wahlfrei**
range (a wide ~)	**eine große Anzahl**
to receive	**empfangen**
recent	**hier: neu**
to refer to	**verweisen auf**
register	**Register, Speicher**
to reinsert	**wieder einstecken**
to remove	**entfernen**
requirement	**Anforderung**
responsible	**verantwortlich**
screen	**Bildschirm**
to search	**suchen**
to seat	***hier:* einpassen**
to secure	**(ab)sichern**
to select	**auswählen**
separate	**getrennt**
setting	**Einstellung**
severe [sɪ'vɪə(r)]	**schwer, ernsthaft**
to ship	**verfrachten**
silicon	**Silizium**
slave	**Sklave**
to slide	**schieben**
speed	**Geschwindigkeit**
start-up	**Start, Inbetriebnahme**
static	**elektrostatisch**
static electricity	**statische Aufladung**
storage space	**Speicherplatz**
to store	**speichern**
to suggest	**vorschlagen**
telephone line	**Telefonleitung**
temporary	**zeitweilig**
to touch	**berühren**
transfer	**Übertragung**
to transmit	**übertragen**
uni-directional	**in eine Richtung gehend**
to unplug	**herausziehen, entfernen**
vacant ['veɪkənt]	**frei**
via [vaɪə]	**über**
whereas	**während**

Additional Vocabulary Computer Hardware

brightness	**Helligkeit**
cable connector	**Kabelverbinder**
clock	**Taktgenerator**
counter	**Zähler**
crash	**Systemabsturz**
dot-matrix printer	**Nadeldrucker**
extensible	**erweiterbar**
frame	**Rahmen**
hub	**Hub, Netzknoten**
interface	**Schnittstelle, Anschluss**
malfunction	**Funktionsstörung**
mouse button	**Maustaste**
mouse pointer	**Mauszeiger**
network	**Netzwerk**
to network	**vernetzen**
network	**Netzwerk**
optical fibre ['fəɪba(r)]	**Lichtwellenleiter**
port	**Anschluss(buchse)**
portable	**tragbar**
power cord	**Netzkabel**
troubleshooting	**Störungssuche**
unplugged	**nicht ange-schlossen**
user's manual	**Benutzerhandbuch**

6 Software

This unit introduces computer software. It describes some of its advantages and disadvantages and shows an example where software is absolutely necessary today.

Kinds of computer software

Introducing the situation

Kristin has started her apprenticeship as a technical draftswoman. She has just bought her first computer because a big part of her job involves working with it. The shop where she bought the computer offers a lecture on computers for free, which Kristin attends. The instructor is informing the participants about software.

"Good evening Ladies and Gentlemen. Welcome to our course tonight. I will give you a short overview of the software a computer needs and application software that can be installed on it. Each computer needs an OS. The two letters stand for operating system. The operating system is necessary to tell your computer what to do. It is a kind of communication language between you and your computer.
The operating system makes it also possible to handle the peripheral devices, such as printer, mouse, monitor and so on. The advantage of an OS is, that you, as a user do not need much technical knowledge because the software handles input as well as output.
The three most commonly used operating systems are Windows versions designed by Microsoft, MAC OS versions designed by Apple Macintosh and Linux, which is based on Unix and available for free.
If you use the Internet a lot, and you want to protect yourself from certain web sites or against hackers, you should install a firewall. Like the name says it works like a wall against – in your case – attacks from the world wide web.
Application software is necessary to work on special tasks. Normally you buy standardized software. This kind of software has been developed for a wide market. It is copied million times and sold everywhere in the world. This is the reason why it is quite cheap.
Standard application software, for example, includes word processing, which is necessary for writing letters or designing leaflets. Kids find it a lot more interesting to do their learning and preparations for school with the help of the computer. Maybe they have to do a presentation or need to do some calculations. Then they can use a spreadsheet program or a presentation graphics package. If you want to use the Internet or exchange e-mails with people all over the world, you need communication software to use an online service."

Activity 1 Vocabulary

Match the English with the German words. Copy the list into your exercise book.

1. operating system
2. application software
3. input
4. spreadsheet
5. word processing
6. peripheral devices
7. presentation graphics

a) Tabellenkalkulation
b) Textverarbeitung
c) Anschlussgeräte
d) Anwendersoftware
e) Präsentationsgrafik
f) Eingabe
g) Betriebssystem

Activity 2 Definitions

Find words in the text that fit the following definitions.

1. explaining what the subject is about without giving all the details
2. getting things ready before you actually start
3. letter to be sent without envelope and stamp
4. paper with information about a special subject on it
5. network over which data can be sent around the world

Activity 3 Questions

Translate the following questions into English and ask your neighbour them. He/she should answer in complete sentences. Switch roles.

1. Welches Betriebssystem ist auf deinem Rechner installiert?
2. Welche Anwendersoftware hast du installiert und was machst du damit?
3. Welche Software hast du zwar auf deinem PC installiert, aber noch nie genutzt?
4. Wie viel Zeit verbringst du beruflich vor deinem Computer?
5. Wozu nutzt du das Internet?

Activity 4 Making predictions

Work with a partner and discuss how important computers will be in the future. Think of aspects like computers at school and at work, communication, telecommuting, spare time, everyday life, and society. Present your ideas to the class.

Use phrases like these:

do you really think … I suppose … probably … I am sure … do you really expect … I think

Here is one example:

I suppose more people will communicate via e-mail while they are sitting comfortably at home in front of their computer. They can get an answer to their e-mails very fast, not to say immediately.

The computer system at Kristin's company

Introducing the situation

Kristin thinks the information about software has been quite interesting. At work she meets Ms Brown their system administrator, who is telling her more about software in general and especially about the software they use at the company.

KRISTIN Good morning, Ms Brown.

MS BROWN Hello, Kristin. Nice to meet our new apprentice. You are interested in our computer system?

KRISTIN Yes, that's right. I bought a new computer and attended a course about software. I would like to know a bit more about the computer system at our company.

MS BROWN It is not typical for a young woman. Is it?

KRISTIN I think that nowadays it is almost impossible to do your job without knowing at least something about computers.

MS BROWN You are quite right. Okay then, let's get started …

Ms Brown shows Kristin around and explains the company's computer system to her.

MS BROWN … Our company has a so-called Intranet. This network connects the workstations in our company. It requires a reliable software that can easily be handled by the employees. Another important aspect of software are the costs. You must consider that software changes rapidly and has to be updated regularly. Sometimes we have to buy a completely new software after a short period of time. That means each employee needs retraining.
Software offers a lot of possibilities. For example, every employee has a password. It allows or refuses access to files and data. So data protection is guaranteed according to the needs and tasks of each single employee and customer of our company. Of course there are security risks and the system is not totally safe against attacks from outside.

KRISTIN Isn't there any system that is more reliable?

MS BROWN Maybe there is. Linux is an operating system that has been developed in Finland. Its security standard is higher. The "I love you" virus, which caused quite a lot of damage a couple of years ago, could not affect it. But so far it is not in wide use in business.

Activity 5 Understanding the text

Read the following statements. Are they true or not? Correct the false ones.

1. Kristin is a trainee.
2. Kristin is used to working with computers.
3. The company has its own internet.
4. The company's workstations are networked.
5. Hardware has to be replaced often.
6. The company must buy new software once a year.
7. Some employees get a password.
8. The trainees have access to all data.
9. The employees must regularly attend courses to refresh their knowledge.
10. The company's system eliminates security problems.

Activity 6 Working with words

Replace the words in bold type with one of the following words in the box below.

1. The Intranet **connects** the workstations in our company.
2. Each **employee** needs retraining.
3. Software must be **updated** regularly.
4. There is the possibility to allow or to refuse people **access** to files.
5. It requires **reliable** software.
6. You must consider that software changes **rapidly**.
7. Kristin **attended** a course about software.
8. Ms Brown met the new **apprentice**.
9. Our specialized software **offers** a lot of possibilities.

Use these words:

renewed ... stable ... staff member ...frequently ... took part in ... links ...
trainee ... provides ... admission

Activity 7

Find words in the text that fit the following definitions.

1. to go to a course
2. something that is not normal
3. to say 'no' to something
4. program that can destroy data on your computer
5. somebody who buys something from a company
6. to tell somebody something so that she/he can easily understand
7. a combination of numbers and letters that gives access to a computer
8. to design new products

CAD – Kristin's new subject

A week later Kristin comes home from vocational school. She looks through the worksheets she has got at school. There are some about the basics of CAD (computer aided design). She starts reading.

The basics of CAD

With CAD you can make two-dimensional drawings or create three-dimensional objects. You can store and save your drawings in files. You can bring them back on-screen and change them, for example, or use parts of them again for further drawings.

There are different possibilities to put in commands. At the top of the screen you can find the menu bar. At the bottom of the screen you have a command line. The more commands you know by heart the faster you can work. On the left side of the screen you can place a toolkit. In the lower left corner you see the coordinate system icon. CAD programs use the WCS (world coordinate system) that ensures an exact and precise drawing method.

There are drawing commands for creating lines, circles, rectangles and so on. A very important aspect of CAD, however, is editing. It offers a trained user a lot of possibilities to draw quickly.

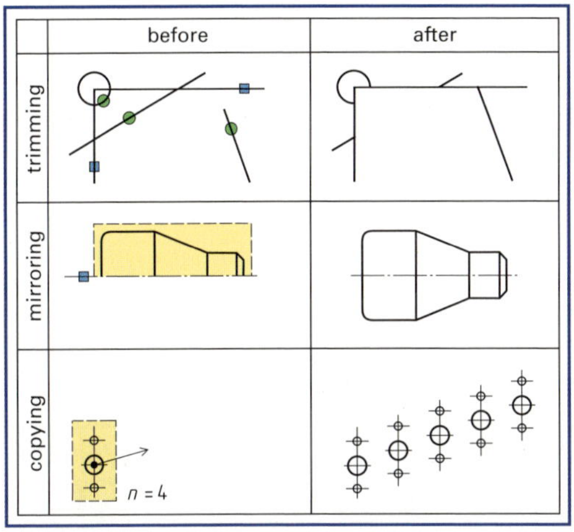

"Trimming" enables you to take away parts of lines in a drawing or to make them longer to the point where the lines meet another object. The command "Mirroring" makes the objects move around an axis. "Copying" leaves the object in its place but creates the same object at any other place in your drawing.

CAD drawings are made up of different layers. You could, of course, create your drawing completely on the screen like on a piece of paper. It is, however, much easier to organize the drawing by using layers. These layers are like transparent sheets which are put on top of each other. All together they show the finished drawing.

You can turn layers on or off. You can use each layer separately. You can assign each layer to a special line type, colour and thickness of line. This helps you while working on-screen. One of the main aspects, however, to organize layers is the thickness of lines for plotting the drawing.

A great advantage of CAD programs is the fact that they are vector oriented. If you have got e. g. 600 mm on screen, you also have got 600 mm on paper. It is therefore possible to program a CNC machine (CNC = computerized numerical control) with data from the CAD drawing. Companies can save a lot of money by using CAD programs.

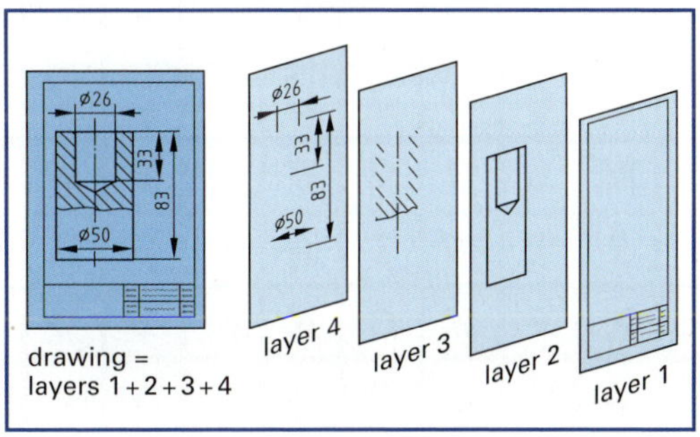

Activity 8 Understanding the text

Answer the following questions.

1. What are the advantages of CAD according to the text?
2. There are different possibilities to put in commands. Name them.
3. What are layers in a CAD program?
4. What is the advantage of using layers?
5. What does editing mean? Find examples.
6. What is a vector-oriented program?
7. Why can companies save a lot of money when they use CAD programs?

Activity 9 Working with words

Find the correct words in the text. Copy the sentences into your exercise book.

1. To create lines and circles there are •••[1].
2. At the bottom of the screen you can find the •••[2].
3. At the top of the screen is the •••[3].
4. CAD drawings are made up of •••[4].
5. It is possible to •••[5] a CNC machine with •••[6] from the CAD drawing.

Activity 10 Word search

Twelve words from the text are hidden in the following chart. They can occur in all directions.

a) Find the words and copy them into your exercise book.

b) Use each word in a sentence.

K	P	M	N	Z	O	J	S	C	V	I	C	O	N	X	P	E	W
P	T	Q	D	J	M	Z	F	H	L	I	O	B	Y	O	M	T	L
I	R	V	A	L	Y	C	F	Y	R	I	M	R	T	B	C	E	A
B	I	O	A	E	A	W	I	C	C	V	M	W	P	I	Y	E	C
L	M	C	G	J	O	Y	L	Y	O	P	A	O	A	G	E	H	I
V	M	L	Q	R	V	E	E	W	R	W	N	E	E	R	C	S	R
O	I	T	W	I	A	L	S	R	D	G	D	H	L	N	L	V	E
Y	N	P	K	C	X	M	D	G	C	U	T	J	M	O	H	C	M
A	G	N	L	P	Y	G	S	F	A	O	X	K	E	Y	V	A	U
D	M	T	D	R	I	H	L	N	D	I	M	E	N	S	I	O	N

2D and 3D

In the text about CAD two and three dimensional drawings are mentioned. The following list shows some of the most important shapes. The related adjectives occur in technical texts quite often.

2 D SHAPES			3 D SHAPES		
Shape	**Noun**	**Adjective**	**Shape**	**Noun**	**Adjective**
	square	square	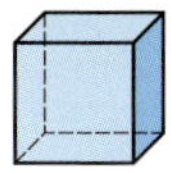	cube	cubical
	rectangle	rectangular		rectangular solid	rectangular
	circle	circular		cylinder	cylindrical
	semicircle	semicircular	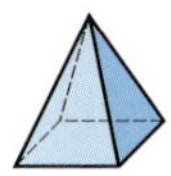	pyramid	pyramidical
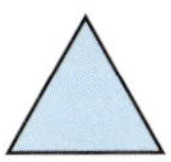	triangle	triangular	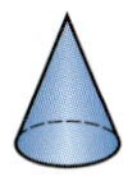	cone	conical
	rhombus	rhomboid		sphere	spherical
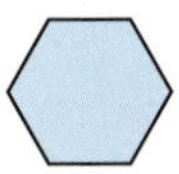	hexagon	hexagonal	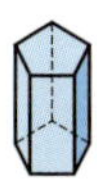	prism	prismatic

Activity 10 Practice

a) Draw 2 D or 3 D shapes according to the following instructions.

1. Draw a square 40 mm by 40 mm. On the top there is a triangle with a height of 20 mm. The angle at the top of the triangle is exactly 90 degrees. The two sides connecting it to the square have equal lengths. At the bottom of the square, 10 mm from the right side line, there is the right side line of a rectangle, which is 20 mm high. It is 12 mm wide.
2. Draw a rectangular solid. It is 86 mm by 15 mm by 10 mm. On top of it there is a cylinder 20 mm high and its diameter is 10 mm. It is in the middle. On each side of the cylinder is a cube with a length of 10 mm.

b) Make drawings with the 2 D and 3 D shapes. Ask your neighbour to describe them.

Vocabulary Unit 6

access	Zugriff
according to	entsprechend
actually	tatsächlich
administrator	Verwalter, Administrator
admittance	Zulassung, Zugriff
advantage	Vorteil
to affect	beeinträchtigen, (ein)wirken, beeinflussen
angle ['æŋgl]	Winkel
application software	Anwenderprogramm
apprenticeship	Ausbildung
to assign [ə'saɪn]	zuordnen
attack	Angriff
to attend a course	an einem Kurs teilnehmen
at least	wenigstens
at the bottom	unten
at the top	oben
axis	Achse
to be familiar with	vertraut sein mit
by heart	auswendig
CAD (computer aided design)	computergestütztes Zeichnen
CAM (computer aided manufacture)	computergestützte Herstellung
circle	Kreis
circular	kreisförmig
CNC (computer numeric control)	computergestützte Maschinensteuerung
command	Befehl
command line	Befehlszeile
communication software	Datenübertragungssoftware
cone	Kegel
conical	kegelförmig
conclusion	Schlussfolgerung
corner	Ecke
to create	erstellen, erschaffen
cube [kju:b]	Würfel
cubical	würfelförmig
couple of	einige
data ['deɪtə]	Daten
data protection	Datenschutz
damage	Schaden
to damage	beschädigen
to describe	beschreiben
to develop	entwickeln
device [dɪ'vaɪs]	Bauelement, Vorrichtung, Gerät
disadvantage	Nachteil
to draw	zeichnen
drawing	Zeichnung
editing	Editieren (Zeichnungselemente ändern)
employee [ˌɪmplɔɪ'i]	Angestellter
to enable	befähigen, ermöglichen
to enclose	einschließen, beilegen, beifügen, enthalten
enclosed	beiliegend
to ensure	sicher stellen, gewährleisten
envelope	Umschlag
equipment	Ausrüstung, Ausstattung
to exchange	austauschen
to expect	erwarten
file [faɪl]	Datei
to finish	beenden
frequently	häufig, oft
further ['fɜːðə(r)]	weiter, mehr
graphical user interface	graphische Benutzeroberfläche
to handle	handhaben, behandeln
height	Höhe
hexagon	Sechseck
hexagonal	sechseckig
icon	graphisches Symbol
importance	Wichtigkeit
input	Eingabe
knowledge	Wissen
layer	Schicht
length	Länge
menu bar	Menüleiste
mirroring	Spiegeln
to network	vernetzen
to occur	geschehen, auftreten
on-screen	auf dem Bildschirm
on the left side	links
on top of	oben auf, über
operating system	Betriebssystem
output	Ausgabe
overview	Überblick
participant	Teilnehmer

Vocabulary Unit 6

peripheral device	Peripheriegerät, Anschlussgerät
possibility	Möglichkeit
preparation	Vorbereitung
probably	wahrscheinlich
protection	Schutz
quite [kwaɪt]	ziemlich
rectangle	Rechteck
rectangular	rechteckig
rectangular solid	Quader
to refuse [re'fjuːz]	verweigern
reliable [rɪ'laɪəbl]	verlässlich
to replace	ersetzen
risk	Risiko
to save [seɪv]	sichern
screen	Bildschirm
security [sɪ'kjʊərətɪ]	Sicherheit, Schutz
semicircle	Halbkreis
semicircular	halbkreisförmig
separately	getrennt
sheet	Blatt
society	Gesellschaft
spare time [speə(r)]	Freizeit
sphere [sfɪə(r)]	Kugel
spherical	kugelförmig
square	Quadrat, quadratisch
stable	stabil
stamp	Briefmarke
to store	speichern
to suppose	annahmen, vermuten
technical draftswoman	technische Zeichnerin
thickness	Stärke
three-dimensional	dreidimensional
trainee	Auszubildende(r)
transparent	durchsichtig
triangle ['traɪæŋgl]	Dreieck
triangular	dreieckig
trimming	Trimmen
toolkit	Funktionen, Hilfsprogramme
topic	Thema
two-dimensional	zweidimensional
to update	aktualisieren
vocational school	Berufsschule
word processing	Textverarbeitung
worksheet	Arbeitsblatt
workstation	Arbeitsplatz am Computer

Additional Vocabulary

anpassen	to adapt
Betreff	subject
Daten eingeben	to enter data
Datenbank	database
Datenübertragung	data transmission
Echtzeit	real time
Empfänger	recipient
Fehler (techn.)	error
Fehler, Misserfolg	failure
Fehlermeldung	error message
Garantie	warranty
Handbuch	manuel
identifizieren	to identify
kabellos, schnurlos	cordless
kostenlose Software	freeware
lokales Netz, LAN	LAN (local area network)
spionieren	to spy
teilen	to share
verbinden	to link
Verbindung	link
vereinbar	compatible
verschlüsseln	to encrypt
Verschlüsselung	encryption
Virus	virus
vorübergehend	temporarily

7 Power Tools and Machines

In this unit you will get some information about the most common machines and power tools. You will also learn to name the main parts of commonly used power tools and how to handle them properly to avoid accidents. In addition you will learn to understand instruction manuals.

Portable electric power tools

Power tools are very common nowadays, at work and in private households. The following text gives you some information about the most common electrically driven power tools. You will learn to identify them, how to use them properly and how to apply safety measures.

Portable electric power tools

Portable power tools are tools that can be moved from place to place. Some of the most common power tools that we use at work or at home are electrically powered and include electric drills, belt sanders, grinders and circular saws, keyhole saws and electric planes. In addition there is a large variety of cordless tools of which the most popular ones are the cordless drill and screwdriver. Nowadays, there is a special tool for each job, and every year new tools are developed and brought on the market.

The following pictures show a small selection of frequently used power tools.

Activity 1 Tools and their applications

Find the names of the electric tools shown in the pictures with the help of the text and explain what you would do with them.

Activity 2 Matching technical terms

Match the parts of the electric drill according to the numbers and give their German names.

a) drill bit
b) chuck
c) rotating direction switch
d) power cord
e) trigger
f) handle
g) chuck key

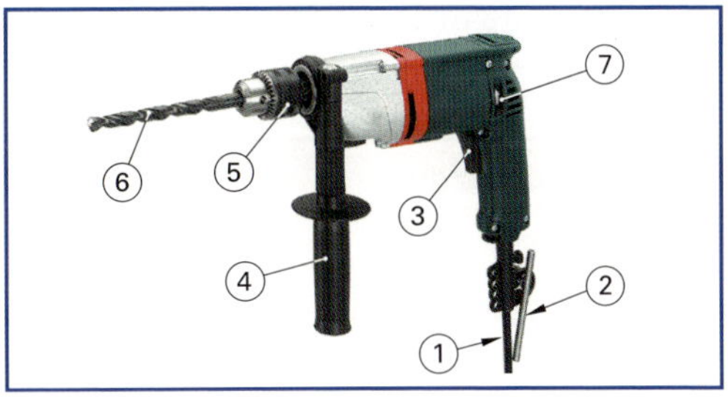

Electric drills

The portable electric drill is probably the most frequently used power tool of all. Although it is especially designed for drilling holes, you can adapt it for different jobs by adding different fitments. Sanding, sawing, screw driving and paint mixing are examples of possible applications. Nowadays there is a large variety of electric drills. It is possible to drill holes of up to 25 mm diameter.

The revolutions per minute (rpm) and the power which the drill delivers are most important when choosing a drill for a certain job. The speed of a drill motor has to be decreased with the increase in size of the drill bit. The larger units are designed to operate larger cutting tools or to drill in hard materials. Each of these factors requires a slower speed. Modern electronically controlled electric drills are equipped with an infinitely variable speed control. It allows the adjustment of the revolutions per minute to the required cutting speed.

The chuck is the clamping device into which the drill bit is inserted. Nearly all electric drills are equipped with a three-jaw chuck. The more modern electric drills have a hand-type chuck that can be tightened or loosened by hand. For the older ones a chuck key will be required.

Always remove the key immediately after you have used it. Otherwise it will come loose when the drill motor is started and may cause serious injury to you or another person. The chuck key is generally fixed at some part of the drill, but if not, make sure you put it in a safe place where it will not get lost. All portable electric drills used nowadays have a momentary contact trigger located in the handle. The trigger is pressed to start the electric drill and is released to stop it. A trigger latch can be used to keep the trigger in the pressed position.

Activity 3 Understanding the text

Answer the questions on the text.

1. Why is the electric drill such an important tool?
2. Why do the larger electric drills usually have lower revolutions per minute?
3. What are the advantages of electronically-controlled electric drills?
4. What is the chuck used for?
5. Why is it important to remove the key from the chuck immediately after use?
6. How is an electric drill started?

Activity 4 Describing an action

With the help of the picture of the electric drill and the technical terms for the special parts describe how to change the drill bit.

Use these words:

chuck key ... chuck ... plug ...power source ... drill bit ... to insert ... to remove ... to tighten ... to loosen ... to fasten

Portable circular saw

The portable circular saw has become very popular as a wood working tool because it saves time and labour, works precisely and is easy to handle.

There is a wide range of sizes of portable electric saws. They are constructed in a way that they may be used as a carpenter's handsaw, both at the job site and on a bench in the woodworking shop.

The portable electric saw is started by pressing a trigger inserted in the handle and is stopped by releasing it. The saw runs only when the trigger is held.

Most saws can be used for crosscutting or for ripping. The ripsaw guide can be adjusted by two nuts at the base of the saw. (see picture on the right) When the guide is inserted in the rip guide slot to the desired dimensions, the nuts are tightened to hold it firmly in place.

Generally, before crosscutting, a guideline should be marked across the board. Place the front of the saw base on the work piece so that the guide mark on the front plate and the guide line on the workpiece are aligned. Before you start the saw it must not touch the workpiece. Then start the saw and allow the cutting blade to revolve at full speed. Now push the saw forward slowly. If the saw stalls, pull it back but do not release the trigger. You can continue when the saw has reached cutting speed again.

The bottom plate of the saw is wide enough to provide the saw with a firm support on the workpiece being cut. The blade of the saw is protected by a spring guard which opens when cutting and snaps back into place when the cut is finished. Different saw blades are available for cutting all kinds of material; e.g. solid wood, plywood, chipboard and plastics.

Activity 5 Matching exercise

The picture shows a portable circular saw. Match the following terms to the different parts of the saw.

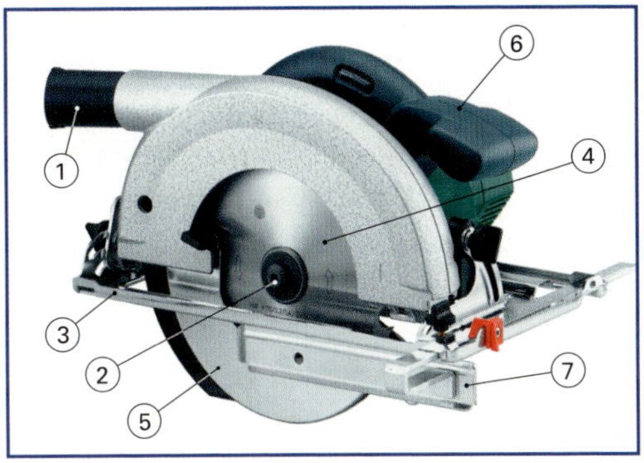

a) saw blade
b) handle
c) ripsaw guide
d) front plate
e) saw dust ejection
f) saw clamp screw and flange
g) spring guard

Activity 6 Describing an action

Fill in the missing words in the text about changing the saw blade.

Changing the saw blade.
First disconnect the •••1. Remove the •••2. Use the •••3 which is provided for this purpose.
Then •••4 the flange. Now take off the •••5. Attach the new saw blade and make sure that the •••6 show in the proper cutting direction. They must point … towards the front of the •••7. Tighten the •••8 and clamp the •••9 with the •••10.

Activity 7 Describing an action

After reading the text "Portable Circular Saw" (page 70) again describe how to make a crosscut. Use your own words.

Use these words:

first … after that … then … if this is finished … later … in the end … finally

Start like this:
First you should draw a guideline across the board. …

Unit 7

Safety regulations

Safety regulations for the use of power tools cannot be emphasized enough. There are several general safety measures to observe in operating or maintaining power equipment.

- Never operate power equipment if you are not thoroughly familiar with its controls and operating procedures. If in doubt ask someone who knows for operating instructions.
- All portable tools should be inspected before use to see that they are clean and in a proper state of repair.
- Before the power tool is connected to the power supply, make sure that the switch is in the "OFF" position.
- When operating a power tool, give it your FULL and UNDIVIDED ATTENTION.
- Fasten all loose sleeves and other parts of clothes.
- Do not remove any safety guards and use safety shields or safety glasses when necessary.
- Do not in any way disturb another person while he or she is operating a power tool.
- After having used the power tool, turn it off, unplug the power supply, wait for the rotation of the tool to stop and then clean the tool. Remove all waste and scraps from the work area and store the tool in its assigned place.
- Never plug the source cord of a portable electric tool into an electric power source until you have made sure that the source provides the voltage and type of current (alternating or direct) called for on the nameplate of the tool.
- If an extension cord is required, always connect the cord of the portable electric tool into the extension cord before the plug is inserted into a suitable outlet.
- Make sure that the power cord never comes into contact with sharp objects.
- power tools must always be treated with respect and handled properly.

Always remember:

1. Electricity strikes without warning.
2. Every electrical circuit is a potential source of danger and must be treated as such.
3. Make no electrical repairs yourself if you are not qualified to do so.
4. Sparking electric tools should never be used in places where flammable gases or liquids or exposed explosives are present.
5. Power tools must always be disconnected before parts are changed.

Activity 8 Understanding safety regulations

Answer the following questions.

1. Why are safety regulations very important when you work with electric power tools?
2. What should you do if you are not familiar with operating a new power tool?
3. In what conditon should power tools be before you use them?
4. Explain why it is important to fasten loose sleeves!
5. Why should you wait until the rotation has come to a stop?
6. Why can it be dangerous if the power cord comes into contact with sharp objects?
7. What should you pay special attention to when working with electric power tools in places where explosives are present?

Activity 9 Safety signs

Safety information must be given in a way that everybody can understand. Therefore it is given in the form of pictures. There are signs that tell you what you must or must not do. Others tell you to be careful and show you how to protect yourself against certain dangers.
There are four categories of signs: prohibitions signs, mandatory signs, warning signs, and information signs. The following picture gives a small selection of signs of each category.

Look at the following safety signs which you can find in the work place and describe what they mean in your own words.

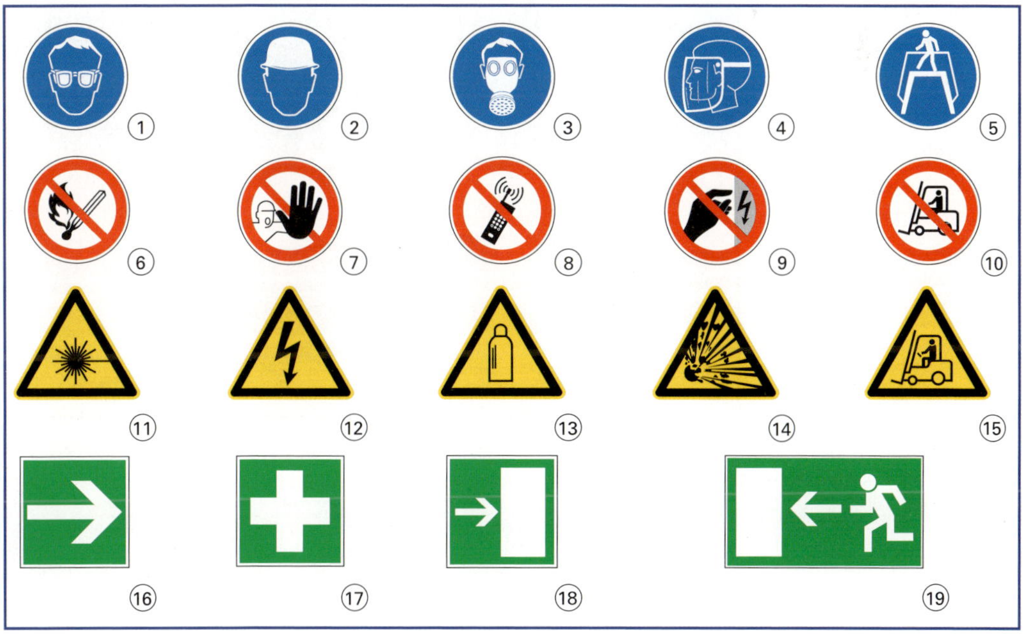

Shaping metal

There are two methods of shaping metal: chipless shaping and shape cutting chipping technology. Apart from the methods of shaping metal with the help of hand tools there are some very important and effective methods of giving a piece of metal its shape with the help of machines. In the following text we will have a short look at two of the most important methods of metal-cutting manufacturing. In mechanical engineering turning and milling are frequently used manufacturing methods of shaping a piece of metal. These two methods have several things in common but also some very significant differences.

Universal centre lathe

The picture below shows a small centre lathe. This type of machine is very versatile and can be found in almost every metal processing workshop. It is used for turning, that means it produces work pieces which are symmetrical to their axis of rotation. Very often these are cylindrical workpieces of different diameters and lengths.

Activity 10 Matching the parts of a lathe

Look at the picture and match the German expressions with the English terms.

a) chuck
b) position display
c) tailstock
d) carriage feed shaft
e) lead shaft
f) emergency switch
g) cross slide
h) feedgear levers
i) safety cover
j) head stock
k) swarf tray
l) engine frame
m) revolution levers

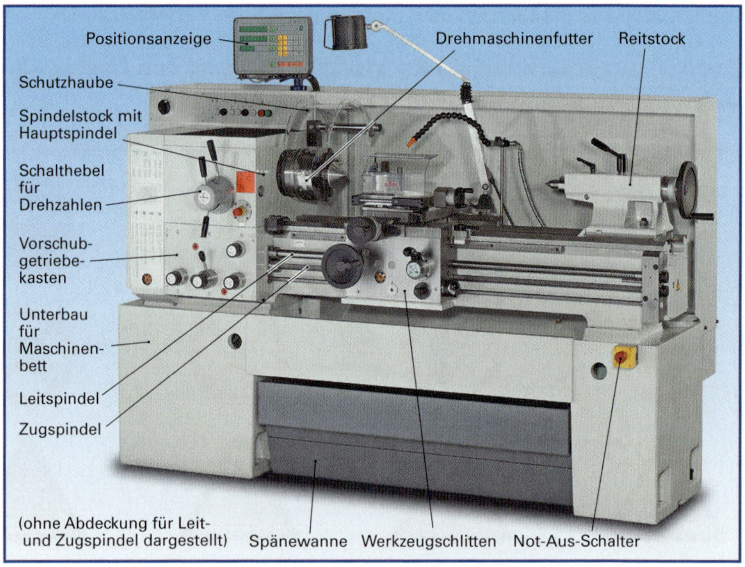

Universal milling machine

In the picture you can see a universal milling machine. This type of machine has a milling head which can be pivoted between 0° (vertical position) and 90° (horizontal position) in order to give the milling tool the optimal position with respect to the work piece. Such a machine can be used to produce work pieces with flat or curved surfaces. The universal machine table can be pivoted into almost every angle position with respect to the tool. The milling cutter usually has several cutting edges and is clamped in the milling spindle. The cutting process is performed by the rotating milling tool, whereas the feed movement and infeed is performed by the movement of the workpiece. The cutting conditions depend on the rotation in relation to the feed movement. You can find details in the chapter 11 **Working on Metal**.

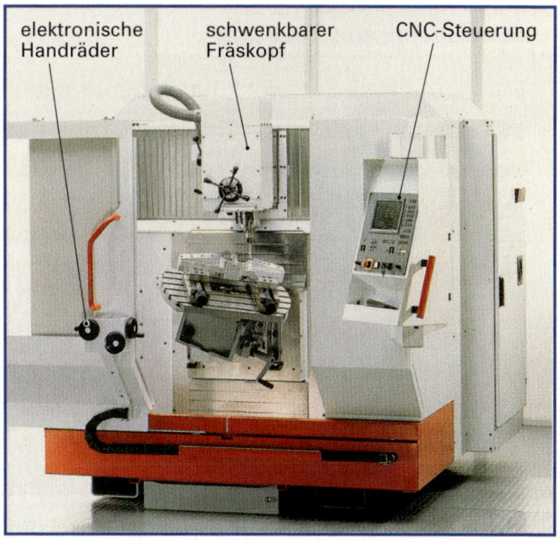

Activity 11 | Understanding the text

Answer the following questions on both texts about shaping metal.

1. What is the difference between chipless shaping and shape cutting chipping technology?
2. What are the most important manufacturing methods of shaping a metal work piece?
3. What kind of work pieces can be produced by turning?
4. Which movements do the tool and the work piece perform in the turning process?
5. What shapes of work piece can be produced with the help of a modern universal milling machine?
6. What can you say about the milling head of a universal milling machine?
7. Which movements do the tool and the work piece perform in the milling process?
8. How is the milling cutter fixed?
9. What are the main differences between a lathe and a milling machine?
10. What do both machines have in common?

In the training workshop

Introducing the situation

John and Frank are working in the in training workshop. Mr. Smith, their instructor, comes to them and tells them that one of the old milling machines in the training workshop does not work properly. He asks them to find out what is wrong with it and, if possible, to repair it.

JOHN I think the best way to start with is to have a look at the instruction manual first.

MR. SMITH Good idea. You can find it on the shelf next to the desk in my office.

JOHN Shall I get it from there?

MR. SMITH Yes, please. I'll be with you in a few minutes. *(John goes to the office and returns with the book.)*

JOHN Here it is. Now let's go to the milling machine and try to find out what's wrong with it.

FRANK There are three of them. Which one is it?

JOHN Mr. Smith said it was the one in the middle over there. *(John points to the milling machines at the side of the training workshop.)*

FRANK I hope you have worked with this machine before and you know how to operate it.

JOHN Yes, certainly. But to be honest, I hate this old machine. It breaks down almost every week. Let's start the machine. *(John presses the switch and starts the motor.)*

FRANK The spindle starts turning, so it's not an electrical problem. Let's find out if the transverse drive works.

JOHN Let's see. We must push this lever clockwise completely to the rear and at the same time turn the hand wheel.

FRANK O.K. It works. So there is nothing wrong with it.

JOHN Then let's try the longitudinal drive.

FRANK The manual says that there are two different ways of moving the longitudinal adjustment:

1. By hand, with the help of this cranked handle,
2. By means of the automatic feed, which is engaged by pushing the two arm crank towards the machine.

JOHN Manually it is possible to move the longitudinal adjustment, but there is something wrong with the automatic feed.

FRANK Is there anything wrong with the adjustable stops? Are they in the wrong position?

JOHN No, they are in the right position. So, there must be a fault in the drive of the automatic feed system. I guess it is the belt.

MR. SMITH Have you found the mistake?

JOHN Well, I think it is the belt for the longitudinal feed.

MR. SMITH I think so, too. All right then. Get to work and repair it.

Activity 12 | Understanding the dialogue

Answer the following questions on the text "In the training workshop" in complete sentences.

1. What information does Mr. Smith give to the two apprentices?
2. What does John think is the best way to start?
3. Where can John and Frank find the instruction manual?
4. Which machine does not work properly?
5. Why does John not like the old milling machine?
6. How do the two apprentices start the machine?
7. How do the trainees find out that it is not an electrical problem?
8. What two ways are there to move the longitudinal adjustment?

Activity 13 | Translation

Translate the following sentences into English.

1. Das Handbuch für die Fräsmaschine liegt im Regal in Herrn Smith's Büro.
2. In der Lehrwerkstatt gibt es drei alte Fräsmaschinen.
3. John hat schon oft an der Fräsmaschine gearbeitet und weiß wie sie bedient wird.
4. Der Hauptschalter muss in Position 1 gebracht und dann der Knopf gedrückt werden.
5. Dieser Hebel muss im Uhrzeigersinn bis ganz nach hinten geschoben werden.
6. Es ist kein elektrisches Problem, weil die Spindel sich zu drehen beginnt.
7. Im Handbuch steht, dass es zwei verschiedene Methoden der Längsverstellung gibt.
8. Es stimmt etwas nicht mit dem automatischen Vorschub.
9. Die Endanschläge sind an der richtigen Stelle.
10. Die Auszubildenden finden heraus, dass der Fehler im Antrieb des automatischen Vorschubs liegt.

Activity 14 | Making questions

The following sentences are answers to questions that Frank asks John. Write down Frank's questions. Use the question words in brackets.

1. The manual for the milling machine lies in Mr. Smith's office. (Where)
2. There are three milling machines in the workshop. (How many)
3. John knows how to operate the machine. (What)
4. You start the machine by pressing this button. (How)
5. I hate this machine because it breaks down very often. (Why)
6. There is something wrong with the automatic feed. (What)
7. Mr. Smith will give us a new belt. (Who)

Replacing the belt

Introducing the situation

After John and Frank have found the defect at the milling machine, they are preparing to change the belt.

FRANK	There is a chapter in the manual which describes how to change a belt.
JOHN	Good, can you please read it out.
FRANK	Yes, but you must help me if I don't understand everything.
JOHN	Okay. What does it say, how do we have to proceed?
FRANK	The instruction says, to replace the belts, proceed as follows: Stop the machine and raise the cover and open the door. Turn the handle upwards to release tension in the belts. Change the belts. Turn the handle downwards, check the tension of the belts and close the cover and the door before restarting the machine.
JOHN	Wait a minute. Does the manual say anything about the size of the belt?
FRANK	Yes, the size of the belt for the milling spindle is 17/11 x 2413 mm and the belt for the feed box has got size 13/8 x 1475 mm.
JOHN	Okay. What do they say about the adjustment?
FRANK	First adjust the milling spindle belt tension by means of the belt tightener. There is a warning here, too.
JOHN	Read it out to me.

WARNING: The motor and its platform should be suspended by the tightener and not by the belt. The handle should always be in the vertical position. Adjust the tension of the feed box belt by displacing the box vertically. For this purpose the four fixing bolts of the box should be loosened slightly.

JOHN	Now, is everything clear?
FRANK	Not quite. What does **to release tension** mean?
JOHN	It means to reduce the tension or take it away completely.
FRANK	Okay. To make sure that I understand everything correctly I should translate the instructions into German.
JOHN	Good idea.

Activity 14 Translation

Study the dialogue between Frank and John again and translate the instructions for replacing the belt into German.

Vocabulary Unit 7

accident	Unfall
to adapt	anpassen
to add	hinzufügen
to adjust	einstellen
adjustable	einstellbar
adjustment	Einstellung
advantage	Vorteil
to aligne	fluchten, ausrichten
although	obwohl
application	Anwendung
to apply	anwenden
apron ['eɪprən]	Schürze
assigned	vorgegeben
to attach	befestigen
available [ə'veɪləbl]	verfügbar
to avoid	vermeiden
base	Basis
to be familiar with	vertraut sein mit
belt-sander	Bandschleifer
bench	Werkbank
both... and	sowohl... als auch
to break down	versagen
carpenter	Zimmermann
carriage	Schlitten
to cause	verursachen
certain(ly)	gewiss, sicherlich
chipboard	Spanplatte
to choose	(aus)wählen
chuck	Futter
chuck key	Futterschlüssel
circuit	Leitungskreis
circular saw	Kreissäge
to clamp	spannen
clockwise	im Uhrzeigersinn
to come loose	verloren gehen
common	gebräuchlich
to connect	verbinden
cord	Kabel
cordless	ohne Kabel
cranked	gekröpft
crosscutting	Schnitt quer zur Faser
current	Strom
cutting speed	Schnitt-geschwindigkeit
to decrease	verringern
to deliver	liefern
to design	entwerfen

to develop	entwickeln
device	Apparat, Gerät
diameter	Durchmesser
to disconnect	trennen
to distinguish	unterscheiden
to disturb	stören
drill bit	Bohrer
electric plane	Elektrohobel
emergency switch	Notausschalter
to emphasize	betonen
to engage	an-, einstellen
engine frame	Maschinengestell
engineering	Maschinenbau
to equip	ausstatten
equipment	Ausrüstung
exposed	offen
extension cord	Verlängerung
feed	Vorschub
feed gear levers	Vorschubgetriebe-hebel
feed shaft	Zugspindel
finally	schließlich
firmly	fest
fitment	Zusatzeinrichtung
flange	Flansch
frequently	häufig
grinder	Schleifmaschine
guideline	Anrisslinie
hand wheel	Handrad
the handle	der Handgriff
head stock	Spindelstock
honest	ehrlich
to identify	identifizieren
immediately	sofort
in addition	zusätzlich
to include	einschließen
increase	Zunahme
infinitely	stufenlos
injury ['ɪndʒərɪ]	Verletzung
to insert	einsetzen
to inspect	überprüfen
instructor	Ausbilder
instruction manual	Bedienungshand-buch
job site	Baustelle
joiner's shop	Tischlerwerkstatt
keyhole saw	Stichsäge
labour ['leɪbə(r)]	Arbeit
lead shaft	Leitspindel

Vocabulary Unit 7

linking words	verbindende Worte
to be located	liegen (Stadt)
location	Ort, Platz
longitudinal	Längs-
lumber	Bauholz
main parts	Hauptteile
to maintain [meɪn'teɪn]	warten, pflegen
manual	Handbuch
to match	zusammen bringen
measure	Maßnahme
mechanical engineering	Maschinenbau
momentary contact	Impuls
nowadays	heutzutage
nut	(Spann-)Mutter
to observe	beachten
otherwise	anderenfalls
paint mixing	Farbe mischen
to pivot	schwenken
plywood	Schichtholz
to point	zeigen
popular	beliebt
portable	tragbar
postion display	Positionsanzeige
power cord	Elektrokabel
power tool	angetriebenes Werkzeug
practice	Verfahren, Methode
precisely	genau, präzise
present	gegenwärtig
probably	wahrscheinlich
procedure	Vorgehensweise
proper(ly)	richtig, passend
to protect	schützen
to provide	versehen mit
purpose	Zweck
qualified	qualifiziert
range	Bereich
regulations	Vorschriften
to release	freigeben
to remove	entfernen
to require	erfordern
revolutions	Umdrehungen
ripping	Längsschnitt
ripsaw guide	Führungsanschlag
rip guide slot	Nut für den Führungsanschlag
safety cover	Schutzhaube
safety guard	Schutzeinrichtung
safety glasses	Schutzbrille
safety shield	Schutzshild
sander	(Sandpapier)Schleifer
to saw	sägen
saw dust ejection	Späneauswurf
scrap	Abfall, Schrott
screw driver	Schraubendreher
section	Abschnitt
selection	Auswahl
shelf	Regal
sleeve	Ärmel
size	Größe
to snap back	zurückschnappen
socket	Steckdose
solid wood	Vollholz
source	Quelle
spark	Funke
spring guard	Federabdeckung
to stall	stecken bleiben
state of repair	Zustand
to stow	verstauen
to strike	zuschlagen
supply	Versorgung
support	Unterstützung
swarf tray	Spänewanne
switch	Schalter
tailstock	Reitstock
thoroughly ['θʌrəlɪ]	sorgfältig
three-jaw	Dreibacken-
to tighten	spannen, festziehen
tool	Werkzeug
transverse	Quer-
trigger latch	Knopf zum Halten des Schalters
trigger	Auslöseschalter
undivided	ungeteilt
to unplug	Stecker entfernen
upwards	aufwärts
usually	gewöhnlich
variety	Vielfalt
various ['veərɪəs]	verschieden
width	Breite
wrench	Schraubenschlüssel

8 Environment

This chapter deals with environmental questions and problems. From time to time you should recall the problems humankind causes on this planet. Keeping the earth habitable is incredibly important. We each have an obligation to protect our environment for ourselves and for future generations.

Environmental problems

Unit 8

Activity 1 Getting into the unit

Have a look at the picture above, which shows some examples of air pollution and then answer the following questions.

1. Which sources of air pollution can you see in the picture? Which of them are natural and which are man-made?
2. What do you know about the effects of emissions on human beings, plants, and buildings?

An interview

Introducing the situation

Regina's class is taking part in a contest about environmental protection. Each student has to contribute something. Regina has to interview people. She wants to find out what people are willing to do to protect their environment. One of her interview partners is Koryn, her American exchange partner.

REGINA Hey, you're wearing quite an interesting T-shirt today. It fits my topic. As you know I have to write about environmental problems. You have got them in the States, too, haven't you?

KORYN Yes, we have. And we have got to work on topics about environmental questions.

REGINA You can be one of my interview partners.

KORYN Sure. What would you like to know?

REGINA When the sun shines do you use your bicycle instead of a car?

KORYN As you know it is quite hot in Arizona and I like my air-conditioned car. Sometimes, however, I walk to school or go by bike, mainly in winter. It depends a little on the time I have left in the morning. If I stay in bed too long, well, you know …

REGINA Sure I do. Do you drive in car pools?

KORYN Yes, of course, we do, we save gas and it's a lot more fun. We do not only drive in car pools to school but we also pick up friends when we go somewhere in our spare time.

REGINA Do you use rechargeable batteries?

KORYN For my flashlight I use rechargeable batteries. On special occasions I sometimes buy some extra batteries.

REGINA Do you leave your appliances on stand-by?

KORYN Well, to be honest, most of the time I forget to switch them off or I want to use, for example, my TV later again. Do you really think that switching off a TV saves that much energy?

Activity 2 Partner work

Find and ask questions.

1. Make a list of Regina's questions.
2. Think of further questions you could ask in an interview.
3. Ask one or more classmates all these questions and present the answers you have collected to the class.

Environmental impacts on air

Air pollution is a major environmental problem of mankind. Toxic pollutants are contaminating the atmosphere. This is a global problem because there are no boundaries in the atmosphere like the borders of a country. Even in regions without any industry, for example, the Antarctic, analytical measurements have proved that the air is polluted.

The consequences of air pollution are very dangerous . Everybody knows that the hole in the ozone layer is getting bigger. Chlorofluorocarbons (CFCs) are mainly responsible for damaging the ozone layer. Even though statesmen from the whole world decided years ago that CFCs had to be reduced, it will still take decades to stop their production completely. Then it will take decades before the ozone layer will have recovered. Meanwhile people have to take care, for example, not to stay in the sun too long because of the danger of skin cancer.

Even bigger problems are the exhaust fumes of cars. They contain carbon monoxide, nitrogen oxides and hydrocarbons. Almost three quarters of all carbon monoxide emissions are produced by cars mainly while waiting at traffic lights. In wintertime careless car owners let their engines run to get rid of the ice on their windscreens. At the same time they are producing great amounts of exhaust fumes which are affecting the environment. Catalytic converters, as well as cars with lower fuel consumption, are helping to reduce emissions. On the other hand, there are still more and more cars registered in every country each year. The results of the exhaust fumes are smog and acid rain which damage plants and buildings. Smog means a high concentration of ozone and other poisonous substances in the air. In Germany students are not allowed to do sports outside in summer when the concentration of ozone in the air is too high. Drivers of older vehicles have to leave their cars at home when the ozone concentration exceeds a certain amount.

Carbon dioxide emissions derive from the burning of mineral oil, gas, and coal, the sources of our energy. It is responsible for the greenhouse effect and global warming. The result is an increase in the temperature on earth and the rise in the sea level. In future countries are likely to suffer from heavy storms with large rainfalls. People, especially farmers in many parts of the world, will have to face the negative effects of climate change.

Activity 3 Understanding the text

Answer the following questions.

1. Why is air pollution a global problem? Find an example in the text that supports your conclusion.
2. Why are CFCs dangerous for the atmosphere?
3. Why is the hole in the ozone layer dangerous for the health of people?
4. What are the consequences of the exhaust fumes of cars?
5. What has been done so far to reduce the emissions of exhaust fumes of cars?
6. What are the consequences if the ozone concentration gets too high?
7. What is mainly responsible for the greenhouse effect and global warming?
8. What are the consequences of the greenhouse effect and global warming?

Activity 4 — Working with words

a) Find the missing words in the text and complete the sentences.

1. •••[1] are helping to reduce emission as well as cars using less petrol.
2. Students are not allowed to do sports outside when the •••[2] of ozone in the air is too high.
3. Years ago it was decided that CFCs had to be •••[3].
4. •••[4] in regions without any industry have proved that the air is polluted.
5. A lot of carbon monoxide is produced by cars waiting at •••[5].

b) Find the 12 hidden words. Make sentences and put as many of the found words as possible into one sentence.

V	P	R	M	O	Z	Y	S	A	X	E	P	V	B	N	C	S	E
R	Q	W	E	H	E	L	I	H	W	N	A	E	M	B	E	S	T
A	L	L	N	N	M	K	Y	E	I	E	V	D	L	U	P	I	N
I	O	B	G	U	W	I	N	T	E	R	T	I	M	E	C	Y	E
H	R	M	I	T	U	O	B	A	Z	G	A	R	E	V	I	R	D
P	T	A	N	S	Y	S	U	L	K	Y	B	F	N	O	R	M	U
L	E	O	E	V	E	R	Y	B	O	D	Y	I	X	K	A	I	T
I	P	M	U	A	L	C	O	N	S	E	Q	U	E	N	C	E	S

Activity 5 — Consequences of air pollution

Air pollution and its consequences are mentioned in the following two columns. Combine the consequences with the causes and copy the correct sentences into your exercise book.

Consequences	Causes
1. warms up the atmosphere	a) smog
2. melts icebergs	b) acid rain
3. raises the water level	c) greenhouse effect
4. causes skin cancer	d) destroyed ozone layer
5. affects the soil for plants	
6. damages old buildings	
7. contains poisonous substances	
8. makes people ill	

Activity 6 Environmental impacts on buildings

a) Complete the text with the words from the box below.

•••[1] rain develops when the oxides of nitrogen or sulphur come in contact with rain water. The nitric acid and sulphuric acid in rain damage plants and affect buildings.

The cathedral of St Peter in Regensburg is made of sandstone and •••[2]. Most of the parts of the western façade and the northern tower are made of sandstone. The acids in the rain dissolve the porous sandstone. That has made it •••[3] to work on the cathedral constantly.

The destruction of the sandstone becomes visible when you look at the •••[4] figure from the northern •••[5], the prophet Amos (see picture above). Today you can find the old figure in the Regensburg museum. The new •••[6], shown in the picture below, is made from limestone which is more resistant to acid rain.

Because of the consequences of acid rain, the church building, its towers and especially the figures are under constant construction. There are rare occasions when there is no •••[7] around at least at parts of the cathedral. Renewal is permanently necessary. A special group of people, •••[8], are employed to take care of the •••[9], clean and replace the destroyed parts.

A couple of years ago there was an •••[10] to protect the façade of another famous church in Regensburg from fading away. A glass construction was built around the portal with its precious stone •••[11]. People thus hoped to save them. Not everybody agreed with this procedure. Some people said that the building should have been left alone. Do you think old buildings should be protected and saved for future generations?

Use these words:

damages ... figure ... carvings ... original ... scaffolding ... limestone ... façade ... stone-masons ... attempt ... necessary ... acid

b) Make passive sentences. Say what should (not) be done, must (not) be done, or ought (not) to be done to minimize air pollution and its negative effects.

Here is an example:

Glass constructions **should be used** to protect precious parts of buildings.

Environmental impacts on water

A few years ago scientists said that the next world war would take place because of a shortage of water. People might say that this is nonsense because about 80 % of the surface of our planet is covered with water. That is true but almost all of it is salt water which cannot be consumed. There are, of course, desalination plants which can turn salt water into drinking water. Every drop of water produced by these plants, however, is very expensive. Water is essential for life and the question is who can afford to pay a high price for it. We can live without a car, a house, clothes, and even food for quite some time but we cannot live without water. Still we keep on wasting and poisoning this precious substance. Each of us consumes about 100 litres a day but only a small amount (about 4 litres) is needed for cooking and drinking. The rest is used for washing, flushing the toilet, cleaning cars, watering the lawn, or filling up swimming pools.

Activity 7 Statements

Are the following statements true or false? Correct them if necessary.

1. There is enough drinking water everywhere.
2. People waste water.
3. Desalination plants produce drinking water cheaply.
4. We only consume four litres of water a day.
5. Most of the earth's surface is covered by fresh water.

Unit 8

Activity 8 From ground water to drinking water

Use the passive constructions in the box to complete the text.

Most water from your tap originates from ground water. Rainwater is not pure enough. After the rain drops have hit the ground, the water drips through the soil for 30 days. It •••1 by minerals and the organic substances •••2 by bacteria. Then the water •••3 to the water works. There carbon dioxide •••4 because the pipes •••5 by rust. Finally a third cleaning stage •••6. The water •••7 again with help of carbon. Then your glass •••8 with clean drinking water.

Use these words:

can be filled ... is pumped ... is filtered (2) ... are eaten ... would be destroyed ... has to be passed ... is extracted

Activity 9 Comprehension

a) How could we reduce water consumption? Think of possibilities and discuss them in class.

b) Write an article for your school magazine. Convince people not to waste water.

Continuing the interview

Introducing the situation

In the afternoon Regina and Koryn meet again. Koryn is interested in the interviews. They get into talking about environmental questions.

KORYN Hi. How was school?

REGINA Fine.

KORYN What about your interviews?

REGINA I'm getting along.

KORYN Is really everybody interested in this subject?

REGINA Not everybody. Of course, there are people who say they do not want to be interviewed. Some say that they are not interested in this subject at all. However, most people I asked were helpful and willing to exchange ideas.
Environmental problems have been discussed in Germany for years. Since a new political party came on the scene, the environment has become an important subject. People are more aware now than they were before that the protection of nature is not only essential for the current generation but even more for the future generations. Many schools have competitions about saving energy, reducing and sorting waste. The best schools get prizes. A lot of new jobs have been created dealing with environmental questions and problems.

KORYN I agree that environmental protection is important. I remember one leader of a native American tribe who said that people would only realize that they could not eat money after they had destroyed nature. A friend of mine wants to be an environmental technician. She wants to work in a water treatment plant. I think it's quite a boring job looking at water all day long. My friend is enthusiastic about it though. Americans love plain water for drinking. That's why I guess it's of great importance to purify water and to help to keep it clean.

REGINA A lot of Germans buy their water in bottles. My mother prefers water from the tap. She doesn't like the bubbles. I try to save water because it has become quite expensive. Our water bill is higher now than it was some years ago. I try to save fuel, too. When I bought my car, I tried to find one that consumes less fuel. Like that I can protect the environment and save money. And even though I love to drive fast, I think a speed limit on German motorways would certainly reduce emissions. In other fields I am rather pessimistic. The question is, for example, if there is much sense in sorting waste, if in the end all the waste is burnt in an incineration plant.

Activity 10 Questions

a) Answer the following questions.

1. What does Regina say about the people she wanted to interview?
2. What has happened in Germany to draw people's attention to environmental problems?
3. What are people aware of nowadays?
4. What do German schools contribute to environmental protection?
5. What does Koryn say about the importance of environmental protection?
6. What do the girls say about drinking water?
7. How does Regina try to protect the environment?

b) Form questions. Use the given words. Your classmates can answer by using the information from the text.

1. love/plain water/who
2. get/best schools/what
3. discuss/environmental problems/for years/where
4. can/see/TV/what
5. be like/job/what
6. protect/environment/can/how
7. discuss/environmental problems/how long

Activity 11 A catalytic converter

Find the correct word for each gap.

Regina mentions a •••[1]. It is a part of a car to •••[2] the exhaust emission.
In burning •••[3] substances cannot be burned completely because of a •••[4] of air. In the case of exhaust fumes of cars, there are carbon monoxide and the nitrogen oxides which cause smog, and hydrocarbons which can cause •••[5]. Since in •••[6] powerful car engines there are high combustion temperatures, the carbon monoxide emission is •••[7], but the proportion of nitrogen oxides in the fume is very high.
The •••[8] of the catalytic converter is easy: At temperatures of about 300 °C the compounds of the exhaust fumes are oxidised with the oxygen of the air. The results are carbon dioxide, nitrogen and water.
This reaction is nearly complete, if platinum is used as a •••[9] and if the concentrations of all compounds are optimal. A lambda probe controls the mixture and keeps the •••[10] constant. For the chemical process it is necessary that the fuel air mixture is exactly $\lambda = 1$.

Use these words:

modern ... lack ... catalytic converter ... processes ... value ... catalyst ... low ... principle ... cancer ... reduce

Activity 12 Discussion

a) The picture shows the structure and the mechanism of a catalytic converter. Describe the picture in your own words.

b) Discuss the advantages of a catalytic converter.

c) Are there also disadvantages? Does this technology solve all environmental problems regarding cars or does it cause other problems?

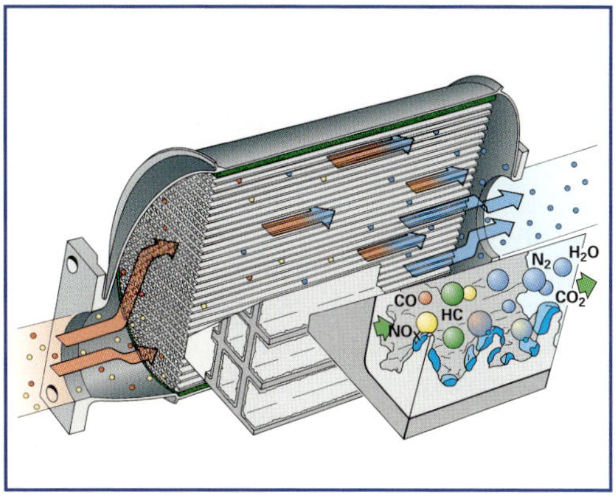

The advantages of the catalytic converter are obvious!

1. Nitrogen oxides are changed into nitrogen. Acid rain cannot be formed anymore.

2. Carbon monoxide is changed into carbon dioxide. Poisonous smog is reduced.

3. Hydrocarbons are burned to carbon dioxide. The probability of cancer is reduced.

Activity 13 Working with words

a) Find the correct words for the following definitions.

1. reddish-brown covering on iron formed when it gets wet
2. place where a large amount of rubbish can be burned
3. money collected by the government
4. worker in the industry with special skills
5. having the characteristics of a substance that can harm or kill

b) Work with a partner. Choose words from the unit. Describe them like in a) and let your partner guess the word. Change roles.

Vocabulary Unit 8

acid	Säure
acid rain	sauerer Regen
to affect	sich auswirken, betreffen
to afford	sich etwas leisten
agriculture	Landwirtschaft
air-conditioned	klimatisiert
air pollution [pə'luːʃn]	Luftverschmutzung
amount	Menge
appliance [a'plaɪəns]	Gerät
approximately	ungefähr
at least	wenigstens
attempt	Versuch
attention	Beachtung, Aufmerksamkeit
to be aware of	bewusst werden
bacteria (pl)	Bakterien
bill	Rechnung
border	Grenze
boring	langweilig
bottle	Flasche
boundary	Grenzlinie
bubble	Luftblase
cancer	Krebs
carbon	Kohlenstoff
carbon dioxide	Kohlendioxid
carbon monoxide	Kohlenmonoxid
careless	nachlässig
car engine	Motor
car pool	Fahrgemeinschaft
carving	Schnitzwerk, Bildhauerarbeit
catalyst	Katalysator (chem.)
catalytic converter	Katalysator (techn.)
cathedral	Dom, Kathedrale
cause	Grund, Ursache
to cause	verursachen
characteristic	Merkmal, Eigenschaft
chemical	chemisch
to choose	wählen
chlorofluorocarbons ['klɔrəˌfluːərə ˌkaːbənz]	Kohlenwasserstoffe
competition	Wettbewerb
to collect	sammeln
column	Säule, Spalte
combustion	Verbrennung
complete	vollständig
compound	Verbindung

consequence	Folge, Konsequenz
to consume	verbrauchen
consumption	Verbrauch
contest	Wettbewerb
to contribute	beisteuern
to convince	überzeugen
couple of	einige
to cover	bedecken
to create	(er)schaffen
damage ['dæmɪdʒ]	Schaden
to damage	beschädigen
to deal with	handeln von
decade	Jahrzehnt
to decide	entscheiden
to depend on	abhängen von
deposition	Ablagerung
to derive from	ableiten, erhalten von
to destroy	zerstören
destruction	Zerstörung
to dissolve	auflösen
distance	Entfernung
to drip	tropfen
effect	Wirkung, Folge
emission	Emission
to endanger	gefährden
enough	genug
enthusiastic	begeistert
environment	Umwelt
environmental protection	Umweltschutz
environmental technician	Umwelttechniker/in
essential	wesentlich
exactly	genau
to exceed	überschreiten
to exchange	austauschen
exchange partner	Austauchpartner/in
exhaust fume [fjuːm]	Abgas
to extract	herausziehen, gewinnen
façade [fə'saːd]	Fassade
to face	vor etwas stehen
to fade away	verschwinden
famous	berühmt
to fit	passen
flashlight	Taschenlampe
to flush	spülen
fuel	Treibstoff

Vocabulary Unit 8

to get rid of	loswerden
global	weltweit, global
greenhouse effect	Treibhauseffekt
ground water	Grundwasser
to harm	schaden
hole	Loch
however	jedoch
hydrocarbon	Kohlenwasserstoff
iceberg	Eisberg
impact	Auswirkung
importance	Wichtigkeit
incineration plant [ɪn'sɪnəreɪʃn]	Verbrennungsanlage
increase	Anstieg, Zunahme
to increase	(an)steigen
iron	Eisen
to kill	töten
lawn	Rasen
lack	Mangel
leader	Führer
limestone ['laimstəʊn]	Kalkstein
little (money)	wenig (Geld)
mainly	hauptsächlich
mankind	Menschheit
meanwhile	inzwischen
measurement	Messung
to mention	erwähnen
mixture	Mischung
motorway	Autobahn
necessary	notwendig
nitric acid	Salpetersäure
nitrogen	Stickstoff
nitrogen oxide	Stickoxid
nowadays	heutzutage
nutrition [njuː'triʃn]	Ernährung, Nahrung
obligation	Verpflichtung
occasion	Gelegenheit
organic	organisch
to oxidise	oxidieren
oxygen	Sauerstoff
ozone layer	Ozonschicht
party	Partei
permanently	dauernd
petrol	Benzin
pipe [paɪp]	Rohr
plain	klar
plant	Pflanze
plant	Fabrik, Werk, Anlage
platinum	Platin

poison	Gift
to poison	vergiften
poisonous	giftig
pollutant	Schadstoff
porous	porös
portal	Eingangsportal
powerful	mächtig
precious	wertvoll
prize	Preis
probability	Wahrscheinlichkeit
probe	Sonde
procedure	Vorgehensweise
process	Vorgang
proportion	Anteil, Verhältnis
to protect	schützen
protection	Schutz
to prove	beweisen
to purify	reinigen
quite	ziemlich
radiator ['reɪdɪeɪtə(r)]	Heizkörper
to raise	heben, erhöhen
rare	selten
to realize	erkennen
reasonable	vernünftig
recall	sich erinnern
rechargeable	wieder aufladbar
recover	sich erholen
reddish-brown	rotbraun
to reduce	verringern, reduzieren
to regard	betrachten
region	Gebiet, Region
renewal	Erneuerung
responsible for	verantwortlich für
rubbish	Abfall
rust	Rost
sandstone	Sandstein
scaffolding	Gerüst
scene	Bildfläche
scientist ['saɪəntɪst]	Wissenschaftler
school magazine	Schülerzeitung
sense	Sinn
severe [sɪ'vɪə(r)]	ernst
shortage	Knappheit
skill	Fähigkeit, Geschick
soil	Erde, Boden
to solve	lösen
to sort	sortieren
source	Quelle

Vocabulary Unit 8

spare time	Freizeit
stage	Stufe
statesman	Staatsmann
stone-mason	Steinmetz
substance	Stoff, Substanz
to suffer from	leiden an
sulphur	Schwefel
sulphuric acid	Schwefelsäure
surface	Oberfläche
to switch off	ausschalten
tap	Wasserhahn
tax	Steuer
thus	so, auf diese Art
topic	Thema
toxic	giftig
traffic-lights	Verkehrsampel
tribe [traɪb]	Stamm
value	Wert
visible	sichtbar
waste	Abfall
to waste	vergeuden, verschwenden
whole	ganz
to water	gießen
water level	Wasserstandslinie
water treatment plant	Wasseraufbereitungsanlage
windscreen	Windschutzscheibe
withdraw	zurückziehen
without	ohne
(the) worst	(das) Schlimmste

British English vs American English

exhaust fume	exhaust gas
motorway	freeway
to oxidise	to oxidize
petrol	gas
sulphur	sulfur
sulphuric acid	sulfuric acid
torch	flashlight
windscreen	windshield

Additional Vocabulary

agenda	Tagesordnung
to aim at	etwas beabsichtigen
biomass	Biomasse
demand	Nachfrage
development	Entwicklung
developing country	Entwicklungsland
drought	Dürre
environmentalist	Umweltschützer
fossil fuel	fossiler Brennstoff
geothermal power	Erdwärme
green product	umweltschonendes Produkt
harmful	schädlich
household	Haushalt
hydroelectric plant	Wasserkraftwerk
to improve	verbessern
industrial nation	Industrienation
to melt	schmelzen
to negotiate	verhandeln
polluter	Umweltsünder
to predict	vorhersagen
priority	Vorrang
public transport	öffentliche Verkehrsmittel
renewable energy	erneuerbare Energie
research	Forschung
resources	Reserven, Hilfsmittel
solar panel	Sonnenkollektor
to swamp	überschwemmen
tidal	Gezeiten-
tidal power plant	Gezeitenkraftwerk
traffic jam	Verkehrsstau
water power	Wasserkraft
wildlife	Tierwelt

9 Energy

In this unit you will learn how electric energy is generated and transmitted. You will also work on alternative sources of energy and you will find out that hydrogen may power cars in the future.

Consumers of energy

Activity 1 Warm up

a) Name the machines and appliances shown in the photographs and the kind of energy they need to work.

b) Think of some more appliances that you use in your daily life and guess their energy consumption.

Unit 9

How electric energy is generated

One of the laws of nature is that energy can neither be created nor destroyed but its form can be changed. We have managed to change the form of energy in such a way that it can do work for us. Energy lights our houses and cities. Energy powers our cars, trains, and planes. It warms our homes, cooks our food and it enables us to listen to the radio and to watch television. Energy powers the machinery in our factories.

Energy is defined as "the ability to do work."

Although most of our vehicles (cars, trucks, planes, ships) are powered by energy that is based on oil, the majority of the devices we use in our households and the machinery that produces the goods in our factories are powered by electric energy.

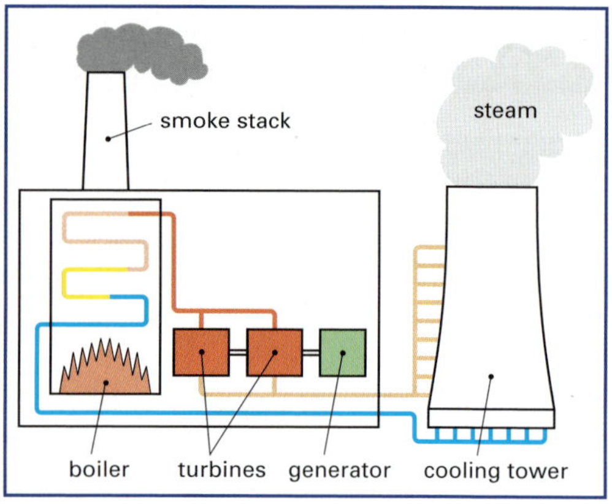

Electric energy is generated in power plants. There are different kinds of power plants, but the biggest and most common ones are big boilers that burn fuel to produce heat energy. This kind of power plant is called a thermal power station. Even nuclear power plants belong to this kind. The heat is used to boil water into steam which then is led to a turbine to make the turbine spin. The turbine's shaft is connected to a generator that changes the mechanical spinning energy into electricity.

Let us look at the cross section of a power plant (picture): In most boilers coal, oil, or natural gas are used to produce heat. Above a hot fire there is a series of pipes with water running through them. The heat energy is conducted into metal pipes, heating the water until it boils into steam. The steam (red line) then goes to the turbines under high pressure. The turbine has many blades that look like the blades of a fan. When the steam hits the blades they spin a shaft that is attached to the bottom of the blades.

The turbine's shaft is attached to the generator which is also made to spin in this way. The generator has a giant magnet inside a stationary ring which is wrapped with a long wire. When the magnet inside the generator turns, an electric voltage is produced in the wire. This process, which is called induction, always takes place when a wire or any electrically conductive material moves across a magnetic field.

After having left the turbine, the steam goes to a condenser where it cools off and so becomes water again. Pumps make it go back to the boiler (blue line) where it is heated again and the process repeats itself over and over. To condense the steam back into water, millions of litres of cooling water are needed every hour. That is the reason why power plants are usually located at rivers or lakes. Big cooling towers are needed to cool off the cooling water. When the hot pipes in the cooling towers come into contact with cool air, vapour in the air is heated and steam is given off above the cooling towers. However, this is not the same steam that is used inside the turbine.

Nuclear power plants work similarly. The difference is that they use uranium as "fuel" to boil water into steam. Inside the reactor of an atomic power plant, uranium atoms are split in a controlled chain reaction. This process is called nuclear fission.

Activity 2 Understanding the text

Answer the following questions on the text.

1. Give examples what we need energy for.
2. How is energy defined?
3. What is a power plant?
4. What is typical about a thermal power station?
5. Describe how the turbine in a power plant is made to spin.
6. What is a generator made of?
7. Why are power plants built near rivers and lakes?
8. What are the cooling towers needed for?
9. Which process in an atomic power plant is called nuclear fission?
10. Why do nuclear power plants belong to the kind of thermal power stations?

How electricity is transmitted

A generator in a power plant generates electricity with a voltage between 10 kV and 30 kV. In our homes we have voltages of either 230 V or 400 V. That means the electricity has to be transformed. However, before it is transformed into the voltages we are familiar with, it is first boosted up by transformers near the power stations. Why?

Electricity often has to travel long distances to the consumers. Therefore it is transported in long cables made of copper or aluminium. Although these metals have a low resistance they do cause unwanted energy losses in the cables. These losses increase as the flow of electric current increases. To keep the losses low, the diameter of the cables of the transmission lines could be increased but this would also rise the price for the cables. The solution is to boost up the voltage. In this way the strength of the electric current can be kept low when a certain amount of energy has to be transmitted.

The cables are fixed at high-voltage poles. It depends on the height of the voltage how big the poles are. Common voltages for the transportation of electric energy in Germany are 380,000 V, 220,000 V, 110,000 V or 10,000 V. In general one can say the higher the voltage the higher are the distances of transmission. The cables go to substations where the high voltage electricity is transformed into lower voltage electricity by transformers. The distribution lines within cities and villages that connect our homes to the substations are underground rather than overhead lines. At our homes the power goes through an energy meter that measures the energy we consume so that the electricity company knows how much energy we have to pay for.

High-voltage pole

Activity 3 Comprehension

The following statements are false. Correct them.

1. The common current at the sockets in our homes is 230 V.
2. Generators boost up the voltages for the transport to the consumer.
3. Electricity is transported in cables made of iron or silver.
4. If the diameter of the cables increases its resistance will rise.
5. Using high voltages can keep the transported energy low.
6. The voltages in the cables depend on the size of the high-voltage poles.
7. Most transmission lines within cities are overhead lines.
8. At our homes the electricity is measured by a transformer.

Activity 4 Working with words

Find words in the texts that match the following explanations.

1. the flow of electricity through a wire
2. factory that generates electricity
3. used to transmit electricity
4. machine whose wheel is turned by water, steam or gas
5. large round building to lower the temperature of water
6. material used in nuclear power plants
7. machine that produces electricity
8. piece of material that attracts iron or steel
9. thin towers used to carry cables
10. electric equipment that changes the height of voltages
11. splitting the nucleus of an atom
12. device that measures the amount of electricity

Activity 5 Translation

Translate the following sentences into English.

1. Energie kann weder erzeugt noch zerstört werden.
2. Elektrizität wird in Kraftwerken erzeugt.
3. Wärmekraftwerke besitzen einen großen Kessel, um Wasserdampf zu erzeugen.
4. Der Wasserdampf wird den Turbinen mit hohem Druck zugeführt.
5. Zum Abkühlen des Wasserdampfes benötigen Wärmekraftwerke sehr viel Wasser.
6. Das ist der Grund, weshalb Wärmekraftwerke an Flüssen oder Seen gebaut werden.
7. In Kernkraftwerken werden Uran-Atome gespalten, um Hitze zu erzeugen.
8. Wenn sich ein Draht quer zu einem magnetischen Feld bewegt, wird in dem Draht eine Spannung erzeugt.
9. Zum Übertragen elektrischer Energie werden sehr hohe Spannungen benötigt.
10. Energie wird in Leitungen übertragen, die an Hochspannungsmasten befestigt sind.

Activity 6 Nuclear fission

Copy the following text into your exercise book and complete it with words from the list below.

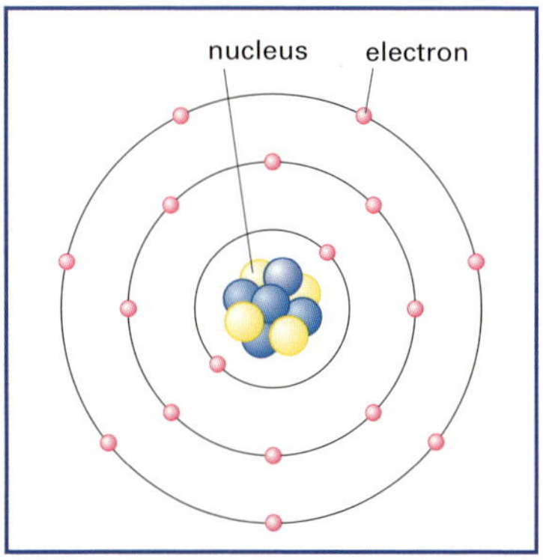

The ancient Greeks believed that the smallest part of nature is an •••[1]. However, 2,000 years ago they did not know that there are even smaller parts in nature. Today we know that atoms are made up of smaller particles: a nucleus of •••[2] and neutrons, surrounded by •••[3] which move around the nucleus much like the earth does around the sun. An atom's nucleus can be •••[4]. When this is done, a huge amount of •••[5] is released. This energy, when let out slowly, can be used to •••[6] electricity. When it is let out all at once, it causes an enormous •••[7] like in an atomic bomb. The word fission means to split. Inside the •••[8] of an atomic power plant, •••[9] are split in a controlled chain reaction.
Chain reaction means that the •••[10] that are released when an atom is split, go off and strike other uranium atoms, splitting those. Those particles given off split still other atoms in a •••[11]. To regulate this process control rods are needed.
The chain reaction gives off •••[12]. This heat energy is used to •••[13] water in the core of the reactor. In other words, nuclear power plants use the chain reaction of atoms to change the energy of atoms into heat energy. The water that surrounds the nuclear core is led to another part of the power plant where it heats another set of pipes which are filled with water. The steam produced in these pipes powers a •••[14] to generate electricity.

Use these words:

chain reaction ... heat energy ... electrons ... atom ... split ... energy ... generate ... uranium atoms ... boil ... particles ... turbine ... explosion ... protons ... reactor

Activity 7 Word Search

Find 12 words related to energy that are hidden across and up and down. Use each word in a complete sentence.

v	k	m	d	x	f	g	t	n	i	k	d	t	s	e	j
o	v	g	r	d	e	p	q	p	m	b	g	g	t	g	z
l	f	y	m	e	n	u	c	l	e	a	r	e	u	p	u
t	t	r	a	n	s	m	i	s	s	i	o	n	l	u	d
a	u	z	g	h	f	p	y	u	h	n	h	e	a	x	g
g	r	w	n	o	i	z	r	v	a	c	n	r	t	f	a
e	b	l	e	n	e	r	g	y	f	f	c	a	b	l	e
u	i	g	t	p	g	j	r	z	t	a	s	t	e	a	m
y	n	i	u	k	d	g	u	b	f	t	z	o	p	m	a
q	e	d	c	w	s	g	u	r	c	u	r	r	e	n	t

Alternative energy sources

When talking about alternative energy sources we might, for example, think of solar energy, hydro energy, geothermal energy, or wind energy. The following photographs show examples of alternative energy sources.

Activity 8 Talking about alternative energy sources

a) Which alternative energy sources do the photographs above refer to?

b) Which alternative energy sources are used …

1. at your house,

2. in your region,

3. in your country?

c) Discuss which alternative energy sources could also be used. Explain why or why not!

Wind energy

Humankind has used wind as a source of energy for thousands of years. The first windmills were probably built in Persia around 900 A.D. In the 19th century there were tens of thousands of windmills in Europe, mainly used to grind grain and to pump water. In recent years, however, another kind of windmill has become very important: windmills that produce electric energy by modern wind turbines. Meanwhile these wind turbines can be seen almost everywhere in Germany, even big wind farms with dozens of wind turbines exist.

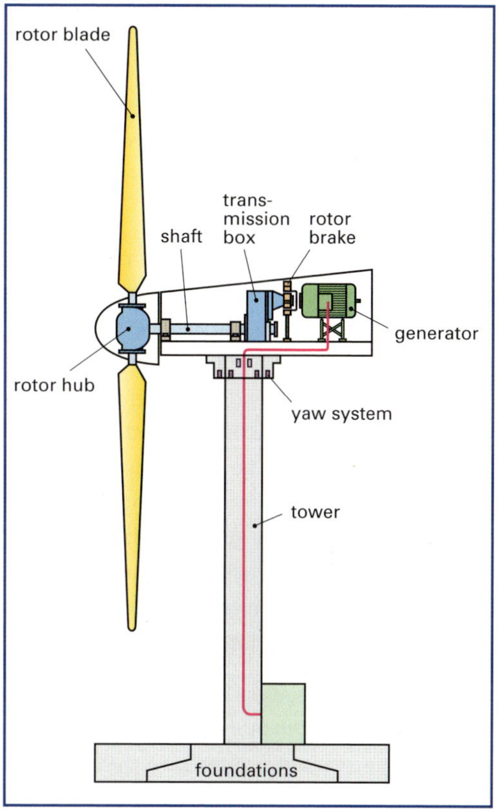

Horizontal axis wind turbine

Wind turbines convert the energy of wind into electricity. Blowing winds make the propeller of the turbine, called the rotor, go round. It consists of either two or three rotor blades which are attached to the rotor hub. The hub is mounted on a turning shaft which goes through a transmission box. The transmission increases the speed of rotation so that the attached generator rotates fast enough in order to produce electricity. The turbines are mounted on top of a tower of steel or concrete. Because of the length of the rotor blades the towers can be quite tall.

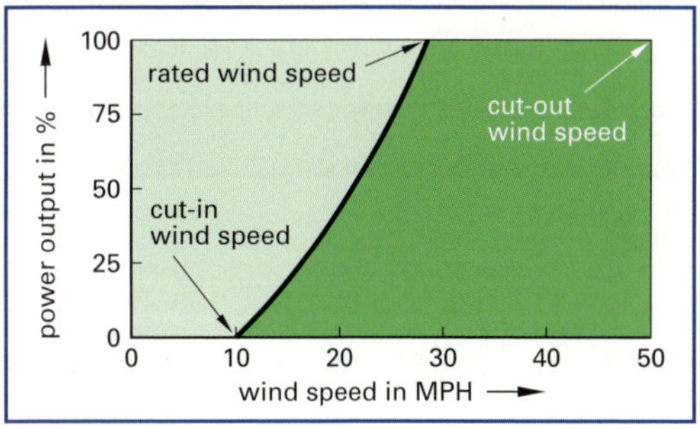

Idealized power curve for a wind turbine

The power output of a wind turbine varies with the wind's speed through the rotor. The ideal wind speed for generating electricity is between six and twenty-five metres per second. In order to operate a wind turbine efficiently an annual average wind speed of four to five metres per second is necessary. As a result extensive measurements have to be carried out before a construction site can be chosen.

Many systems are designed to have a constant power output. This can be achieved, for example, by automatically adjusting the rotor blades to the speed of the wind. In case of a storm a computer, which controls the whole system, puts the blades in a parked position and the generator is switched off.

Wind turbines are generally grouped into two types:

- **Vertical axis wind turbines,** in which the axis of rotation is vertical with respect to the ground
- **Horizontal axis turbines,** in which the axis of rotation is horizontal with respect to the ground

In most cases horizontal axis wind turbines are in operation. Wind generators must always look in the right direction. This means that the blades either face the wind directly or are driven from behind. For this reason the entire housing, called a nacelle, is mounted on a kind of turntable which can be turned by electric motors. The whole system including the necessary brakes, bearings and gears is called a yaw system. With the help of certain sensors that check the direction of the wind, the system always turns the rotor into the best direction.

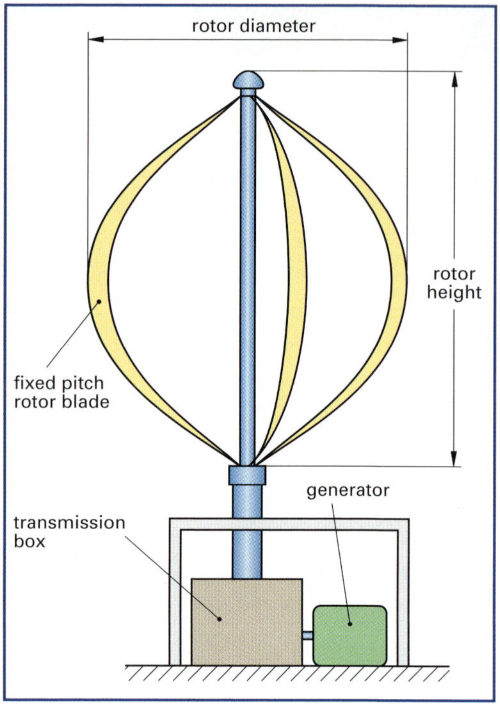

Vertical axis wind turbine

As well as being sited on land, wind farms could also be set up at sea, where strong winds blow more constantly. Off-shore wind power, as it is called, means to fix the bases of the wind turbines firmly to the sea bed, making sure that they can withstand the much more hostile conditions at sea. Denmark and the Netherlands have already planned and set up off-shore wind farms. Vindeby in Denmark, which was the first, has been operating since 1991. The turbines are sited 1.5 to 3 kilometres off the island of Lolland generating up to 5 MW of electricity. However, much bigger ones are in the planning stages.

Activity 9 Comprehension

Answer the questions with complete sentences.

1. Make a list of all rotating parts of a horizontal axis wind turbine.
2. Explain the function of the transmission box.
3. What does the height of the tower of a wind turbine depend on?
4. What is the function of the yaw system?
5. What must be considered before a wind turbine can be put up?
6. List up the advantages and disadvantages of off-shore wind parks.
7. According to the text the ideal wind speed is between 6 and 25 metres per second. Does this correspond to the diagram on the previous page? Explain your answer.
8. What wind speed (in m/s) is necessary to get 75% of the maximum power of a wind turbine?

Activity 10 The Alternative Energy Quiz

How much do you know about alternative energies? By answering the following questions you can collect energy, which will enable you to travel by car. How far? That depends on the amount of Joules you can collect. An average car needs about 250 MJ (J = Joule) to run 100 kilometres.

1. **250 MJ:** Alternative energies are also called ...
   a) available b) renewable c) suitable d) changeable
2. **300 MJ:** Which energy source is not an alternative one?
   a) sun b) wind c) oil d) biomass
3. **350 MJ:** People in industrial countries need about ... more energy than people in Third World countries.
   a) 3 times b) 7 times c) 10 times d) 14 times
4. **400 MJ:** Energy from ocean waves is a form of ...
   a) sun energy b) wind energy c) hydro energy d) geothermal energy
5. **450 MJ:** When hot water comes through a crack in the earth we call it ...
   a) a volcano b) a fountain c) an earthquake d) a geyser
6. **500 MJ:** What tidal range is necessary to use tidal energy economically?
   a) 2 m b) 5 m c) 9 m d) 15 m
7. **550 MJ:** What does "geothermal" energy mean? It means energy from the heat of ...
   a) the sun b) the earth c) the oceans d) tropical plants
8. **600 MJ:** Which is not biomass?
   a) tree branches b) leftover crops c) paper d) tree leaves
9. **650 MJ:** Solar cells are made of ...
   a) germanium b) silicon c) selenium d) carbon
10. **700 MJ:** The efficiency of solar cells is equal to ...
    a) 10% b) 17% c) 20% d) 25%
11. **750 MJ:** Solar cells are not used to power a ...
    a) satellite b) pocket calculator c) watch d) discman
12. **800 MJ:** According to scientist oil will run out in about ...
    a) 10 years b) 20 years c) 40 years d) 70 years
13. **850 MJ:** Which country uses most geothermal energy?
    a) Canada b) Norway c) Switzerland d) Iceland
14. **900 MJ:** The amount of energy that reaches the earth every day is equivalent to how many Hiroshima atomic bombs?
    a) 5000 b) 30000 c) 500000 d) 1000000
15. **950 MJ:** Which particles are responsible for the photovoltaic effect?
    a) neutrons b) quarks c) photons d) electrons
16. **1000 MJ:** Who discovered the photovoltaic effect?
    a) James Watt b) Alessandro Volta c) Edmund Bequerel d) Albert Einstein

Hydrogen – Energy of the future?

Introducing the situation

Robert Plant, editor of the local newspaper, wants to continue his series about alternative energies. To learn more about hydrogen as an energy source he is talking to Dr Peter Frazer, a scientist who has been working on the development of fuel cells for many years.

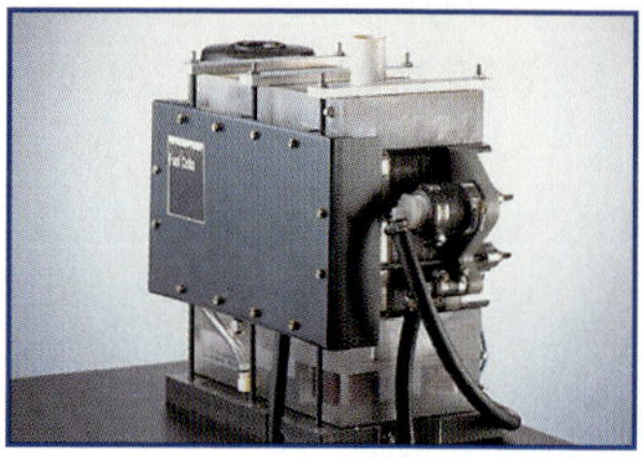

Fuel cell

R. PLANT Air pollution, greenhouse effect, acid rain – only three aspects that show the effects of burning fossil fuels. Factories and power plants but especially cars and trucks emit huge amounts of carbon dioxide (CO_2), the gas that is mainly responsible for heating up the earth's atmosphere. Dr Frazer, you believe hydrogen could help to solve these problems.

DR FRAZER That's right. Many scientists believe that our climate will change dramatically if we don't reduce the emissions of carbon dioxide. Cars have become the most important means of transport and the number of cars producing carbon dioxide is still increasing. It is very difficult to persuade people to use public transport because the car is so convenient and comfortable. This means we urgently need an energy source for cars that is absolutely clean: hydrogen.

R. PLANT How can hydrogen be used to power vehicles?

DR FRAZER Car manufacturers are working on two different systems. Hydrogen can be burned like petrol in an internal combustion engine. When burned in this way, hydrogen mainly turns into heat and water vapour. There is also a small amount of other gases, mostly oxides of nitrogen but the exhausts are free from carbon dioxide! The second system uses fuel cells to generate electricity to power an electric motor.

R. PLANT That means a fuel cell is similar to a battery? What has it got to do with hydrogen?

DR FRAZER Well, in principle, a fuel cell works like a battery but unlike a battery, a fuel cell does not run down or need recharging. It will produce energy as long as hydrogen fuel is supplied. Fuel cells combine oxygen from the air with hydrogen from the vehicle's fuel tank to produce electricity. When oxygen and hydrogen are combined they give off energy and water. In fuel cells this is done without any burning. By the way, fuel cells have been used on spacecraft for many years to power electric equipment.

R. PLANT If this is a well-known technology, why on earth haven't we used it in our cars yet?

DR FRAZER At present, fuel cell vehicles have only been developed as prototypes. Some of these cars can reach a speed of 90 mph and can travel up to about 280 miles before they need refuelling. However, without mass production they will be too expensive. Moreover, it's still a problem to store hydrogen on the vehicle, although it can be stored either as gaseous or liquid hydrogen. To carry gaseous hydrogen, it must be compressed and stored in high pressure containers. Another possibility is to store it in liquid form, which means it must be compressed and cooled down to –217 °C and maintained by a special insulated container. Both methods are common technology but the problem is the size of the containers. You can't sell cars without any luggage space.

R. PLANT — Isn't it very dangerous to carry hydrogen on a car? I remember the "Hindenburg" disaster in 1937 when the whole airship went up in flames because of the huge amount of hydrogen that was stored aboard the ship.

DR FRAZER — Hydrogen is highly flammable, that's right. One of the main problems would occur if there were a leak, but the safety standards are so high that I'm sure this won't happen as long as the guidelines for the handling and storage of hydrogen are observed.

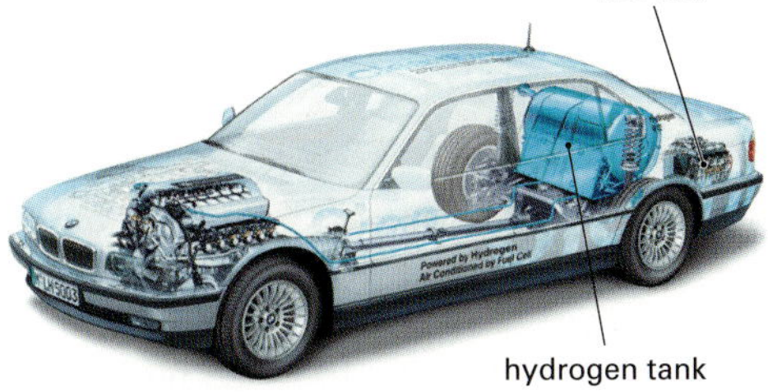

Prototype: Fuel cell car

R. PLANT — One last question, Dr Frazer. Where do we get all the hydrogen from in case this kind of energy will be used on a large scale one day?

DR FRAZER — In general, hydrogen is easy to produce through electrolysis: the splitting of water (H_2O) into oxygen and hydrogen by using electricity. Clean energy sources like the sun, wind or water can supply the necessary energy for this process. Hydrogen can also be extracted from biomass, landfill gas or methanol.

R. PLANT — Thank you very much, Dr Frazer.

Activity II Comprehension

Find questions to the following answers.

1. Carbon dioxide.
2. Cars are so convenient and comfortable.
3. It turns into heat and water vapour.
4. It produces electricity by combining oxygen and hydrogen.
5. In spacecraft.
6. It must be cooled down and compressed. Moreover, a special insulated container is needed.
7. Because the containers are so big that they use up most luggage space in a car.
8. It went up in flames in 1937.
9. You must observe the guidelines for its proper handling and storage.
10. Alternative energy sources can supply the necessary energy for this process.

Activity 12 Working with words

A few days after he had talked to Dr Frazer, the following report is published in the newspaper. Fill in the gaps with words from the text.

Burning •••[1] has caused a lot of environmental problems. Cars and trucks are among the main producers of carbon dioxide, the gas that is said to be responsible for the •••[2]. Dr Frazer, a leading scientist in the development of fuel cells, believes that hydrogen powered cars may help to reduce the amount of CO_2 in our •••[3]. Hydrogen can be used and burnt like petrol in •••[4]. The exhausts then mainly consist of •••[5] and a small amount of other gases, however, there is no •••[6]! Hydrogen can also be used to produce electricity in •••[7]. These cells give off energy when oxygen and hydrogen is •••[8] in them. There are already some prototypes of cars that are powered by •••[9] but the storage of hydrogen on vehicles is still a problem. Firstly, special •••[10] are needed that are still too big because they use up most luggage space. Secondly, hydrogen is a highly •••[11] gas and that means there could be an explosion in case of a leak. Nevertheless, hydrogen will be a clean source of energy for our •••[12] if we use alternative energy sources for the production of hydrogen.

Activity 13 Translation

Translate the Information "Fuel Cells" into German.

INFO: Fuel Cells

A fuel cell consists of two electrodes with an electrolyte between them. When oxygen passes over one electrode and hydrogen over the other, electricity is produced as well as water and heat. Hydrogen fuel is fed into the "anode" of the fuel cell. Oxygen (or air) enters the fuel cell through the "cathode". With the help of a catalyst, the hydrogen atoms split into protons and electrons, which then take different ways to get to the cathode. The protons pass through the electrolyte. The electrons create an electric current that can be utilised to power a consumer. Reaching the cathode the electrons reunite with the hydrogen and oxygen in a water molecule.

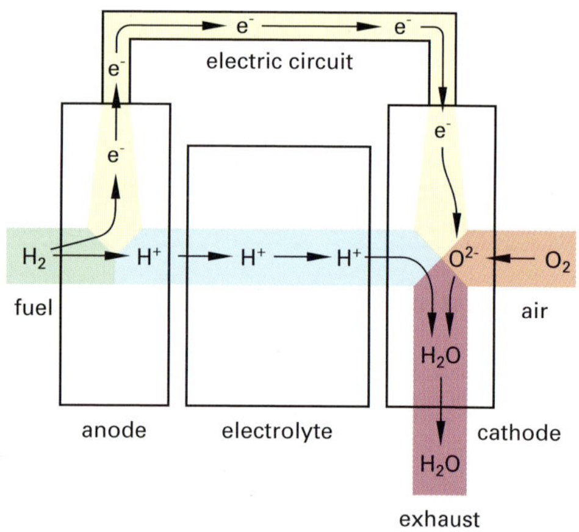

Vocabulary Unit 9

ability	Fähigkeit
to achieve	erreichen
to adjust	einstellen
airship	Luftschiff
ancient	alt
annual	jährlich
appliance	Gerät, Vorrichtung
to attach	befestigen
attempt	Versuch
average	Durchschnitt
bearing ['beərɪŋ]	Lager
blade	(Propeller) Flügel
boiler	Dampfkessel
to boost up	hoch transformieren, verstärken
brake	Bremse
branch	Ast, Zweig
cable	Kabel
catalyst ['kætəlɪst]	Katalysator
chain reaction	Kettenreaktion
climate	Klima
to combine	verbinden
to compress	verdichten
concrete	Beton
condenser	Kondensator
to conduct	leiten
conductive	leitend
to consist of	bestehen aus
constantly	ständig, konstant
construction site	Bauplatz
consumer	Verbraucher
consumption	Verbrauch
to control	steuern
control rod	Regelstab
convenient	bequem
to convert	umwandeln, umformen
cooling tower	Kühlturm
copper	Kupfer
core	Reaktorkern, Eisenkern
crack	Spalte, Riss
cross section	Querschnitt
development	Entwicklung
device	Gerät, Vorrichtung, Bauelement
diameter	Durchmesser
distribution	Verteilung
earthquake	Erdbeben
editor	Redakteur
efficiency	Wirkungsgrad
efficiently	effizient, gut
electrolysis	Elektrolyse
electrolyte [ɪ'lektrəlaɪt]	Elektrolyt
emission	Ausstoß, Emission
to emit	ausstoßen
to enable	ermöglichen
energy loss	Energieverlust
energy source	Energiequelle
entire	völlig, ganz
equivalent to	gleichwertig, gleichbedeutend
exhaust	Abgase, Auspuffgas
extensive	umfangreich
to extract	gewinnen, extrahieren
to face	gegenüberstehen
familiar	vertraut
fan	Lüfter, Ventilator
to feed	zuführen
firmly	fest
flammable	brennbar
fossil fuel	fossiler Brennstoff
fuel cell	Brennstoffzelle
gaseous ['gæsɪəs]	gasförmig
gear	Getriebe, Gang, Übersetzung
gear-wheel	Zahnrad
to generate	erzeugen
geothermal energy	Energie aus Erdwärme
giant	riesig, Riese
grain	Getreide
greenhouse effect	Treibhauseffekt
to grind	mahlen
to guess	vermuten
guidelines	Richtlinien
high-voltage pole	Hochspannungsmast
hostile	feindlich
humankind	Menschheit
hydro energy	Wasserenergie
hydrogen ['haɪdrədʒən]	Wasserstoff
induction	Induktion
insulated	isoliert
internal combustion engine	Verbrennungsmotor
landfill gas	Deponiegas
law of nature	Naturgesetz
leak	Leck
leftover crops	Erntereste
liquid	flüssig
magnetic field	Magnetfeld

Vocabulary Unit 9

majority	Mehrheit
mass production	Massenproduktion
means of transportation	Verkehrsmittel
to measure	messen
measurement	Messung
meter	Zähler
molecule ['mɒlɪkjuːl]	Molekül
to mount	errichten
neither ... nor	weder ... noch
nitrogen ['naɪtrədʒən]	Stickstoff
nuclear fission	Kernspaltung
nuclear power	Atomkraftwerk
nucleus	Atomkern
to observe	beachten
to occur	vorkommen
on a large scale	in großem Umfang
output	(Produktions)Leistung
overhead line	Überlandleitung
oxygen ['ɒksɪdʒən]	Sauerstoff
to persuade	überreden
pipe	Rohr
plug	Stecker
pollution	Verschmutzung, Schadstoffbelastung
to power	antreiben
power plant	Kraftwerk
pressure	Druck
proton	Proton
public transport	öffentliche Verkehrsmittel
to publish	veröffentlichen
to recharge	wiederaufladen
to refuel	auftanken
to release	freisetzen
renewable	erneuerbar
resistance	Widerstand
to reunite	wiedervereinigen
to rotate	drehen, rotieren
rotor blade	Flügelblatt
rotor hub	Rotornabe
sensor	Sensor
shaft	Welle
source	Quelle
to spin	(schnell) drehen, herumwirbeln
to split	spalten
stationary	feststehend
to store	speichern
to strike	treffen auf, stoßen gegen
substation	Umspannwerk
thermal power station	Wärmekraftwerk
tidal range	Tidenhub
to site	anlegen, aufstellen, platzieren
to transform	umformen
transformer	Transformator
transmission	Übertragung, Getriebe
transmission box	Getriebegehäuse
transmission line	Hochspannungsleitung
transmission pole	Hochspannungsmast
to transmit	übertragen
turntable	Drehscheibe
uranium [jʊ'reɪnɪəm]	Uran
urgently	dringend
to utilize	nutzen
vapour ['veɪpə(r)]	Wasserdampf
to vary	verändern
wire	Draht, Leitung
with respect to	in Bezug auf
to withstand	widerstehen
to wrap	(ein)wickeln
yaw system	Windrichtungs-nachführung

Additional Vocabulary

Atommülllagerung	radioactive waste storage
Bohrturm	drilling rig
elektr. Verteilernetz	grid
Energiebedarf	energy requirement
Energieeinsparung	energy conservation
Entschwefelung	desulphurization
Erdgas	natural gas
Gezeitenkraftwerk	tidal power plant
Heizkörper	radiator
Heizöl	fuel oil
Pumpspeicher-kraftwerk	pumping plant and reservoir
Staudamm	dam
Stausee	reservoir
Steinkohlebergwerk	coal mine, pit
Umwälzpumpe	circulation pump
Wärmepumpe	heat pump
Wärmespeicher	heat reservoir
Wärmetauscher	heat exchanger
Wasserkraftwerk	hydroelectric power station

10 Automotive Technology

In this unit you will learn something about the car workshop and components of the car.

The workshop's inside

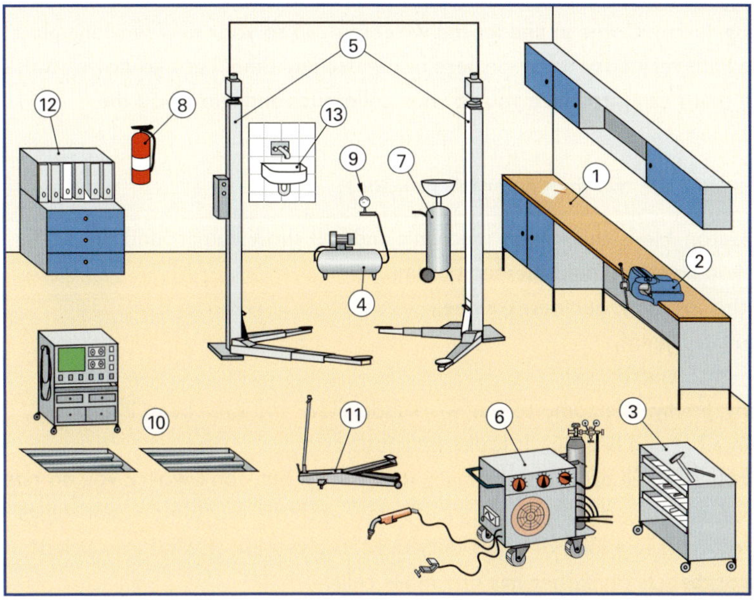

1. Workbench
2. Vice
3. Tool trolley
4. Compressor
5. Car lift
6. Welding machine
7. Engine sump drainer
8. Fire extinguisher
9. Pressure gauge
10. Diagnostic centre
11. Jack
12. Cupboard
13. Washbasin

Activity 1 Working with words

a) Copy the list next to the picture and translate the words into German.

b) Copy the sentences and complete them with the words from the box below.

1. We keep tools in a •••¹.
2. A •••² is needed to hold things.
3. In the •••³ we check the adjustment and condition of the engine.
4. Books and garage manuals are kept in the •••⁴.
5. After work we wash our hands in the •••⁵.
6. We need a •••⁶ to check the pressure of the tyres.
7. A •••⁷ is needed to lift up a car.
8. According to the safety regulations a •••⁸ is needed in a workshop in case of fire.

Use these words:

diagnostic centre ... tool trolley ... vice ... cupboard ... washbasin ... fire extinguisher ... car lift ... pressure gauge

The first day at the workshop

Introducing the situation

Jimmy is nervous. He is 15 years old and he is starting his apprenticeship as a car mechanic today. He arrives at the workshop at 7:30 am. Straight away he goes to the garage owner's office. Mr Hendrix is very busy writing job cards.

JIMMY Good morning, Mr Hendrix.

MR HENDRIX Good morning, Jimmy. Come in and let me welcome you to your new working place. I'm sorry but I am very busy today. So, let's not waste any time. Let's go down to the workshop, so that I can introduce you to your colleagues and show you the workshop.

A few minutes later the two men enter the workshop.

This is Mr Clapton. He is the master mechanic and will show you around the workshop. If you need any help, please ask him.
Mr Clapton, this is Jimmy, our new trainee.
Okay, see you later, Jimmy.

JIMMY See you later, Mr Hendrix.

MR CLAPTON Good morning, Jimmy. Welcome to our workshop. Have you ever been in a garage?

JIMMY Yes, but not in a big one like this. It looks very interesting.

MR CLAPTON If you look around, you'll probably see many new things. But don't worry, you do not have to know everything on the first day. Let's start with the most important things: Over there you can see a kind of heavy-duty table. Do you know what it is called?

JIMMY Sure, it is a workbench. My father has one in his cellar.

MR CLAPTON Fine, and what is mounted on the workbench?

JIMMY That's a vice. It is a device to hold things.

MR CLAPTON Right, Jimmy. Over there you see our mechanic Eric, working underneath a car. He has lifted up the car with a …?

JIMMY I think it's called a car lift.

MR CLAPTON Yes. And where does he keep all the tools?

JIMMY It's called a tool trolley.

MR CLAPTON Very good, Jimmy. I think this is enough for now. Maybe we will talk about some tools later.

Activity 2 Comprehension

Answer the questions in full sentences and with your own words.

1. What does Jimmy start with today?
2. What is Mr Hendrix doing when Jimmy enters the office?
3. What status does Mr Clapton have in the workshop?
4. What equipment does Jimmy's father have in his cellar?
5. Where does the mechanic Eric keep his tools?

The tool trolley's inside

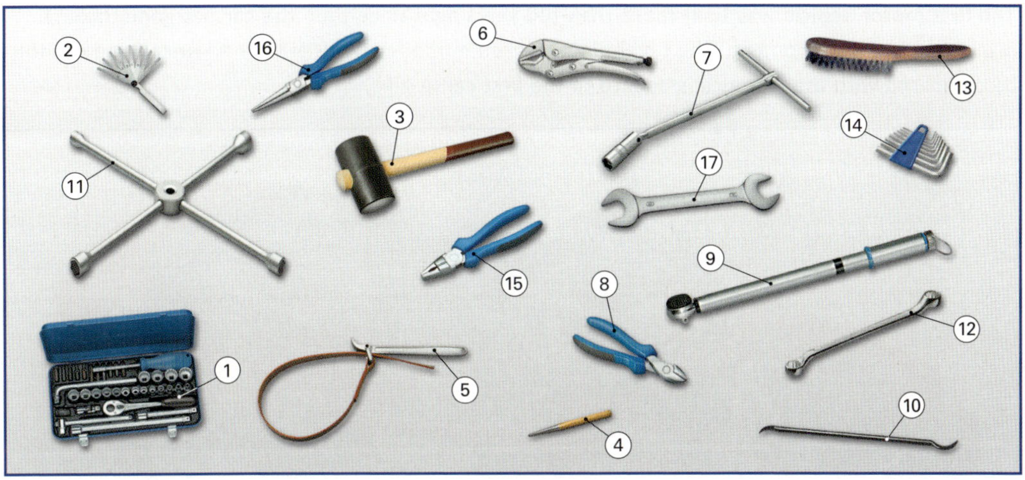

Activity 3 — Working with words

a) Match the following equipment to the numbers given in the picture and translate them.

Use these words:

torque wrench ... feeler gauge ... vice grip pliers ... lever ... set of Allen keys ... rim wrench ... strap wrench (oil filter wrench) ... long-nose pliers ... rubber mallet ... centre punch ... wire brush ... open-ended spanner ... ring spanner ... side cutter ... combination pliers ... socket set ... spark plug wrench

b) Assign the tools from the box above to the following definitions.

The tool you use ...

1. ...if the hexagon is inside the head of the bolt.
2. ...if you want to replace the spark plugs.
3. ...to clean the thread of a bolt.
4. ...to tighten a bolt according to the garage manual.
5. ...for checking the valve gap.
6. ...if you want to shorten a wire.
7. ...to mark the centre of a hole before drilling.
8. ...to loosen the oilfilter.
9. ...to remove the wheel cap.
10. ...to loosen the rim nuts.

c) Choose a tool from the picture above and describe it in full sentences with your own words. Your partner has to find out which tool you are describing. Then change roles.

Car technology

The first motor vehicle was built more than 100 years ago. Since then the car has gone through many stages of development. The technology applied in modern cars is very advanced and cannot be compared with the technical standard of the first car at all.

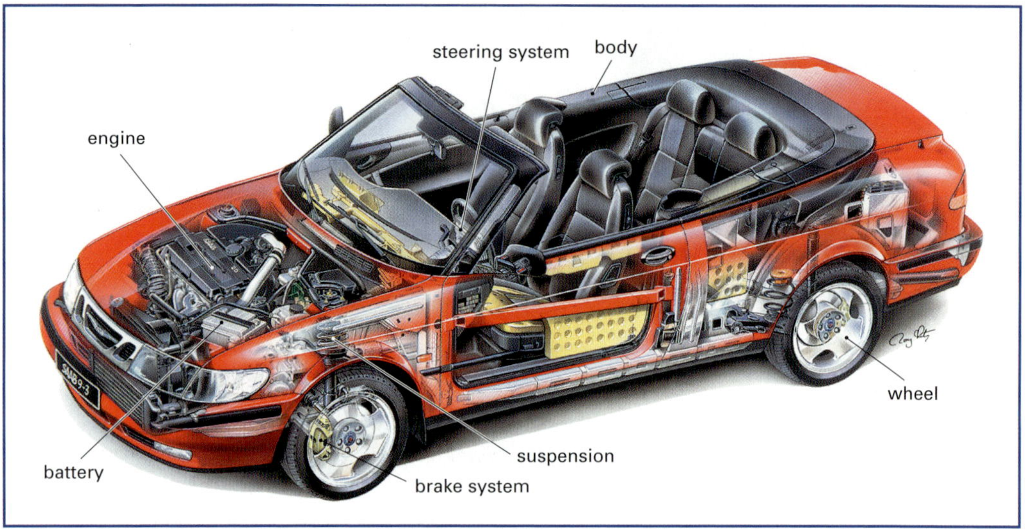

When developing a new car, engineers have to pay attention to the law, pollution, safety, purpose of use, and customers' wishes. The car is subdivided into sections. The basic components of the car are shown in the following flow chart.

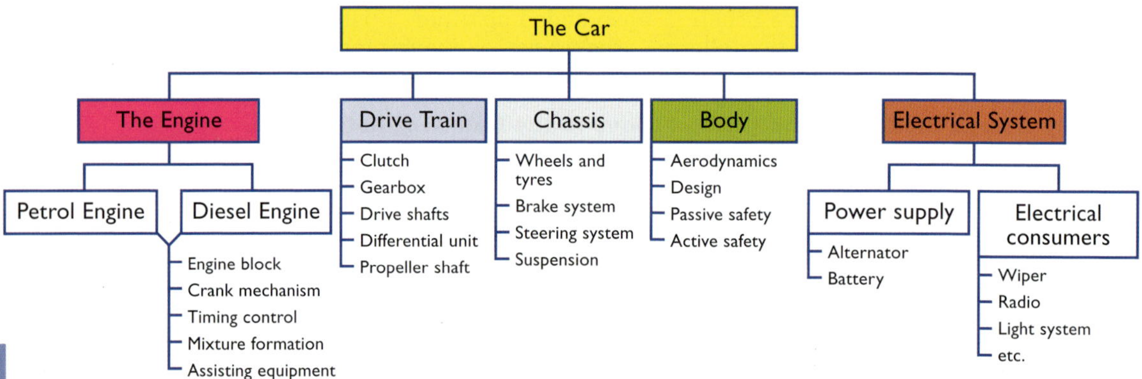

One can imagine, how complicated and expensive it is to produce a car. It is, however, interesting to know how the single components of a car form a unit which allows the car to move. Some facilities are controlled by the driver himself. With others he does not realize when they are in action. These facilities are subdivided in those for the passengers' comfort and safety and those for the reduction of pollution and various other purposes. We distinguish between active and passive safety. Active safety refers to features of the vehicle which reduce the probability of an accident. Passive safety features are intended to protect the passengers in case of an accident.

Activity 4 Vocabulary

a) Look up the following words in a dictionary and write the translation in your exercise book.

1. clutch
2. motor vehicle
3. engine
4. suspension
5. equipment
6. law
7. pollution
8. facility
9. occupants
10. accident
11. passengers
12. components
13. customer
14. design
15. safety

b) Check the words in row 1. to 6. and find out which one does not fit.

	a	b	c	d
1.	drive train	clutch	brake	gearbox
2.	brake	steering	wheel	light
3.	occupant	passive safety	drive shaft	body
4.	engine	timing control	propeller shaft	crank mechanism
5.	power supply	transmission	alternator	battery
6.	suspension	drive shaft	design	car

Activity 5 Understanding the text

a) True or false? Correct the statements that are wrong.

1. The clutch is a part of the engine.
2. The history of the motor vehicle is more than 100 years old.
3. Passive safety means to protect the occupants in case of an accident.
4. Active safety means to protect the occupants in case of an accident.
5. Producing a car is complicated but cheap.
6. The car as such is subdivided into sections.
7. Each facility works independently from the remaining components of the car.
8. Only some of the safety facilities are controlled by the driver himself.

b) Answer the following questions.

1. Which are the five components of the car?
2. What is the difference between active and passive safety?
3. To which component does the brake system belong?
4. What do the engineers have to pay attention to when designing a car?
5. Why is it complicated and expensive to produce a car?

The engine of a car

There are many different kinds of engines. They differ in the way they work, how they convert energy and how they are constructed. The most popular engines are the petrol engine (also known as Otto engine) and the diesel engine. Both engines are "four-stroke engines". Their main parts are similar.

The engine is a device which converts heat energy into mechanical energy to do work. Engines burn fuel internally and therefore they are called "internal combustion engines".

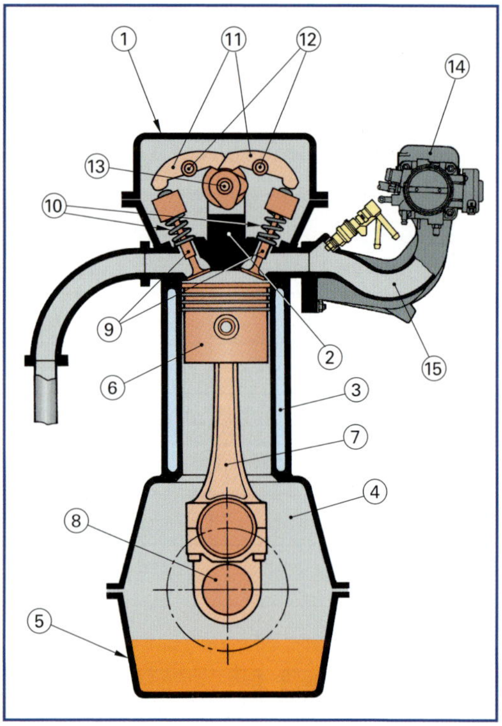

In general an engine is divided into the following sections (see picture):

- **the engine block**
rocker cover (1), cylinder head (2), cylinder (3), crank case (4), oil sump (5)

- **the crank mechanism**
piston (6), connecting rod (7), crankshaft (8)

- **the timing control**
valves (9), valve springs (10), rocker arms (11), rocker shaft (12), camshaft (13), timing gears, timing chain or timing belt

- **the mixture formation**
injection system (14) or carburettor, intake manifold (15)

- **the assisting equipment**
ignition system, lubrication system, cooling system, exhaust system

A piston glides in a cylinder by reciprocal movements. In technical language we say:
The piston moves from "top dead centre" (TDC) to "bottom dead centre" (BDC).

The piston is connected to the crankshaft by a connecting rod. Therefore the reciprocal movement of the piston is converted into a rotating movement of the crankshaft. The crankshaft has got a section which is off-centre from the centre line of the shaft, therefore, it "cranks" when the shaft turns. (When pedalling a bicycle, for example, your leg acts as a connecting rod while the pedal crank and sprocket work like a crankshaft.)

The exchange of gas in the combustion chamber is controlled by valves. The valves are opened by a "cam" from the camshaft. They are closed by the force of the valve springs.

The camshaft is driven by the crankshaft, either by a gear, a chain or a belt. The camshaft rotates half as often as the crankshaft, in other words: the ratio is 1:2.

The air-fuel mixture is ignited either by a spark (petrol engine) or by the heat of the air-fuel mixture, caused by compression (diesel engine). This happens shortly before TDC. Right after

TDC the air-fuel mixture is burned completely and the highest pressure in the cylinder is achieved. Due to the rapid expanding air-fuel mixture the piston is forced toward BDC. The inertia of mass causes the continuation of movement, therefore, the piston comes over to the next power stroke. The exchange of gas (exhaust gas out and fresh gas in) is controlled by the valves.

The picture below shows some details of the four-stroke cycle.

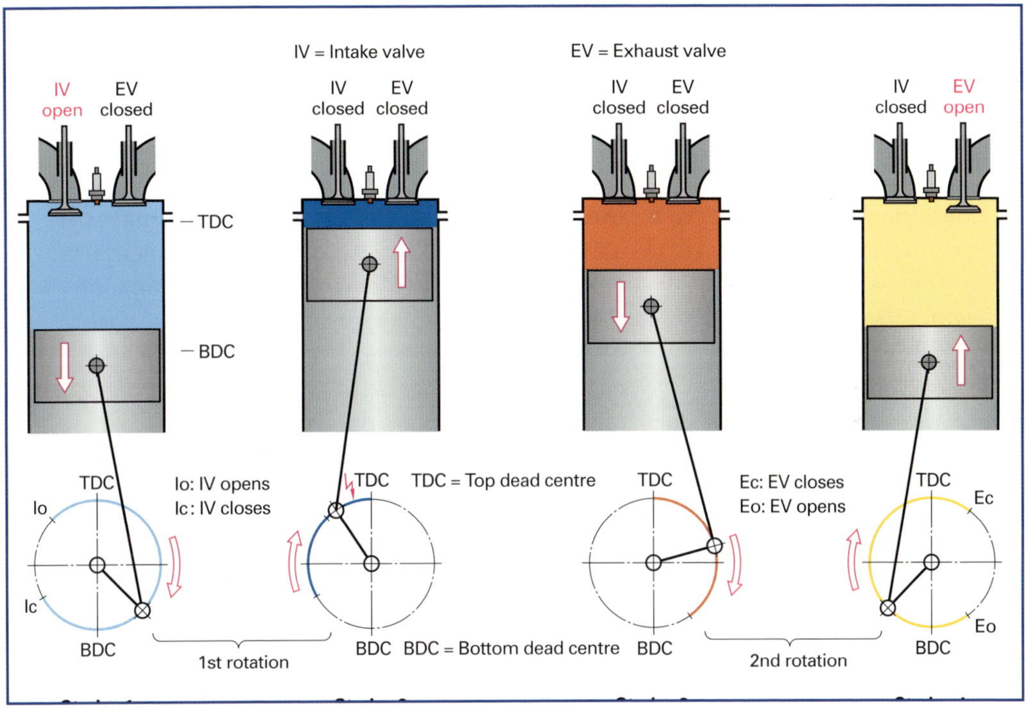

Intake stroke (induction)	Compression stroke	Power stroke	Exhaust stroke
The piston moves from TDC to BDC. The intake valve is open. An air-fuel mixture is drawn into the combustion chamber.	Intake and exhaust valves are closed. The air-fuel mixture gets compressed by the movement of the piston from BDC to TDC. Prior to TDC a spark (or the heat) ignites the mixture.	Both valves are closed. The piston is forced towards BDC by the rapidly burning and vigorously expanding gas.	The exhaust valve is open. The piston moves from BDC to TDC. Therefore the exhaust gas is pushed out of the combustion chamber.

Note the position of the valves in different phases. In the compression stroke the time of ignition is indicated by ϟ.

Activity 6 Comprehension

a) Answer the following questions.

1. In which position is the intake valve during the power stroke?
2. Which are the five components needed to construct an engine?
3. What is the meaning of TDC and BDC?
4. Which parts are connected by the connecting rod?
5. What is the ratio of the camshaft to the crankshaft?
6. What is the second stroke called?
7. Explain what happens during the "compression stroke".
8. Which section does the "rocker shaft" belong to?
9. To which different sections do the camshaft and the crankshaft belong to?

b) Combine the phrases 1. to 6. and the phrases a) to f) to form new sentences.

1. (petrol engine).	a) The piston is connected to the crankshaft
2. by the valves.	b) The camshaft is driven by the crankshaft
3. right after TDC.	c) The air-fuel mixture is ignited by a spark
4. by a connecting rod.	d) The air-fuel mixture is ignited by heat
5. (diesel engine).	e) The highest pressure in the cylinder is achieved
6. by a gear, a chain or a belt.	f) The exchange of gas is controlled

Activity 7 Working with words

Copy the following sentences into your exercise book and complete them with the words from the box below.

1. The air-fuel mixture is •••[1] either by spark or by heat.
2. The camshaft rotates •••[2] as the crankshaft (the ratio is 1:2).
3. A piston is gliding in a cylinder by •••[3] movements.
4. The engine is a device which converts •••[4a] into •••[4b] to do work.
5. The full name of an engine is •••[5].
6. The piston is •••[6] to the crankshaft by a connecting rod.

Use these words:

heat energy … connected … internal combustion engines … half as often … mechanical energy … ignited … reciprocal

Activity 8 Understanding the text

a) Explain the four-stroke principle. Name the strokes in the right order and explain what happens in each stroke.

b) Explain the function of the engine in your own words.

At the vocational training centre

Introducing the situation

Today's subject of the lesson at the vocational training centre is the drive train. Mr Mercury is the teacher for this section.

MR MERCURY: Good morning everybody. Today we will talk about the drive train. Who knows the parts that belong to the drive train?

There is no answer from the students.

MR MERCURY: Well, when we talk about the drive train we talk about the power flow from the engine to the wheels. Which components do you think belong to the power flow?

PETER: Well, I think there is the gearbox, the propeller shaft, the differential unit and the drive shafts.

MR MERCURY: You are right, Peter. But there is still one component missing.

JIMMY: I think, it is the clutch.

MR MERCURY: Good, Jimmy. The components in the correct order of the power flow are the clutch, the gearbox, the propeller shaft, the differential unit and the two drive shafts. Now we want to find out the purpose of each part. Let's start with the clutch. Who can tell us something about the clutch?

MARK: The main purpose of the clutch is to allow a gradual and smooth start from a position at rest. Furthermore the clutch disconnects the engine from the gearbox if we want to change gears.

MR MERCURY: Good. Now, next in line there is the gearbox. Which function does the gearbox have? What do you think, Anne?

ANNE: The gearbox makes it possible to drive at different speed levels. I think from starting off, up to high speeds on the highway or up a hill. When reversing, the rotation is inverted in the gearbox. Nowadays most gearboxes have got five forward gears and one reverse gear.

MR MERCURY: Perfect, Anne. You have a good knowledge about the function of a gearbox. But there are three parts left. Mike, can you explain the remaining parts?

MIKE: I'm not sure, but I'll try. Well, the propeller shaft, or prop shaft, is needed only on rear-wheel and four-wheel driven vehicles. It transmits the rotation from the gearbox to the differential unit. One function of the differential is to change the rotation from lengthwise to crosswise. The other function is to equalize the differences of the outer and the inner wheel when going around a corner. Going around a corner means that the outer wheel has to cover a longer distance than the inner one. Finally we have got the drive shafts. They transmit the rotation from the differential unit to the wheels. Therefore we have one at each side.

MR MERCURY: Very good, Mike. Thanks to you all. You gave us very good explanations.

Activity 9 Working with words

Match the following equipment to the numbers given in the picture and translate them.

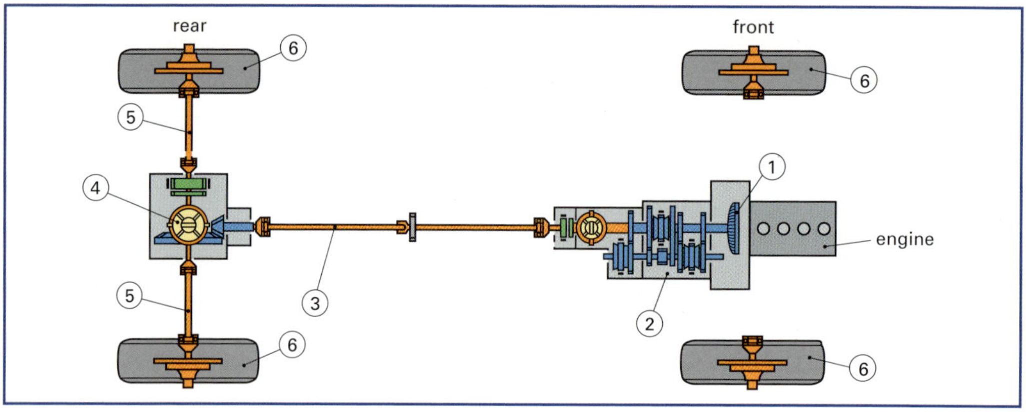

Use these words:

drive shafts ... gearbox ... wheels ... differential unit ... clutch ... propeller shaft

Activity 10 Understanding the text

a) Name the five components of the drive train and set them in the correct order of the power flow.

b) True or false? Correct the statements that are wrong.

1. Mike is sure about the purpose of the propeller shaft, the differential and the drive shafts.
2. The clutch connects the gearbox to the differential unit.
3. The clutch disconnects the engine from the gearbox.
4. The engine is a component of the drive train.
5. The correct order in the drive train according to the power flow is: clutch, gearbox, propeller shaft, differential unit, drive shafts.
6. One function of the differential unit is to change the rotation from lengthwise to crosswise.

c) Answer the following questions.

1. What is the main purpose of the clutch?
2. Which vehicle type needs a prop shaft? Explain why.
3. What is the difference between the prop shaft and the drive shaft?
4. What is the function of the gearbox?
5. What is the function of the drive train?
6. Which part of the drive train is responsible for the adaptation of the wheel rotation in a curve?

The brake

We need a facility to reduce the speed of a vehicle. The brake is used, for example, to prevent an accident or when stopping at a red traffic light. Even the brake has gone through different stages of development. While constructing the brake system the engineers have to pay attention to the type and weight of the vehicle, the maximum speed, the design and the law.

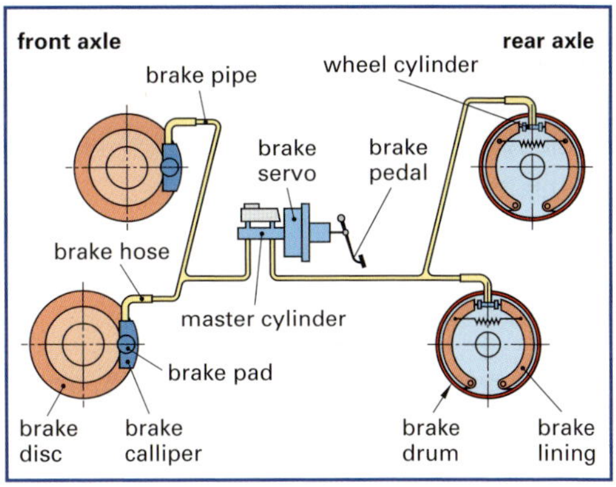

Modern cars are equipped with hydraulic brake systems. According to the law an additional mechanical brake system is also necessary.

Brake systems are available as drum brakes or disc brakes. More and more modern vehicles are equipped with disc brakes on all wheels. But still a combination of disc brakes on the front axle and drum brakes on the rear axle is very common. Whatever system is used, the power from the brake pedal is transmitted to the wheels via brake fluid.
For normal practical purposes, the hydraulic brake fluid may be regarded as incompressible.

When the brake pedal is pressed, the brake fluid is displaced from the brake master cylinder into the wheel cylinders via brake pipes and brake hoses. This causes a movement of the pistons in the brake callipers which press the brake pads towards the brake discs. The function of the drum brake is quite similar.

Note the different names of the parts!

Parts of the disc brake	Corresponding parts of the drum brake
brake calliper brake pads brake disc	wheel cylinder brake linings brake drum

Friction can cause extremly high temperatures! Brake fluid is hygroscopic. This means that brake fluid absorbs humidity from the atmosphere. A mixture of brake fluid and water is very dangerous. If the mixture gets hot, the water evaporates and steam bubbles develop. Since steam is compressible, there is no direct transport of the displacement from the master cylinder to the wheel cylinders.

It is recommended to change the brake fluid once a year, for your own safety and for the safety of other people.

Due to the high temperature caused by the force of friction the brake lining and the brake pad materials are worn out. Furthermore the diameter of the brake drum expands, therefore, the gap between the brake lining and the brake drum increases. This effect reduces the braking force. It is called "brake fading".

Activity 11 Vocabulary

a) Look up the following words in a dictionary and write the translation into your exercise book.

1. master cylinder
2. brake booster/brake servo
3. brake disc
4. brake pad
5. brake calliper
6. brake hose
7. brake pipe
8. brake drum
9. brake shoe/brake lining
10. wheel cylinder
11. brake fluid

b) Check the words in row 1. to 6. and find out which one does not fit.

	a	b	c	d
1.	brake pad	brake disc	master cylinder	brake calliper
2.	brake	brake fluid	light	safety
3.	hygroscopic	wheel cylinder	300 °C	humidity
4.	brake drum	displacement	wheel cylinder	master cylinder
5.	brake fluid	every year	brake pipe	replace
6.	brake fading	wheel cylinder	high temperature	force of friction

Activity 12 Comprehension

a) True or false? Correct the statements that are wrong.

1. Brake fluid does not have to be changed regularly.
2. The function of the drum brake and the disc brake is quite similar.
3. All cars are equipped only with a mechanical brake system.
4. Old brake fluid reduces the safety of the car.
5. A combination of a disc brake and a drum brake is still very common.
6. Friction can cause extremely high temperatures.
7. When constructing a brake system the maximum speed of a vehicle does not matter.
8. Steam is incompressible.

b) Answer the following questions.

1. What kind of brake systems are modern vehicles equipped with?
2. What do engineers have to pay attention to when constructing a brake system?
3. What is the difference between disc brakes and drum brakes?
4. Which parts does the disc brake system need?
5. How does the power from the brake pedal reach the wheels? Explain the process.
6. Explain what the brake fluid is required for.
7. Why is a mixture of brake fluid and water very dangerous?
8. What does "brake fading" mean?

Vocabulary Unit 10

to absorb	aufsaugen
air filter	Luftfilter
air-fuel mixture	Luft-Kraftstoff-Gemisch
Allen key	Innensechskant-schlüssel
alternator	Generator, Licht-maschine
apprenticeship [ə'prentɪʃɪp]	Lehre, Ausbildung
approximately	ungefähr
assisting equipment	Hilfseinrichtungen
atmosphere	Atmosphäre
axle ['æksl]	Achse
bolt	Bolzen, Schraube
bottom dead centre	unterer Totpunkt
brake	Bremse
brake calliper	Bremssattel
brake disc	Bremsscheibe
brake drum	Bremstrommel
brake fading	Bremsfading
brake fluid	Bremsflüssigkeit
brake hose	Bremsschlauch
brake lining	Bremsbelag
brake pad	Bremsklotz
brake pedal	Bremspedal
brake pipe	Bremsleitung
brake servo	Bremskraftverstärker
brake shoes	Bremsbacken
brake system	Bremsanlage
camshaft ['kæmʃa:ft]	Nockenwelle
car lift	Hebebühne
carburettor	Vergaser
centre punch	Körner
centre line	Mittellinie
chain	Kette
clutch	Kupplung
combination pliers	Kombizange
combustion chamber	Verbrennungsraum, Brennkammer
compression	Kompression, Verdichtung
compression stroke	Verdichtungstakt
compressor	Kompressor
connecting rod	Pleuelstange
consumption	Verbrauch
continuation	Fortsetzung
to convert	umformen, umwandeln
cooling system	Kühlsystem

corner	Ecke
crank case	Kurbelgehäuse
crank mechanism	Kurbeltrieb
crankshaft ['kræŋkʃa:ft]	Kurbelwelle
crosswise	quer
cylinder	Zylinder
cylinder head	Zylinderkopf
to design	konstruieren
design	Konstruktion, Bau-form, Ausführung
development	Entwicklung
device	Gerät, Vorrichtung, Bauelement
diagnostic centre	Diagnosezentrum
differential	Differential
to disconnect	trennen
to displace	verschieben
drive shaft	Antriebswelle
drive train	Antriebstrakt
engine	Motor
engine block	Motorblock
engine sump drainer	Altölbehälter
to equalize	ausgleichen
equipment	Ausstattung
exhaust fumes	Abgase
exhaust stroke	Ausstoßtakt
exhaust system	Auspuffsystem
to expand	ausdehnen
facility	Einrichtung, Leich-tigkeit
feature	Merkmal
feeler gauge	Fühlerlehre
fire extinguisher	Feuerlöscher
formation	Bildung
four-stroke engine	Viertaktmotor
four-wheel drive	Allradantrieb
friction ['frɪkʃn]	Reibung
garage manual	Werkstatt-Handbuch
garage owner	Werkstattbesitzer
gear	Getriebe, Gang, Übersetzung
gearbox	Getriebe(gehäuse)
gear wheel (gear)	Zahnrad
gradual	allmählich
heat resistance	Hitzefestigkeit
heavy-duty	strapazierfähig
hexagon ['heksəgən]	Sechskant
humidity	Feuchtigkeit

Vocabulary Unit 10

hydraulic brake system	hydraulische Bremsanlage
hygroscopic	wasserziehend
to ignite [ɪg'naɪt]	entzünden
ignition system	Zündsystem
incompressible	nicht komprimierbar
independence	Unabhängigkeit
inertia [ɪ'nɜːʃə]	Trägheit
injection system	Einspritzsystem
intake manifold	Ansaugstutzen
intake stroke	Ansaugtakt
internal combustion engine	Verbrennungsmotor
to invert	umkehren
item	Gegenstand
jack	Wagenheber
job card	Arbeitskarte
lengthwise	der Länge nach
lever	Hebel, Brechstange
long-nose pliers	Schnabelzange
to loosen	lösen, lockern
lubrication system	Schmiersystem
mixture formation	Gemischaufbereitung
motor vehicle	Kraftfahrzeug
mounted	montiert
nut	(Schrauben)Mutter
off-centre	außermittig
oil sump	Ölwanne
open-ended spanner	Maulschlüssel
operation	Funktionsweise
to pay attention	beachten
piston ['pɪstən]	Kolben
pollution	Verschmutzung, Schadstoff-belastung
power flow	Kraftfluss
power stroke	Arbeitstakt
pressure gauge	Druckmanometer
to prevent	verhindern
propeller shaft	Kardanwelle
purpose of use	Einsatzzweck
ratio ['reɪʃɪəʊ]	Verhältnis
rear-wheel drive	Heckantrieb
reciprocal movement	Hin- und Herbewegung
to recommend	empfehlen
to reduce	verringern
to refer to	Bezug nehmen auf
requirement	Bedarf
reverse gear	Rückwärtsgang
rim	Felge
rim wrench	Radkreuz
ring spanner	Ringschlüssel
rocker arm	Kipphebel
rocker cover	Ventildeckel
rocker shaft	Kipphebelwelle
rotating movement	drehende Bewegung
rotation	Umdrehung
rubber mallet	Gummihammer
safety	Sicherheit
section	Abschnitt, Teil
side cutter	Seitenschneider
socket set	Steckschlüsselsatz
spark	Funke
spark(ing) plug	Zündkerze
spark plug wrench	Zündkerzenschlüssel
speed	Geschwindigkeit
sprocket ['sprɒkɪt]	Kettenrad
steam bubbles	Dampfblasen
steering	Lenkung
status	Stellung, Rang
strap wrench	Bandschlüssel
stroke	Takt
to subdivide	unterteilen
suspension	Federung, Aufhängung
thread [θret]	Gewinde
to tighten	festziehen
timing	Steuerung
timing control	Ventilsteuerung
tool trolley	Werkzeugwagen
top dead centre	oberer Totpunkt
torque wrench [tɔːk]	Drehmoment-schlüssel
trainee	Auszubildende(r)
to transmit	übertragen
valve	Ventil
valve gap	Ventilspiel
valve spring	Ventilfeder
vice [vaɪs]	Schraubstock
vice grip pliers	Gripzange
vocational training	Berufsausbildung
welding machine	Schweißgerät
wheel	Rad
wheel cylinder	Radbremszylinder
windscreen wiper	Scheibenwischer
wire	Draht
workbench	Werkbank
workshop manager	Werkstattleiter

11 Working on Metal

In this unit you will learn about the terminology of a twist drill and you will get some information about how to grind the point of a twist drill. In the second section you will get some insight into the milling process and milling tools. In the third section you will learn something about turning and lathes.

Drilling

Making a hole in a piece of metal is generally a simple operation but in most cases it is an important and precise job. There is a large number of different tools and machines available, so that holes can be made quickly, economically and accurately in all kinds of material. In order to use these tools efficiently, it is important to become familiar with them. The most common tool for making holes in metal is the **twist drill**.

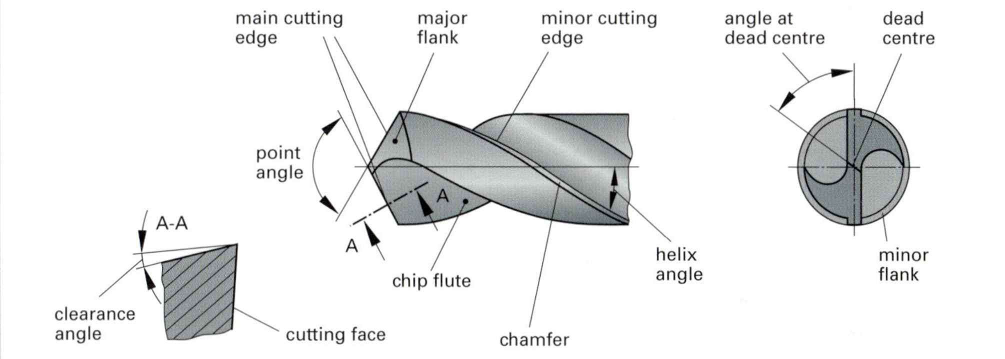

It consists of a cylindrical piece of steel with spiral grooves. One end of the cylinder is pointed while the other end is shaped so that it can be attached to a drilling machine. The grooves, usually called flutes, are cut into the steel cylinder. The main parts of a twist drill are the body, the shank, and the point. The chisel edge, also called the dead centre, of a twist drill is the sharp edge at the extreme tip of the drill. It should always be in the exact centre of the axis of the drill. The point is the complete cone-shaped end of the drill. The lip or cutting edge of a drill is that part of the point that actually cuts away the metal when drilling a hole. It is usually as sharp as the edge of a knife. A normal twist drill has two cutting edges.

The lip clearance of a drill is the surface of the point that is ground away of the back of the cutting edge of the drill. The strip along the inner edge of the body is called the chamfer. It is the largest diameter of the drill and extends to the whole length of the flute. The diameter at the end of the body is smaller than the diameter at the point. This allows the drill to revolve without grating when drilling deep holes. The shank is the part of the drill which fits into the socket, spindle, or chuck of the drill press.

Activity 1 Matching exercise

Look at the drawing of the twist drill and match the English expressions of the parts of the drill with the German ones in the following list.

a) Hauptschneide
b) Hauptfreifläche
c) Spitzenwinkel
d) Freiwinkel
e) Querschneide
f) Nebenfreifläche
g) Spanfläche
h) Führungsfase
i) Spannut
j) Querschneidenwinkel
k) Nebenschneide

Sharpening of twist drills

In order to produce a hole properly there are certain requirements which are of greatest importance in twist drill grinding:

1. equal-length cutting lips
2. correct clearance behind the cutting lips
3. correct chisel-edge angle
4. equal and correctly sized drill-point angles

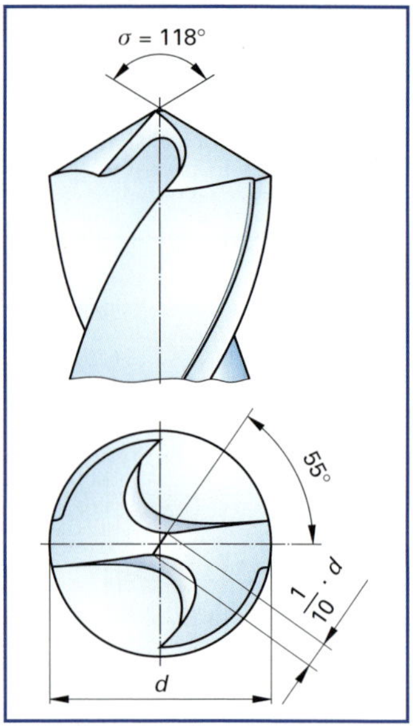

These four requirements are equally important when grinding either a regular point or a flat point which is used for drilling hard and tough materials. The figure on the right shows the correct specifications for grinding a regular point twist drill. To sharpen twist drills, first get the grinder ready. If necessary, dress the face of the grinding disc so that it is clean, a true circle, and square with the sides. Before starting the grinder, adjust the tool rest to 1 mm from the face of the wheel. This is an important safety measure which helps to keep the drill from wedging between the tool rest and the face of the wheel.

Sharpening a twist drill by hand is a skill that is mastered only after a lot of practice and careful attention to the details. Therefore, whenever possible, use a tool grinder in which the drill is properly positioned, clamped in place and set with precision for the various angles. Grinding with the machine will enable you to sharpen the drills accurately. As a result, they will last longer and will produce more accurate holes.

Whether you sharpen a drill by hand or by machine, it is very important that the temperature at the point is kept down. If the point gets hot, it approaches the temperature at which the temper of the steel will be lost. Keep the point cool enough to be held in your bare hand. Do this by making a few light passes over the grinding wheel. Take a few seconds to let the point cool down and repeat alternate grinding and cooling.

If you notice that there appears a blue temper colour at the point, it is too late. You have lost the temper and the steel is now too soft to maintain a cutting edge.

Then the only thing you can do is to continue the sharpening process to remove the soft tip. First sharpen one lip and then the other, until you have finally ground away the soft tip of the drill.

Activity 2 Understanding technical descriptions

Read the text carefully and answer the following questions.

1. What conditions must a correctly ground point of a twist drill fulfil?
2. What point angle must a correctly ground point for normal steel have?
3. What should you do before you start grinding the point?
4. Why must you avoid that the point gets hot?
5. How can you avoid that the tip of the twist drill gets hot?
6. What must you do if the temper of the point has been lost?

Drilling thin materials

When drilling thin materials the chisel edge may break through before the outer corners of the drill are cutting. This causes burrs on the underside of the work, snatching of the drill with possible breakage and holes that are not round. Better results can be achieved by using flatter point angles of 140° or more and thinning the chisel edge almost to a point to reduce end pressure and help penetration.

There are three examples of different kinds of twist drill points:

Web Thinning

Repeated sharpening, which shortens the drill, or the fact that the remaining length of the broken drill has been re-sharpened, results in an increase in the web thickness at the point. As a result, the web should be thinned to approximately 10% of the drill diameter using a shaped grinding wheel with a thickness of half the flute width. Excessive thinning may weaken the drill causing splitting up of the web.

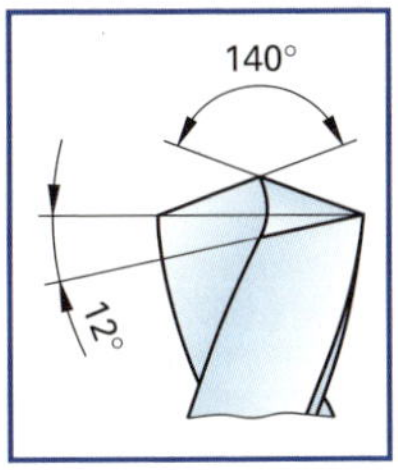

Flat Point Angles

A flat point angle up to 140° inclusive can be advantageous to high tensile steel. It also helps to reduce burrs at the underside when thin materials are drilled. This angle causes the cutting lips to become concave which weakens the outer corners. It is preferable to use specially designed drills for the more difficult materials.

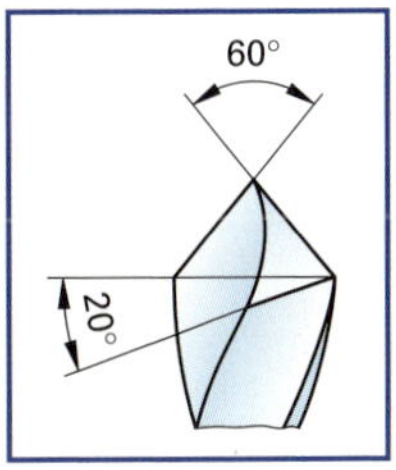

Acute Point Angles

Point angles down to 60° can be used to reduce the tendency of brittle materials, such as hard plastic materials, to flake away on the underside as the drill breaks through. When you grind an acute angle the result is a convex cutting edge.

Activity 3 Finding information in a text

Read the text and answer the following questions.

1. Why should the web of a twist drill be thinned after repeated sharpening?
2. How can the web be thinned?
3. What result can a too thin web have?
4. What advantages can flatter point angles have?
5. What does a flat point angle lead to?
6. For what reasons can drills have a point angle of about 60°?

Milling

Milling is another very important metal cutting shaping process. It produces flat or curved surfaces. With modern computer numerical controlled (CNC) milling machines a wide variety of different forms can be produced, including three dimensional and other complex shapes.

The milling cutters have cutting edges which are wedge shaped. Depending on the tool diameter the number of cutting edges varies considerably. Milling cutters with small diameters have only few cutting edges; those with larger diameters have more. Each cutting edge can be considered as a single chisel (see picture below). The cutting motion is performed by the milling cutter, whereas the feed and the infeed are performed by the workpiece which is usually clamped on the machine table.

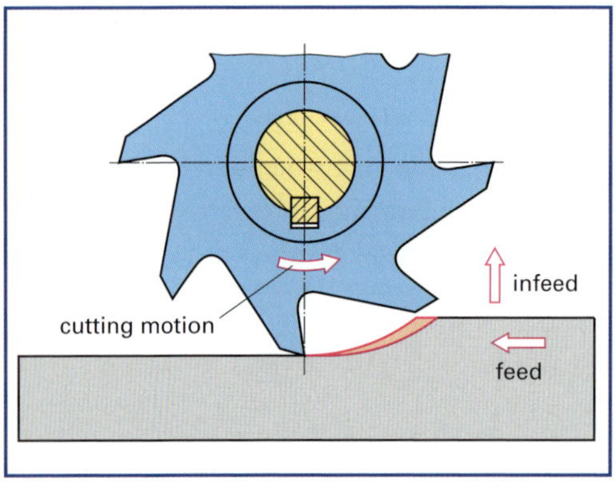

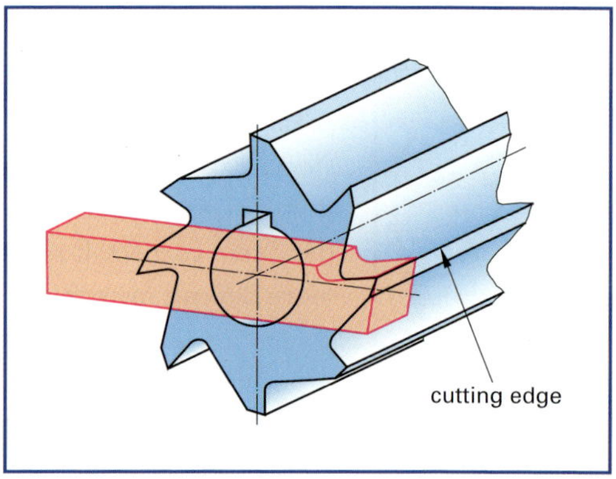

Activity 4 Defining technical terms

Find words in the text above that fit the following definitions.

1. a very important metall shaping process
2. having a shape that is rounded and not straight
3. the top layer of a piece of material
4. words for the acronym CNC
5. a thin line cut into a surface
6. a piece of metal that has a thick edge and a pointed edge
7. a straight line going from one side of a circle to the other passing through the centre
8. a metal tool with a wedged edge
9. the speed with which the workpiece moves towards the tool

Cylindrical milling

In cylindrical milling the axis of the milling tool is parallel in relation to the surface of the workpiece. Only the cutting edges at the circumference take part in the cutting process. According to the direction of the feed in relation to the rotation direction there are two types of cylindrical milling: up-cut milling and synchronous milling. Both in up-cut milling and synchronous milling the chip is comma-shaped.

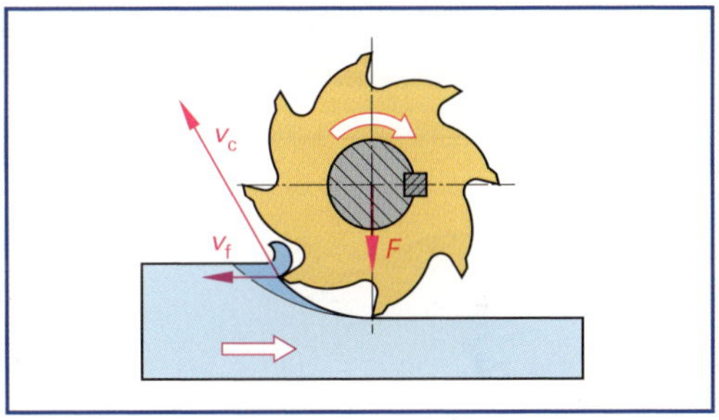

Up-cut milling

In **up-cut milling** the rotation of the milling tool is directed against the feed direction. Before the tool starts cutting, the cutting edge slides across the surface of the workpiece and compresses it. The comma-shaped chip reaches its maximum thickness when the cutting tool leaves the workpiece. The cutting pressure then reaches its peak. The sliding of the cutting edges lead to a considerable wear and tear of the lip clearance surface. As a result the milled surface tends to be wavy. Because of this, up-cut milling is an advantage only if the workpiece has a hard surface.

In **synchronous milling** the cutting edge starts cutting abruptly. While forming the comma-shaped chip, the cutting force and chip thickness decrease. As a result a smoother surface can be achieved. Milling machines for synchronous milling must have a machine table drive without any slackness. Otherwise the milling tool tends to wedge the workpiece between the work table and the tool. The surface that can be achieved is smoother and more even than in up-cut milling. In addition, the cutting speed can be almost twice as high in synchronous milling.

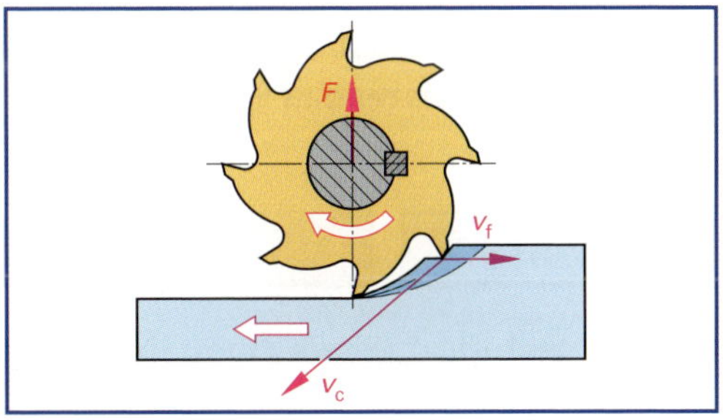

Synchronous milling

Activity 5 Understanding technical descriptions

Answer the following questions on the text.

1. What is the main difference between up-cut milling and synchronous milling?
2. What kind of chips do both methods produce?
3. What is the advantage of synchronous milling?
4. Why does up-cut milling produce a wavy surface?
5. Under which condition is up-cut milling an advantage?

Activity 6 Giving explanations

Explain the following technical terms in your own words.

1. up-cut milling
2. infeed
3. synchronous milling
4. feed direction
5. chip
6. smooth surface
7. diameter
8. cone
9. cylinder
10. lip clearance area

Face milling

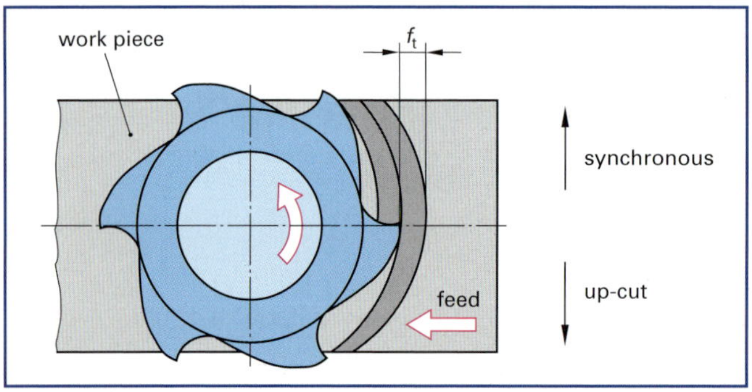

In face milling the milling tool axis is vertical in relation to the surface of the workpiece. With a symmetrical position of the tool axis the effects of up-cut and synchronous milling can be neglected.

There is a number of advantages in face milling compared to cylindrical milling:

- There are always several teeth in operation. This results in a smooth running and a high cutting performance.
- Hard metal tips for high cutting speeds can be changed easily.
- The chip thickness remains almost constant during the cutting process.

Activity 7 Describing a technical process

Use the technical terms given in the texts above to describe the differences between cylindrical milling and face milling as far as cutting movement, feed direction and the number of teeth in operation are concerned.

Activity 8 | Translation

Translate the following text into English.

Beim Fräsen erfolgt die Spanbildung durch die kreisförmige Bewegung des Werkzeugs und durch die geradlinige Vorschubbewegung und Zustellbewegung des Werkstücks. Es ist für die Spanbildung von großer Bedeutung, in welchem Verhältnis Vorschubbewegung und Schnittbewegung zueinander stehen. Wenn Vorschub- und Schnittbewegung gegeneinander gerichtet sind, spricht man von Gegenlauffräsen. Wenn Vorschub- und Schnittbewegung gleich gerichtet sind, nennt man dies Gleichlauffräsen.

Turning

Turning is a metal cutting shaping process with a geometrically defined cutting edge and a circular cutting movement. The cutting tool consists of a chisel with only one cutting edge. In general it is fixed in the tool clamp on the cross slide. The workpiece is usually clamped in a three-jaw chuck. Depending on the shape of the workpiece there are also other types of chuck that can be installed on the lathe spindle.

The turning principle

The shape of the workpiece is the result of the combination of the different movements in the turning process:

The **cutting motion** is carried out by the workpiece. The cutting speed v_c is measured in m/min and depends on the revolutions per minute and the diameter of the workpiece. It has to be adjusted with respect to the material being cut and the material of the cutting chisel.

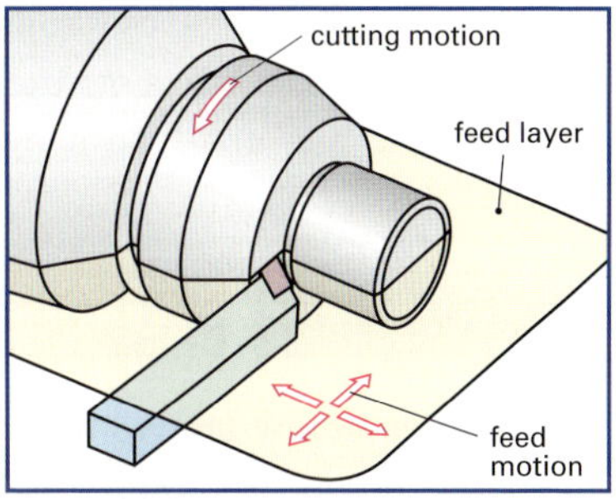

The turning principle

The **feed motion** and infeed are carried out by the cutting tool. The feed is measured in mm/revolution and the infeed is measured in mm.

Shapes of the workpieces

The shapes of the workpieces produced in the turning process can vary considerably. The shape of the surface produced in the turning process is another important characteristic to distinguish the various turning methods. As has already been mentioned, all shapes symmetrical to the rotation axis can be produced. The main types are, however, cylindrical and flat shapes. Cylindrical shapes are formed by cutting parallelly to the rotation axis and flat shapes by cutting at a right angle to the rotation axis. Cones are produced by cutting parallel with and at right angles to the rotation axis at the same time. Apart from these there are lots of other shapes that can be produced on a lathe. Male and female threads are often part of a complex workpiece and can be produced on a lathe with the appropriate cutting tool.

Activity 9 Working with words

Find words in the text about turning (page 127) which fit the following definitions or explanations.

1. a small piece of metal which is cut off in the turning process
2. the sharp part of a tool that cuts material
3. formed with an exact and fixed chisel angle
4. a turning cutting movement
5. the part of a lathe that carries the top slide and tool clamp
6. the part of a lathe that holds the workpiece
7. a machine for producing workpieces symmetrical to the rotation axis
8. the outer form of a workpiece
9. the number of circular motions of the workpiece per minute
10. a straight line going from one side of a circle to the other side
11. the length in mm which the tool passes when the workpiece turns around its axis once
12. the length in mm which defines the width of a chip
13. the outside or top layer of a workpiece
14. in the shape of a cylinder
15. a workpiece with a round base and sloping sides and a point at the top
16. a spiral line cut into a cylindrical bolt to hold a nut

Activity 10 Asking questions and finding answers

The picture below shows two apprentices at a lathe. Look carefully and ask questions about what the students are doing. Ask your classmates to answer the questions.

Example:

What is the apprentice on the right doing?
He is watching his workmate.

Use the following words to help you:

to watch ... to measure ... to wear goggles ... to produce a workpiece ...
to operate the lathe ... aluminium chips ... to lie on the top slide

Vocabulary Unit 11

according to	nach, gemäß
accurately ['ækjərətlɪ]	akkurat, genau
to achieve [ə'tʃi:v]	erreichen
acronym	Abkürzung
actual	tatsächlich, eigentlich
acute [ə'kju:t]	spitz(winklig)
additional	zusätzlich
to adjust	einstellen
advantage [əd'vɑ:ntɪdʒ]	Vorteil
alternate	abwechselnd
angle ['æŋgl]	Winkel
apart from	außer, abgesehen von
application	Anwendung
to apply	anwenden
to approach	sich nähern
appropriate	angemessen
approximately [ə'prɒksɪmətlɪ]	annähernd
to assist	unterstützen
to attach	befestigen
to avoid	vermeiden
axis	Achse
bare hand	bloße Hand
blue temper	blaue Anlauffarbe
breakage	Bruch
brittle	spröde
burr	Grat
by means of	mit Hilfe von
to carry out	ausführen
case	Fall
to cause	verursachen
certain	gewiss, bestimmt, zuverlässig
chip	Span
chisel	Meißel
circular	kreisförmig
circumference	Umfang
to clamp	spannen
clearance ['klɪərəns]	Spiel (techn.), Spielraum
clearance surface	Freifläche
clockwise	im Uhrzeigersinn
to combine	kombinieren, zusammensetzen
common	gebräuchlich, gewöhnlich
to compare	vergleichen
to compress	zusammendrücken, zusammenpressen

concave ['kɒnkeɪv]	konkav
condition	Bedingung
cone	Kegel
to consider	betrachten
to consist of	bestehen aus
convex ['kɒnveks]	konvex
cross slide	Werkzeugschlitten
curved [kɜ:vd]	gekrümmt
cutting face	Spanfläche
cutting force	Schnittkraft
cutting lip	Schneidkante
cutting motion	Schnittbewegung
cylindrical	zylindrisch
dead centre	Querschneide
definite	definitiv
depending on	in Abhängigkeit von
to define	bestimmen
diameter	Durchmesser
difficult	schwierig
discontinuous	unterbrochen
distinction	Unterscheidung
up-cut milling	Gegenlauffräsen
downwards	abwärts
to dress	vorbereiten, abziehen
drill	Bohrer
drilling	Bohren
economically	wirtschaftlich, sparsam
efficient [ɪ'fɪʃnt]	wirkungsvoll
equal	gleich
excessive	ausgedehnt
face milling	Stirnfräsen
face	Vorderseite, Stirnfläche, Gesicht
familiar	gewohnt, vertraut
feature	Merkmal
feed	Vorschub
feed direction	Vorschubrichtung
female thread [θred]	Innengewinde
fixed	fest
to flake away	ausbröckeln
flat point	flache Spitze
flute	Spannut
flute width [flu:t widθ]	Spannutbreite
to fulfil	erfüllen
gauge [geidʒ]	Lehre (Messgerät)
generally	im Allgemeinen
geometrically defined	geometrisch bestimmt
to grind	schleifen

Vocabulary Unit 11

grinding disc	**Schleifscheibe**
grinder	**Schleifgerät**
groove [gruːv]	**Nut**
hard metal tip	**Hartmetallplättchen**
helix angle ['hiːlɪks]	**Drallsteigungswinkel**
high tensile steel	**Stahl mit großer Streckgrenze**
hole	**Loch**
importance [ɪm'pɔːtns]	**Bedeutung, Wichtigkeit**
important	**wichtig**
in general	**im Allgemeinen**
infeed	**Zustellung**
in order to	**um … zu**
in relation to	**im Verhältnis zu**
inclusive	**einschließlich**
to increase	**erhöhen, vergrößern**
insight	**Einblick**
kind of	**Art, Sorte von**
land	**Führung am Bohrer**
large	**groß**
lathe [leið]	**Drehmaschine**
layer	**Lage, Schicht**
length	**Länge**
lightly	**leicht**
to maintain [meɪn'teɪn]	**beibehalten**
male thread	**Außengewinde**
margin	**Rand**
measure ['meʒə(r)]	**Maß, Maßeinheit, Maßnahme, Ausmaß**
to mention ['menʃn]	**erwähnen**
motion	**Bewegung**
to mill	**fräsen**
milling	**Fräsen**
necessary	**nötig**
to neglect [nɪ'glekt]	**vernachlässigen**
nomenclature [nə'menklətʃə(r)]	**Nomenklatur, Fachsprache**
to obtain	**erhalten**
pass	**Durchgang**
penetration	**Durchdringen, Eindringen**
to perform	**ausführen**
peripheral speed	**Umfangsgeschwindigkeit**
point	**Spitze, Punkt, Einzelheit**
point angle	**Spitzenwinkel**
pointed	**spitz**
precise	**präzise, genau**
preferable	**vorzuziehen**
pressure ['preʃə(r)]	**Druck**
procedure	**Verfahren**
properly	**regelrecht, richtig**
radiused	**abgerundet**
to recommend	**empfehlen**
to reduce	**verringern**
regular point	**normale Spitze**
to remain	**bleiben**
repeated	**wiederholt**
to require	**erfordern, benötigen**
requirement	**Anforderung**
to result in	**führen zu**
result	**Ergebnis**
rotation axis	**Rotationsachse**
rotation	**Drehung**
section	**Abschnitt**
several	**einige**
shank	**Schaft**
shape	**Form**
to sharpen	**schärfen**
sharpness	**Schärfe**
simple	**einfach**
slackness	**(techn.) Spiel**
to slide	**(auf)gleiten, schieben**
smooth	**glatt**
to snatch off	**wegreißen**
spiral ['spaɪərəl]	**spiral(förmig)**
to split up	**aufspalten**
square with	**im rechten Winkel zu**
steel	**Stahl**
step	**Schritt**
straight [streɪt]	**gerade**
successful	**erfolgreich**
surface ['sɜːfɪs]	**Oberfläche**
synchronous milling	**Gleichlauffräsen**
to take place	**stattfinden**
to temper	**anlassen, härten, tempern**
to tend	**neigen**
tendency	**Neigung**
thickness	**Dicke**
to thin	**ausspitzen, ausdünnen**
three-jaw chuck	**Dreibackenfutter**
tool	**Werkzeug**
tool clamp	**Werkzeughalter**

Vocabulary Unit 11

tool rest	Werkzeugauflage
top view	Draufsicht
tough [tʌf]	zäh
towards	auf etw. zu
true circle	rund
twist drill	Spiralbohrer
to turn	drehen, drechseln
underside (lower surface)	Unterseite
up-cut milling	Gegenlauffräsen
variety [vəˈraɪətɪ]	Vielfalt
various	verschieden
wavy	wellig, gewellt
to weaken	schwächen
wear and tear [wɜə(r)]	Verschleiß
web thinning	Ausspitzen
web	Bohrerseele, Gewebe
wedge shaped	keilförmig
to wedge [wedʒ]	festklemmen
whereas	wohingegen
wide	breit
with respect to	im Hinblick auf

Additional Vocabulary

Außengewinde	male thread
Biegung, Abkantung	bend
Blech	sheet metal
Durchgangsbohrung mit Gewinde	tapped through hole
Durchzug (techn.)	extrusion
Falz	lock seam
Feingewinde	fine screw thread
Gewinde	thread
Gewindeschneideisen	tap and die set
Gewindestange	threaded rod
Gussform	mould
Innengewinde	female thread
Kieme, Lüftungsschlitz	louver
Kühlmittel	coolant
linksgängiges Gewinde	left-hand thread
löten	to solder
Matritze	die
Messing	brass
metrisches Gewinde	metric coarse thread
Plasma-Schutzgas-schweißen	plasma MIG welding
rechtsgängiges Gewinde	right-hand thread
Reibung	friction
Scharnier	hinge
Schneidspalt	kerf
Schraubverschluss	screw lid
Schutzgasschweißen	gas-shielded welding
Verkleidung (techn.)	trim
Verschleiß	abrasion
Windeisen	tap holder

12 Electrical Engineering

In this unit you will get information about measurement technology, electric motors, and electronic components. You will also learn something about the dangers of electricity and how mobile telephoning works.

Measuring instruments

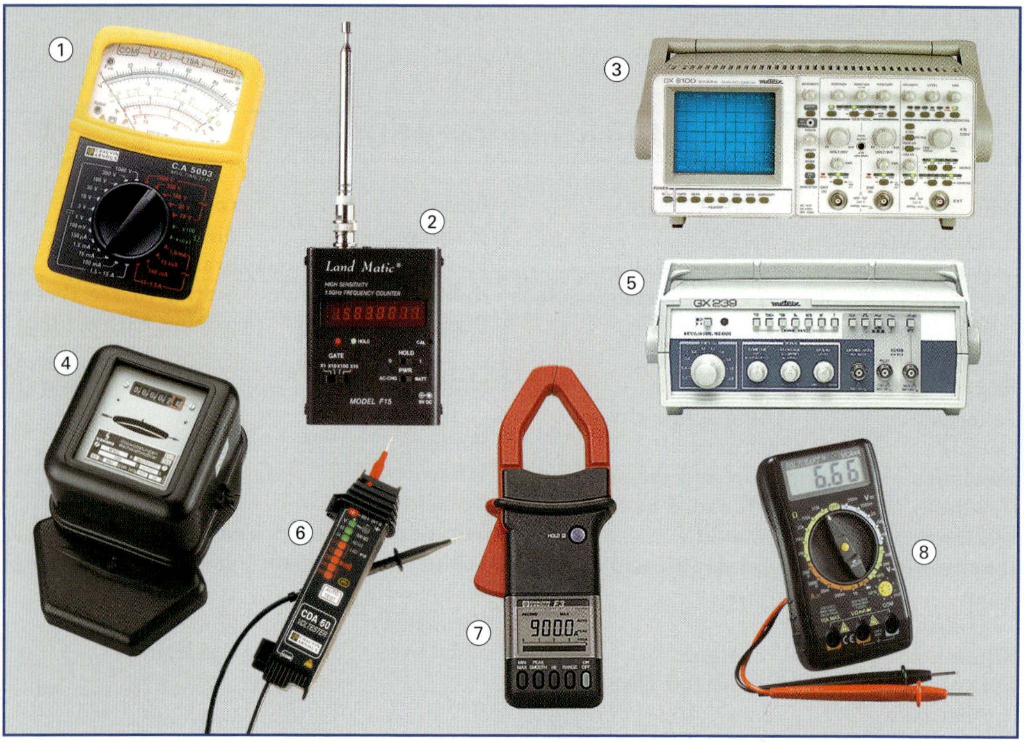

Activity 1 Working with measuring instruments

a) Find the English expressions for the measuring instruments shown in the picture above.

b) Tell your partner what you can do with these instruments.

Use the following words:

oscilloscope ... frequency counter ... voltage tester ... clamp ammeter ... analog multimeter ... energy meter ... digital multimeter ... function generator ... check ... test ... measure ... count ... continuity ... frequency ... voltage ... resistance ... electric current

Digital multimeters

Digital multimeters are used to measure voltage (both AC and DC), electric current, and resistance. Many have a diode test function, too. The more advanced ones can also measure capacitance, frequency, temperature, and transistor gain. Latest developments even offer an auto range function and an RS 232 interface.

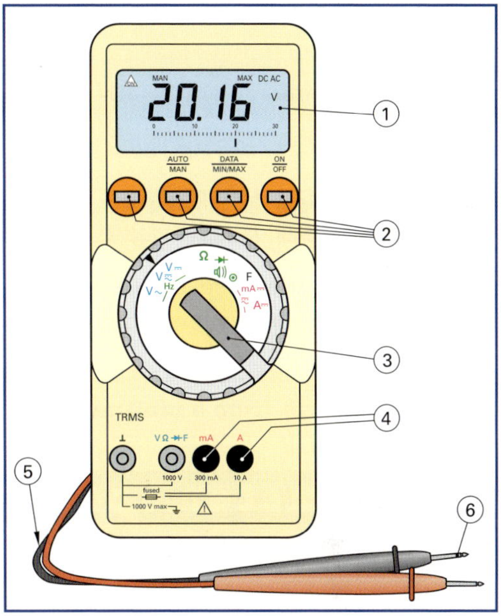

Digital multimeters change analog measured quantities into digital ones. Compared to an analog multimeter this means a better resolution as well as an easier reading. Moreover, it is possible to store the measured data and if there is an appropriate interface you can connect a computer or a printer to the multimeter.

The picture below shows a schematic diagram of a digital multimeter. The central unit is an analog digital converter (AD-converter). AD-converters need voltages as an input signal. That means digital multimeters must have a transformer for measuring resistance or electric current. Precision resistors do this job when measuring electric current (they change the electric current into voltage), a constant-current source is needed when resistance is measured.

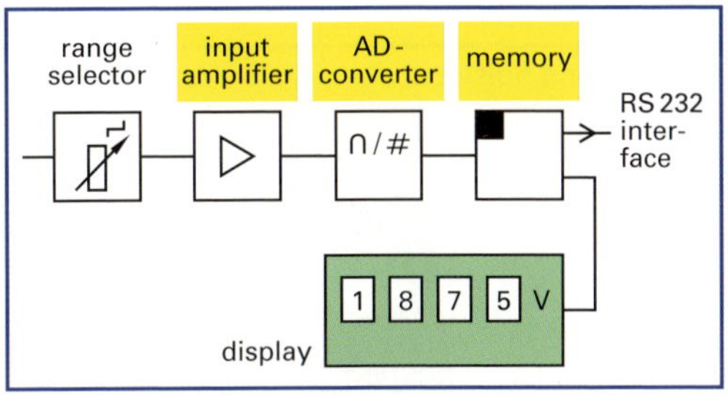

Digital Multimeter: block diagram

When measuring voltage, the input signal first goes to a changeable voltage divider (range selector) and then to an amplifier that helps to create a very high input impedance for this kind of measuring. Moreover, the value of the input impedance does not change when the range selector is turned.

To display the measured values either 7-segment, 14-segment or dot-matrix displays are used. As well as digits, dot matrixes can also display letters and symbols. The displays are usually LCDs (liquid crystal displays), however, LEDs (light emitting diodes) are also possible. The advantage of an LCD is that it consumes very little electric energy.

Common multimeters have a maximum reading of either 1999 or 19999. Since the first figure can only show a "1" or "0" we talk about a 3 1/2 or 4 1/2 digit display, however, there are also displays that show 5 1/2 or even 6 1/2 digits.

Unit 12

Activity 2 Parts of a multimeter

Match the following parts of a multimeter with the numbers given in the picture (page 133):

a) measuring line
b) LCD display
c) probe tip
d) connecting socket
e) function keys
f) function switch

Activity 3 Dialogue

You want to buy a used multimeter from a colleague. However, before buying it, you want to know more about its specifications (specs).

Work with a partner. Ask and answer questions about the multimeter. The following excerpt from a multimeter's specifications will help you.

Multimeter specifications (excerpt)

Display:	3 1/2 digit liquid crystal display (LCD) with a maximum reading of 1999
Polarity:	Automatic, positive implied, negative polarity indication
Overrange:	(1) or (–1) is displayed
Battery life:	300 hours typical with carbon-zinc
Power:	Single standard 9-volt battery
Measurement rate:	2.5 times per second, nominal
Operating environment:	0 °C to 50 °C at < 70 % R.H.
Dimensions:	147 mm (H) x 70 mm (W) x 39 mm (D)
Weight:	Approx. 340 g including battery and holster

DC VOLTS

Ranges:	0,2 V, 2 V, 20 V, 200 V, 500 V
Resolution:	1 mV (on 2 V range)
Accuracy:	± (1.2 % rdg + 1 dgt)
Input impedance:	1 MΩ
Overload protection:	600 VDC or AC rms

AC VOLTS: (50 Hz–500 Hz)

Ranges:	200 V, 500 V
Resolution:	100 mV (on 200 mV range)
Accuracy:	± (2.0 % rdg + 4 dgts)
Input impedance:	450 kΩ
Overload protection:	600 V DC or AC rms

Resistance

Ranges:	200 Ω, 2 kΩ, 20 kΩ, 200 kΩ, 20 MΩ
Resolution:	100 mΩ (on 200 Ω range)
Accuracy:	± (1.5 % rdg + 3 dgts) on 200 Ω range ± (1.5 % rdg + 1 dgts) on 2 kΩ to 2000 kΩ range
Overload protection:	500 V DC or AC rms

Electric motors

There are many different kinds of electric motors, but the basic principle is always the same. Every conventional electric motor consists of a rotor (the rotating part) and a stator. Both the rotor and the stator are magnetic and use the attractive and repulsive forces between magnetic poles to make the rotor spin. Their poles are arranged in such a way that the rotor must move in order to bring its north poles nearer to the stator's south poles and vice versa. As a result, the rotor begins to rotate. Since at least some of the magnets are electromagnets, they are designed to constantly change their poles. As the rotor's north poles approach the stator's south poles the polarities are reversed, which means the rotor has to continue its rotation to bring its north poles closer to the stator's south poles again. This process of constant attraction and repulsion keeps the rotor turning.

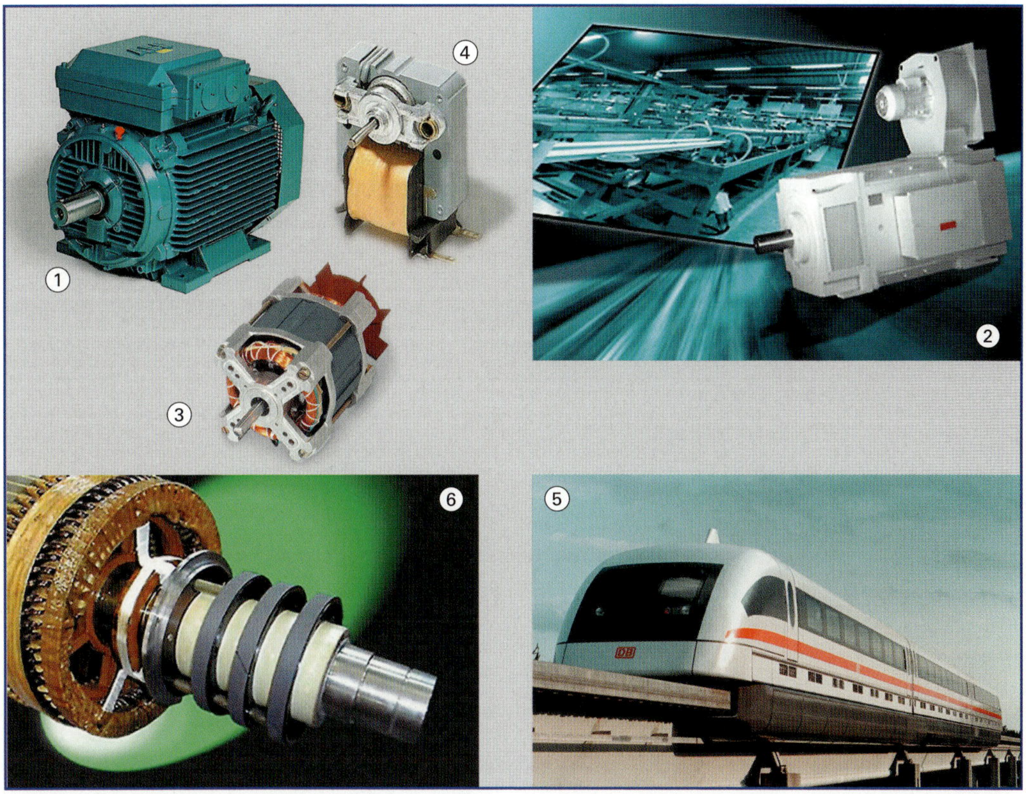

Activity 4 Matching exercise

a) What kind of electric motor do the pictures above show or refer to?

Use these words:

slip ring motor ... linear motor ... DC motor ... capacitor motor ...
shaded-pole motor ... squirrel-cage motor

b) Find examples where these motors are used.

Squirrel-cage motors

Squirrel-cage motors belong to the group of three-phase asynchronous motors. They are the most important of these kinds of motors because their production is inexpensive, and they are robust, cheap and relatively small. Moreover, they are almost maintenance free. These motors are used, for example, to power machine tools or blower fans in agriculture.

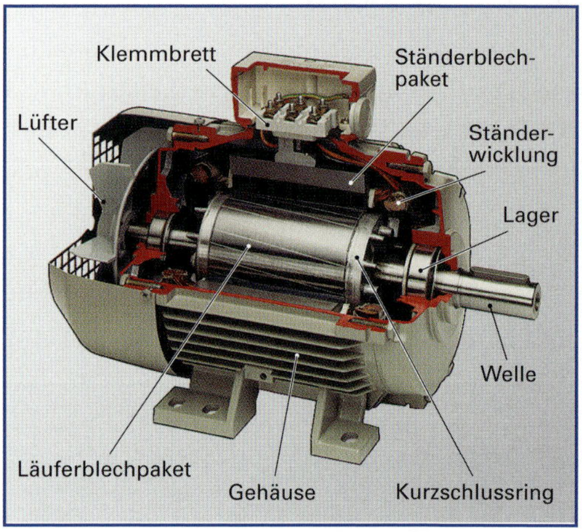

The stator of a squirrel-cage motor consists of the casing, the stator lamination pack, and the stator winding. The rotor with its rotor lamination pack is attached to the shaft. Slots inside the rotor pack contain bars made of copper or aluminium that are short circuited by rotor end rings at both ends. The bars and the rotor end rings together are shaped like a cage, which gave this kind of motor its name. Both stator pack and rotor pack are made of insulated layers of magnetic sheet steel to suppress eddy currents.

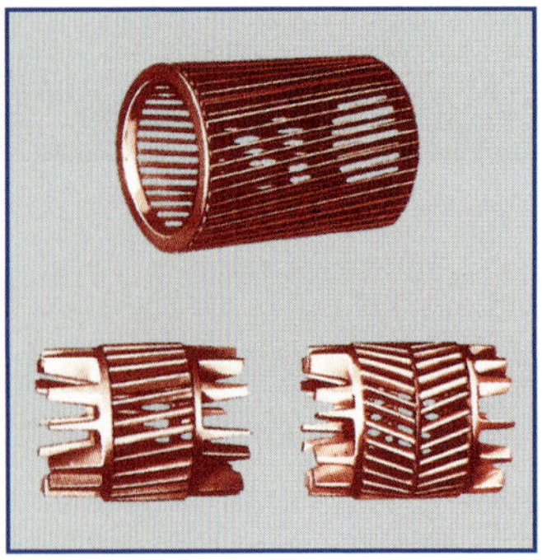

Types of cages

A set of stationary electromagnets in the motor's stator is used to produce the magnetic field, which is rotating rapidly around the motor's central component – the rotor. The magnetic field causes currents to flow in the bars so that they also become magnetic. In this way the rotor is dragged along with the rotating electric field of the stator. However, the rotation speed of the rotor lags behind the rotating field of the stator, the speeds are asynchronous. They must be asynchronous, otherwise no electric field would be induced in the rotor and it would not spin. This difference in speed is called the slip.

As long as there is no load at the shaft there is only a small slip. The bigger the load at the shaft, the slower the motor turns; however, the torque it produces at the shaft is higher. If the load exceeds a certain value the motor will stop to turn.

Activity 5 Comprehension

Do the following tasks.

1. Translate the German expressions of the parts of a squirrel cage motor (see picture) into English. Most words can be found in the text.
2. Describe in your own words how the rotor is made to turn.
3. Copy the following table about squirrel-cage motors into your exercise book and complete it.

Advantages	Use	Parts of the stator	Parts of the rotor
robust	?	?	?

Mobile phones

Introducing the situation

Phil has just started his apprenticeship as a radio engineer in Rochester near London. One day, while returning to their company from a customer service call in Camden Street, Phil and his colleague receive a mobile phone call. Because Mark is driving Phil answers the phone.

PHIL: Hello?

JAMES COLLINS: Phil, this is James Collins speaking. Listen, I've got another job for you before you return. Please have a look at Mrs Graham's TV. This is her address: 16 Malcom Drive. You've got that?

PHIL: Mrs Graham, 16 Malcom Drive. What's the matter with her TV?

JAMES COLLINS: She says she's got a black screen but the sound is okay.

PHIL: Alright, we're right on the way.

MARK: Who was it?

PHIL: Our boss. We've got to look at Mrs Graham's TV first before going back to the company. You've heard the address.

MARK: Yeah. This job used to be less stressful before everybody started using these mobile phones.

PHIL: But isn't it great that you can make phone calls wherever you are and whenever you want?

MARK: Sometimes it's quite useful, for example, when you're trapped in a traffic jam and you've got a date with your girlfriend or if there is an accident and you need to call an ambulance. However, I'm sure, for most people it's just a modern toy.

PHIL: Mr Collins will certainly consider it as a very useful invention. By the way, what I don't understand is how the system knows where you are. Mr Collins could also have reached us in Manchester or Liverpool.

MARK: That's right. Your mobile phone tells it to the system. It permanently communicates with the BTS of the cell you're just in.

PHIL: BTS? Cell? What do you mean?

MARK: BTS stands for Base Transceiver Station. It is responsible for handling all telephone calls in its area. This area is called a cell. The whole country is divided into areas that look like the cells of a honeycomb with a BTS in its centre.

PHIL: Ah. And our BTS has told Mr Collins' telephone where we are.

MARK: No, unfortunately it's not that simple. Every user of a mobile phone is registered in his Home MSC, which is the abbreviation for Mobile Switching Centre. When Mr Collins dialled our number he was first connected to the Home Switching Centre of our mobile

Transmission Tower

phone. An MSC has got the information if a user has switched on his phone and if so, where he is. As a result the MSC could route the call to the BTS of the cell we are in.

PHIL Great, but many people move around and probably leave a cell. Why isn't the call disconnected then?

MARK The users are handed over to the neighbouring cell. A BTS constantly checks the quality of the signals it receives from a mobile phone. The quality decreases the further off you are from the BTS. If the quality falls below a certain level, the system tells the neighbouring BTS, which receives a stronger signal, to take the call over. This is something the user doesn't notice.

PHIL Quite clever. And this even works if you leave the country.

MARK Sure. You simply lock yourself into the system of the country your are in and your system at home is informed where you can be reached.

PHIL Not bad. Look, next right is Malcom Drive. No. 16 is …

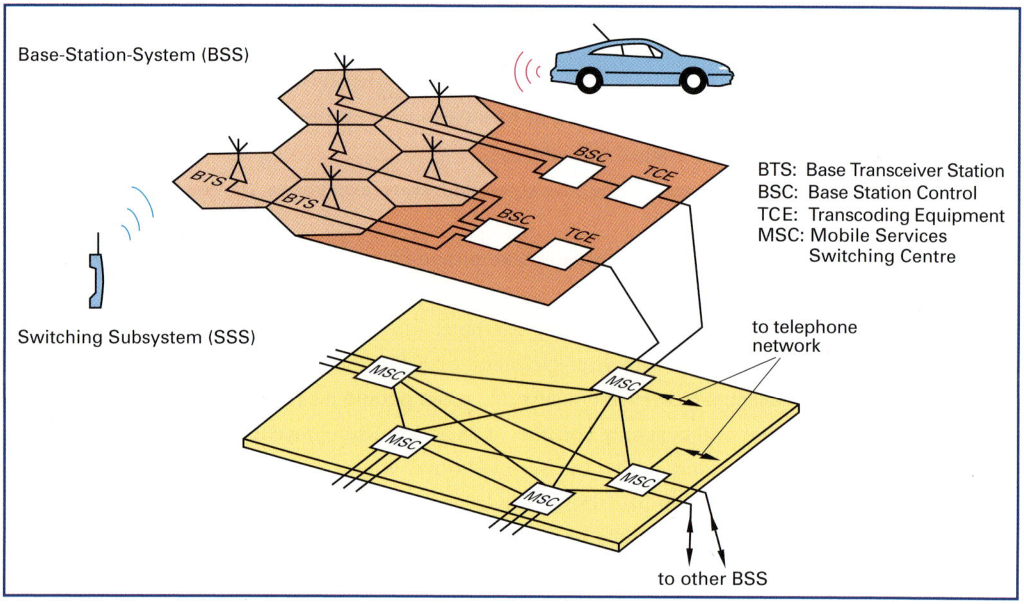

Activity 6 Comprehension

Answer the following questions.

1. Why does James Collins call Mark and Phil?
2. What does Mark think about mobile phones?
3. What is a BTS and what is its function?
4. Which part of the system has got the information about whether a user is available and where he is?
5. What is meant by handover and how does it work?
6. Do you have a mobile phone? How do you use it?
7. You are on a trip, let's say near Kassel, and you want to call a friend on her mobile phone near Kiel. Explain how the connection is established.

Protection against electric shock

Electricity can be dangerous. If a person touches a live wire, his body becomes a resistor that is part of an electric circuit through which an electric current is driven. According to Ohm's law, the height of the current depends on the voltage that is applied to the resistance. The effects on the human body vary considerably: A person might only feel an unpleasant prickling or experience something more serious like muscle cramps and burns. The most dangerous result, however, could be ventricular fibrillation which often leads to death. Two factors mainly determine how seriously the human body will be injured (see also the info box on page 141):

- the value of shock current that is flowing,
- the length of time it flows.

To prevent people from being electrocuted there are a wide range of precautions, some of which will be described in the following text.

If a person gets an electric shock, (s)he must be in contact with a live conductor. Two types of contact are classified: direct contact or indirect contact. Direct contact means that someone touches a conductor that he should have expected to be live, for example, after having removed the plate of a switch. Indirect contact means that a person touches something that is totally unconnected (for example the metal casing of an electric motor) but has become live as a result of a fault.

Protection against direct contact

Preventing direct contact usually means ensuring that people cannot touch live conductors. The standard method is to insulate live parts and to make sure that the insulation withstands almost any chemical, mechanical and thermal use. Moreover, the insulation must not be removable except by destroying it. Another method is to use safety barriers or obstacles to prevent that a person gets to near to an electrical installation.

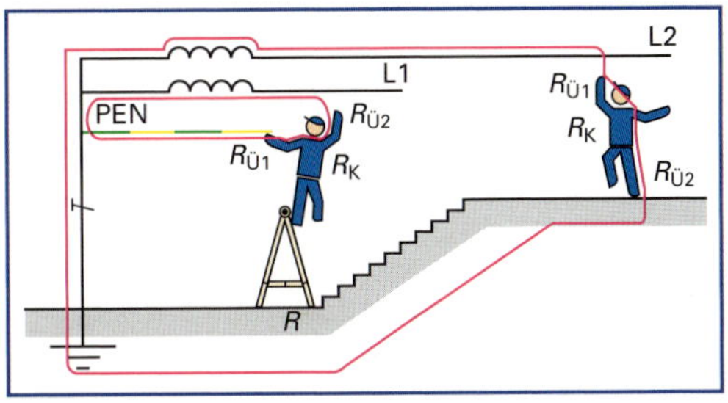

Direct Contact

Protection against indirect contact

There are several methods that can prevent people from receiving an electric shock after coming in contact with a conductor that normally would not be live. All these methods protect against a dangerous fault current flowing through the human body. One very common method is to make sure that the potential difference between the parts, that a person may touch simultaneously, is so low that it cannot cause a dangerous current. Moreover,

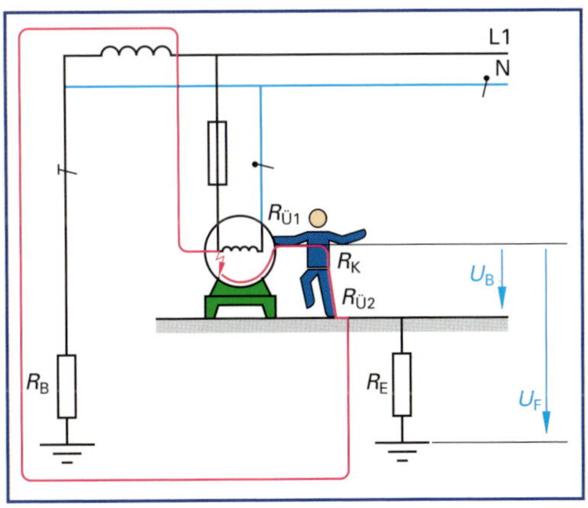

Indirect Contact

the power supply must be shut off within a safe time. This is the function of the yellow-green protective conductor (PE) in our houses. In case of a fault (e.g. body contact between a live conductor and the casing of a motor) a person who touches the casing is not endangered because the casing is connected to the protective conductor which has earth potential. This prevents a dangerous potential difference between the person's hand, that touches the casing, and his feet, that are earthed by the floor (earth potential). In other words, the human body is short circuited by the protective conductor. As a result a fault current will flow through the protective conductor and not through the person's body. Since this method must also provide a low impedance of the earth fault loop, the fault current will be so high that a protective fuse will blow immediately.

Of course a person could also touch a live part with his one hand and some kind of metalwork, e.g a radiator, with the other simultaneously. This would cause a fault current from one hand to the other via the person's heart which is even more dangerous. In order to prevent such situations, all metal parts of a house like pipes, bath tubs etc. are also connected to earth.

A different method uses double insulation which means that there is a second layer of insulation to make sure that there can never be a contact to live parts. This method is used with household appliances, TV-sets, radios etc. (class II equipment).

Unit 12

Protection against direct as well as against indirect contact

There is no need for special means of protection if a system works with low voltages, for example, 6 V, 12 V or 25 V. Well known examples are small power tools, toys or instrument and control circuits. Depending on certain specifications the following methods are applied:

- Protection by separated extra-low voltage (SELV)
- Protection by protective extra-low voltage (PELV)
- Protection by functional extra-low voltage (FELV)

INFO: The effects of electric shock

All movements of the human body are controlled by the nervous system which carries electrical signals between the brain and the muscles. The signals are electro-chemical in nature with values of a few millivolts. If an external current is imposed on these signals, the muscles receive much stronger signals than those they usually get. This causes uncontrolled movements and pain and the person is unable to counter the effects of the shock current. A good example is the "no-let-go" effect which means that a person who has touched a live conductor may not be able to release the conductor because he cannot control the movements of his muscles.

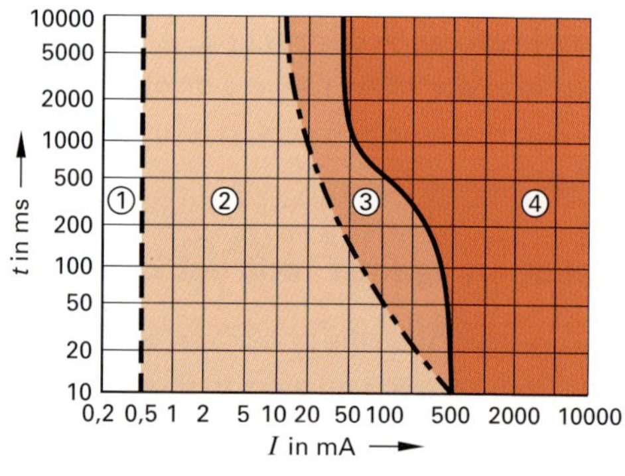

1. No reaction of the human body
2. No dangerous effects
3. Muscle cramps; danger of ventricular fibrillation
4. Ventricular fibrillation possible; mortal effects probable

Electronic components

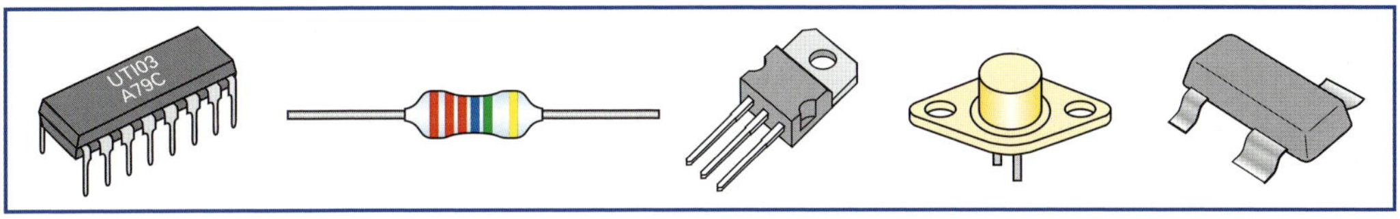

Mr Michael Kating of EuroTechnologies has sent a fax to London Electronics Ltd.

EUROTECHNOLOGIES
Düsselberger Hauptstr. 15
56789 Großenburg

Großenburg, March 17th, 20..

London Electronics Ltd.
27 Avenue Kent
London

Order

Dear Mr Granger,
Thank you for sending us your latest price list. We would like to place an order for

Quantity	Item	Item No.
20	Resistor 3.9 k / 0.25 W / ± 5%	356.786
15	Resistor 15 k / 0.5 W / ± 10%	356.087
5	Resistor 330 Ω / 4 W / ± 20%	357.348
6	Transistor BC 109B	654.888
3	Transistor 2N 2055	654.765
5	SMD Transistor BC 846B	610.564
15	LED / Ø 3 mm / green	487.008
15	LED / Ø 3 mm / red	487.009
2	Jumbo-LED / Ø 10 mm / red	455.832
15	Low-Current LED / Ø 5 mm / yellow	488.012
2	Thyristor TIC 106 E5	277.396
2	Triac TIC 246 M	289.155
1	Thyristor BT 151	247.379
4	Positive voltage regulator 78 S18 (18V/2A)	100.324
10	Electrolytic capacitor 4700 µF / 40 V	776.056

Yours sincerely
Michael Kating

Activity 7 Talking about electronic components

Do the following tasks.

a) Name the electronic components that are shown on the previous page. You find the terms in Mr. Kating's fax.
b) Explain the different specifications of the resistors in the fax.
c) Work in pairs. Make a list of about 10 to 15 electronic components (in German) and translate them into English. Present your list to the class, for example, by putting it on the blackboard. Complete the list with words from other groups.
d) London Electronic Company cannot deliver all components required so Mr Granger calls Mr Kating to talk about alternatives. Work with a partner and write down the telephone conversation between Mr Granger and Mr Kating.

Activity 8 Transistors

Copy the following text into your exercise book and complete it with the words given in the box below.

Transistors are made of semi-conducting material, usually •••[1]. In general, there are two different types of transistors: unipolar and bipolar transistors. Both types have •••[2] legs, however the legs are named differently.

Bipolar transistors consist of three layers of semi-conducting material, either n-p-n or p-n-p. Its electrodes are named basis, collector and •••[3]. The current through the transistor, that is the current from the collector electrode to the emitter electrode, can be •••[4] and varied by the current that flows into its basis. If, for example, the •••[5] signal at the basis has a sinus form, the current through the transistor will also be a sinus.

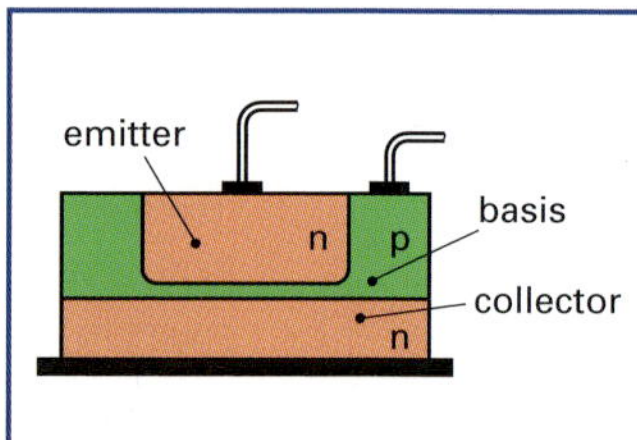

The electrodes of unipolar transistors (FET = **F**ield **E**ffect **T**ransistor) are called gate, source and drain. With FETs the electric current only goes through one kind of •••[6] material, either n or p. It is controlled by an •••[7] which is created by a certain voltage between the gate and the source. Both, bipolar and unipolar transistors, are used as •••[8] and electronic switches.

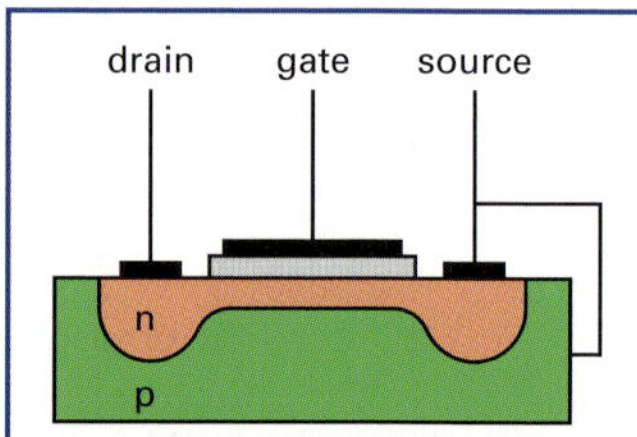

Use these words:

emitter ... input ... silicon ... three ... amplifier ... controlled ... electric field ... semi-conducting

Resistor colour coding system

Resistors are coded by colour bands on their bodies. There are three types of resistor colour coding which provide different information.

3 digits, multiplier, tolerance, thermal coefficient

3 digits, multiplier, tolerance

2 digits, multiplier, tolerance

Table of colour codes

Colour		Digits [1-3]	Multiplier [4]	Tolerance [5]	TC [6]
Black		0	1		
Brown		1	10	1 %	100 ppm
Red		2	100	2 %	50 ppm
Orange		3	1 k		15 ppm
Yellow		4	10 k		25 ppm
Green		5	100 k	0,5 %	
Blue		6	1 M	0,25 %	
Violet		7	10 M		
Gray		8			
White		9			
Gold				5 %	
Silver				10 %	

Unit 12

Activity 9 Defining resistors

a) Find the value of the following resistors.

1. blue / grey / yellow / silver
2. brown / black / black / gold
3. orange / green / red / red
4. yellow / violet / orange / silver
5. white / brown / brown / gold

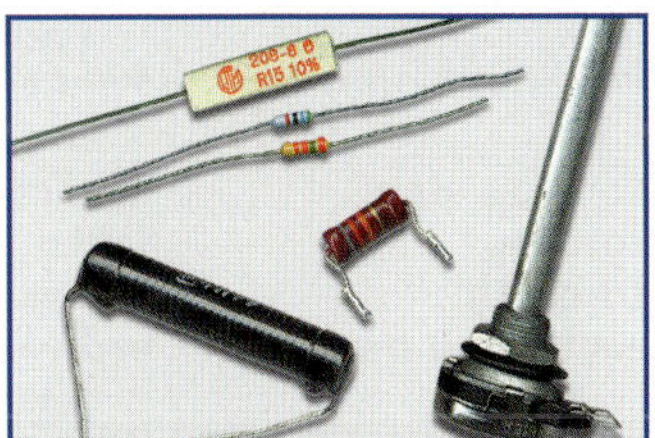

b) Work with a partner. Find the colour code for the following resistors.

a) 120Ω b) 4.7 MΩ c) 68Ω d) 33kΩ e) 820kΩ f) 560Ω g) 1000Ω

Vocabulary Unit 12

abbreviation	Abkürzung
accuracy ['ækjərəsɪ]	Genauigkeit
advanced	fortgeschritten, modern
to apply to	verwenden, anwenden auf
appointment	Verabredung
appropriate	passend
asynchronous	asynchron
attractive	anziehend
auto range	automatische Bereichswahl
bar	Stab, Stange
barrier	Sperre, Schranke
bath tub	Badewanne
to be electrocuted	einen elektrischen Schlag bekommen
to be trapped	festsitzen
blower fan	Gebläse
body contact	Körperschluss
burns	Verbrennungen
cage	Käfig
capacitance [kə'pæsətəns]	Kapazität
capacitor motor	Kondensatormotor
casing	Gehäuse
cell	Zelle
to classify	einteilen, ordnen
clamp ammeter	Stromzange
colleague	Kollege
component	Bauteil
connecting socket	Anschlussbuchse
to consider	eingehend betrachten, sorgfältig ansehen
considerably	beträchtlich
constant-current source	Konstantstromquelle
control circuit	Steuerstromkreis
conventional	herkömmlich
converter	Wandler
to decrease	fallen, abnehmen
to determine	bestimmen
to dial	wählen (Telefonnummer)
dot-matrix display	Punktmatrix-Anzeige
to drag along	mitschleppen
to drop	fallen
to earth	erden
earth-free bonding	erdfreier Potentialausgleich
eddy currents	Wirbelströme
electric shock	elektrischer Schlag
electrical separation	Schutztrennung
electrolytic capacitor [ɪˌlektrɒ'lətɪk kə'pæsɪtə]	Elektrolytkondensator
to endanger	gefährden
energy meter	kWh-Zähler
to ensure	sicherstellen
excerpt	Auszug
fault current	Fehlerstrom
frequency counter	Frequenzzähler
function generator	Funktionsgenerator
function key	Funktionstaste
function switch	Umschalter für Messfunktionen
fuse	Sicherung
holster	Halfter, Tasche
honey comb	Bienenwabe
impedance of the earth fault loop [ɪm'piːdens]	Schleifenimpedanz
input impedance	Eingangswiderstand
instrument circuit	Messstromkreis
to insulate	isolieren
invention	Erfindung
to lag behind	hinterherhinken
layer	Schicht
linear motor	Linearmotor
live wire	spannungsführende Leitung
load	Last
machine tool	Werkzeugmaschine
magnetic sheet steel	Elektroblech
maintenance-free	wartungsfrei
measurement technology	Messtechnik
measuring line	Messleitung
metalwork	Metallarbeit
muscle cramp	Muskelkrampf
non-conducting location	nicht-leitende Räume
obstacle	Hindernis
operating level	Betriebsspannung
overload protection	Überlastschutz
permanently	ständig
potential difference	Potentialdifferenz
precision resistor	Präzisionswiderstand
precaution	Sicherheitsmaßnahme
to prevent	verhindern
prickling	Kribbeln, Stechen
probe tip	Messspitze
protection	Schutz
protective conductor	Schutzleiter
R.H. (relative humidity)	relative Luftfeuchtigkeit
radiator	Heizkörper
radio engineer	Rundfunktechniker
range	Bereich

Vocabulary Unit 12

range selector	Messbereichsumschalter
to receive	empfangen
to register	registrieren
repulsive	abstoßend
resistance	Widerstand
resolution	Auflösung
to reverse	umkehren
robust	robust
rotor end ring	Kurzschlussring
rotor lamination pack	Läuferblechpaket
to route	führen, weiterleiten
schematic diagram [skiːˈmætɪk ˈdaɪəgræm]	Schaltplan
screen	Bildschirm
semi-conducting material	Halbleitermaterial
shaded-pole motor	Spaltpolmotor
to short circuit	kurzschließen
short circuit	Kurzschluss
shut off	abstellen, abschalten
simultaneously [sɪmlˈteɪnɪasli]	gleichzeitig
slip	Schlupf
slip ring motor	Schleifringläufermotor
slot	Nut, Schlitz
specifications	technische Daten
squirrel-cage motor [ˈskwɪrəl]	Käfigläufermotor
stator lamination pack	Ständerblechpaket
stator winding	Ständerwicklung
stepping motor	Schrittmotor
synchronous motor [ˈsɪŋkrənəs]	Synchronmotor
torque	Drehmoment
to touch	berühren
traffic jam	Stau
transistor gain	Transistorverstärkung
unpleasant	unangenehm
ventricular fibrillation	Herzkammerflimmern
voltage tester	Spannungsprüfer
to withstand	widerstehen
zinc	Zink

Unit 12

Additional Vocabulary

AD-Umsetzer	A-D converter
Anlasswiderstand	starting resistance
Antenne	aerial, antenna (AE)
Blindleistung	reactive power
Brückenschaltung	bridge circuit
Dämpfung	attenuation
Drahtwiderstand	wire(-wound) resistor
Drehfeld	rotating field
Drehkondensator	variable capacitor
Dreiphasen-Wechselstrom	three-phase alternating current
Effektivwert	root-mean-square value (r.m.s.)
Einheit	unit
Entladung	discharge
Feldstärke	field strength
Frequenzbereich	frequency range
Funk	radio
Gegenkopplung	negative feedback
Gleichrichter	rectifier
Kaltleiter	PTC resistor
Klemmbrett	connecting terminal plate
Kreisfrequenz	angular frequency
Lager	bearing
Leistungsschild	rating plate
Leiter (elektr.)	conductor
Leuchtstofflampe	fluorescent lamp
Messdaten	readings
Messwerk	measuring system
Mitkopplung	positive feedback
Nebenschlussmotor	shunt motor
Nebenwiderstand	shunt
Neutralleiter	neutral
Parallelschaltung	parallel connection
Platine	PCB (printed circuit board)
Reihenschlussmotor	serial-wound motor
Schaltzeichen	circuit symbol
Scheinleistung	apparent power
Schieberegister	shift register
Schlupfdrehzahl	asynchronous speed
Unterbrecher (elektr.)	contact-breaker
Schwingkreis	resonating circuit
Spannungsteiler	voltage divider
Sperrschicht	junction
Spule	(inductance) coil
Verstärker	amplifier
Wechselrichter	d.c.-to-a.c. inverter
Wirkleistung	effective power

13 Automotive Electric

In this unit you will learn something about electrical systems in motor vehicles particularly the example of the light system and an air bag.

Electrical system

The electrical system is becoming more and more important in modern-day motor vehicles. To name some of the electrical systems we can talk about the power supply-, safety- and security systems, comfort and the board system.

Especially the safety-, security- and the comfort units are increasing in importance almost every day. In addition, electronic controlled fuel systems are inevitable when reducing emissions. Some vehicles carry seventy electronic control units (ECU). ECUs are a kind of on-board computer. One can imagine how complex the electrical system is becoming.

At this point we want to give you a little idea of car electronics by introducing a simple board electrical system, part of the light system and the air bag.

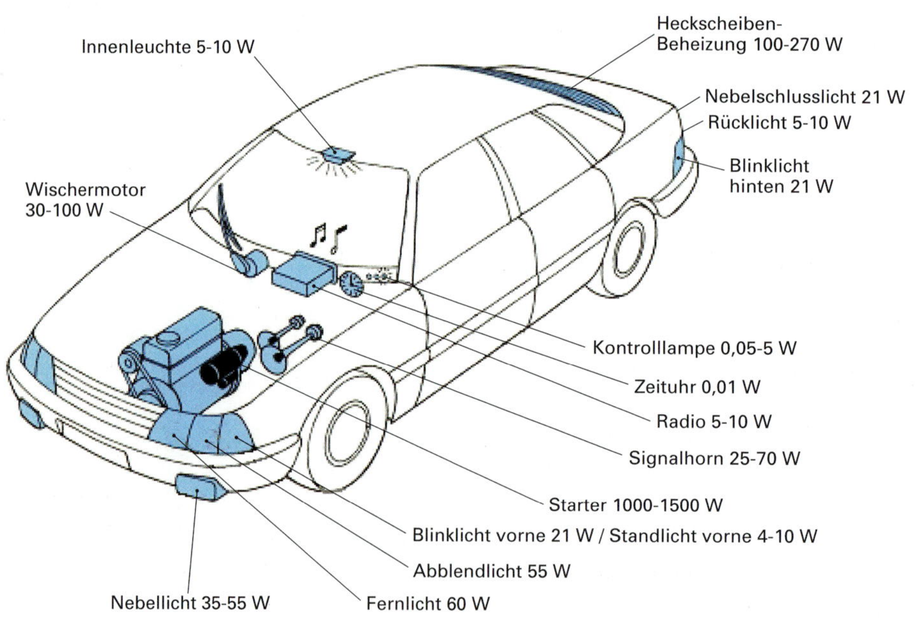

The alternator and the car battery are the main parts of the supply system. The battery is the source of energy when the engine is off. Electrical consumers such as the interior light, parking light, hazard warning lights, etc. are supplied with energy by the battery. Even to start up the engine the starter is taking the energy from the battery.

As soon as the engine is running all electrical systems are supplied by the alternator. Also the car battery gets recharged by the alternator.

The increasing amount of electrical equipment in modern motor vehicles are requiring more energy. To get a little idea of the consumption of some electrical components see the picture on previous side.

When one is driving short distances only and having many electrical users switched on, this can result in an empty battery. Often in winter this happens when the driver turns on the light, heater, radio, wiper, etc. there is not enough time to recharge the battery.

Activity 1 Talking about the electrical system

a) Translate the names from the picture (page 146). Write the names and the translation into your exercise book.

Use these words:

clock ... radio ... horn ... windscreen wiper ... interior light ... main beam ... dipped beam ... clearance lamp ... fog light front ... fog light rear ... reverse lamps ... break light ... indicator light ... rear window defroster ... starter motor

b) List up the electrical users when the car is driven at night and when it is foggy. Add the ignition for the engine and the heater to your list.

c) Find out the summary of the required electrical power of all electrical users when a car is driven during a foggy winter night. Count the ignition with 100 W and the fan of the heater with 300 W.

d) Answer the questions in full sentences and with your own words.

1. Which electrical systems do you find in contemporary motor vehicles?
2. Where does the hazard warning light get the power from when the engine is off?
3. What does ECU stand for?
4. Which electrical system do the alternator and the car battery belong to?
5. Is the power of the alternator always enough to recharge the car battery?
6. How is the starter motor supplied with electrical power?
7. What is essential to reduce emissions?
8. Does the increasing number of electrical users cause any differences? Explain your answer.

Light system and lamps

All motor vehicles must have the prescribed lightning systems, and additional lighting systems that have been declared permissible may also be fitted.

The lighting system in modern vehicles is very advanced. Different light sources are used, e.g. metal filament lamps, halogen lamps, LEDs (light-emitting diode) or gas-discharge lamps.

The lights should signal the intentions of the driver in terms of driving behaviour and make it possible for other road users to see the vehicle.
The functions of lighting systems in the motor vehicle are to illuminate the road ahead with the main-beam headlight or the dipped-beam headlight. Due to the density of today's traffic the dipped-beam is most often used for driving.

For making the contours of the vehicle visible in the darkness the vehicles are equipped with clearance lamps and parking lights as well as reflectors. Other lights like fog lamps or reverse lamps can be added.

To indicate intended manoeuvres to other road users is the purpose of the indicator lamps (direction-indicators) and the break lights.

Several other lights on the dashboard are to indicate switch statuses or to control functions like oil pressure or the generating.

Halogen lamps like the type "H 4" are still very common as light bulbs in head lamps.

The H 4-Lamp is a so called dual-wire lamp. The bulb of the halogen lamp is made of quartz glass. It has very small dimensions so that it can heat up to approximately 300 °C during operation.

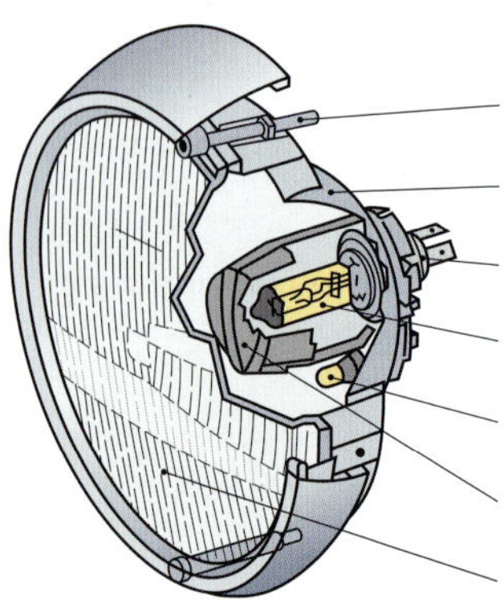

To the left you can see the design of a head light with the H 4 light bulb inside.

The housing holds the reflector with the lens, the light bulb and the headlight adjustment mechanism. The reflector reflects and focuses the light from the bulb.

The lens of most head lights is designed to illuminate the road even when dipped beam is on. The adjusting screw is to set the headlight into a 12% angle of inclination. All in all the result of the cone (beam) of light is as one can see in the picture next side.

The illumination of the road surface is not a matter of the light source only. It depends also on the construction of the reflector and the lens.

Engineers are currently working to find the optimal way of illumination. One step on the way is the cornering light. The system of cornering light enables the adaptation when the car is cornering.

Due to the asymmetric illumination pedestrians who are walking on the side of the road, animals or anything else is seen earlier. The oncoming traffic passes the cone of light for a very short time, therefore the driver is not blinded by the light.

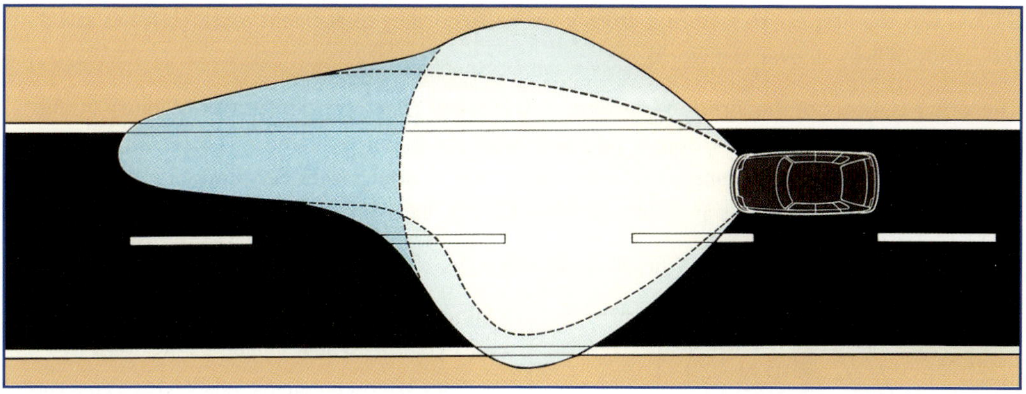

The picture above shoes the light distribution on the road surface produced by an "asymmetrical" dipped beam as seen from bird's eye view.
To check the function of all lights around the car is necessary for your own safety and the safety of others. Be aware that the light on your car is not only to see in the dark, it is important to be seen from other road users as well.

Activity 2 Comprehension

a) Translate the following sentences into English. Write the translation into your exercise book.

1. Das Licht ist nicht nur um zu sehen, auch um gesehen zu werden.
2. Alle Lichter sollten immer vor Fahrtantritt auf Funktion kontrolliert werden.
3. Die Neigung der Hauptscheinwerfer sollte mindestens jährlich kontrolliert werden.
4. H 4 Lampen werden während des Betriebes sehr heiß.
5. Eine H 4 Lampe ist eine „Zweifaden-Lampe", einen Faden für das Fernlicht und einen für das Abblendlicht.

b) Explain to your neighbour the advantage of the asymmetrical dipped beam.

c) Let your neighbour explain to you the necessity of clearance lamps.

d) Answer the questions.

1. What is the function of the headlight?
2. Which additional lights can be fitted on the front of a car?
3. Which headlight beam is currently most commonly used?
4. What are the indicator lamps for?
5. What does the illumination of the road surface depend on?

Airbag

With the airbag a new era of safety in motor vehicles began. Launched in 1981, the Mercedes-Benz S-Class was the first car to feature a driver's airbag. According to accident research it has saved thousands of lives all over the world.

The airbag is a part of the interior safety zone. The safety zone reduces the risk of injury in the interior of the passenger cell through the use of restraint system and impact-protection measures. As the first airbags were installed in the steering wheel only, engineers have continued to develop its technology. Passenger cars are equipped with front airbags, sidebags and windowbags ect.

In the following we will deal with the driver airbag only.

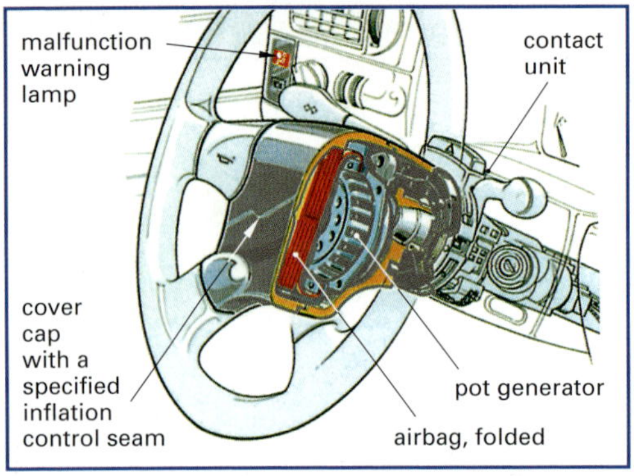

An undeployed airbag is folded tightly within a car's steering wheel behind a cover cap. Its sodium azide-containing inflator (pot generator) is attached to the crash sensor in the steering column. Activated by a crash (as seen on the pictures on page 151), the sensor triggers the inflator to produce an electric spark that ignites the sodium azide, which rapidly produces gas (mainly nitrogen and carbon dioxide) that passes through a filter and inflates the airbag. The airbag is deployed within 30 milliseconds. The gas then is discharged to atmosphere via outlet openings facing away from the occupant's side.

The electrical connection between the gas generator and the ECU is established in the steering-wheel unit by a volute spring in the contact unit.

The airbag prevents the driver's head and his upper body from impacting the steering wheel. While the impact continues and the airbag was fully inflated, it deflates immediately so the driver is able to see out of the windscreen in case further reactions are necessary.

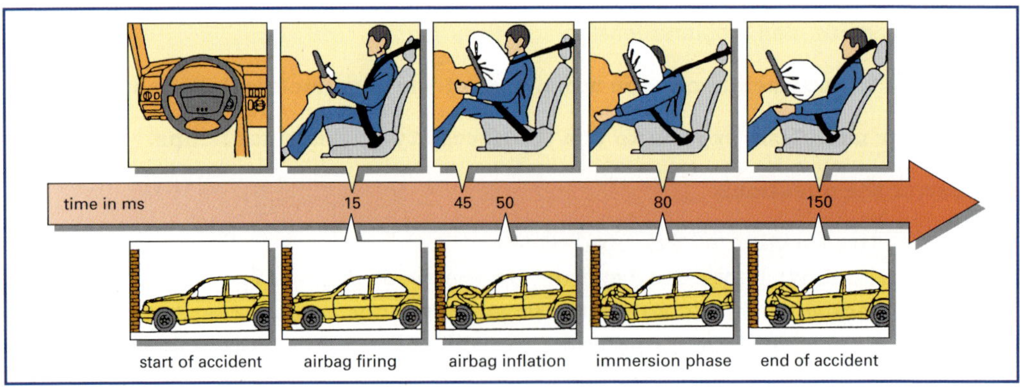

In the picture below you can see a real airbag being deployed. The pictures are taken with a special camera.

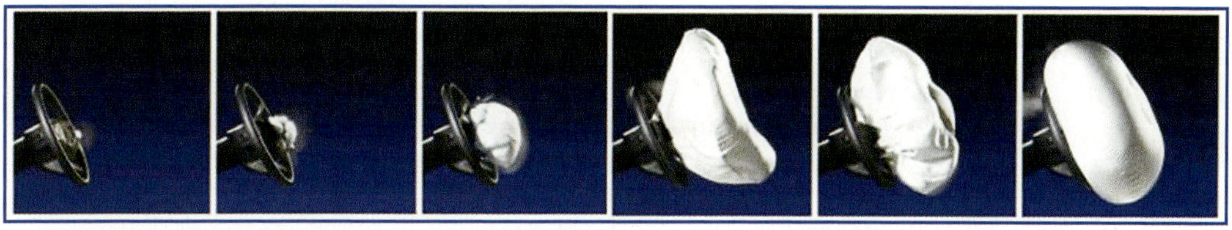

Activity 3 Talking about the airbag

a) Answer the questions.

1. Which safety zone does the airbag belong to?
2. In what part of the car were the first airbags fitted?
3. When was the first production car equipped with an airbag?
4. What time does it take to deploy an airbag?
5. What does the driver's airbag prevent?
6. Are passenger cars still equipped with one airbag only?
7. What is the meaning of "interior safety zone"?
8. How does the airbag get deployed?
9. What happens to the airbag after inflating and why?
10. What happens after the crash sensor gets activated?
11. Which gas is produced after igniting the sodium acid?
12. Where is the gas of the airbag discharged to, so the occupants do not inhale?

b) Explain the five phases shown in the time lab in your own words. Write the explanations into your exercise book.

c) True or false? Correct the statements that are wrong.

1. The airbag does not help anything.
2. The production car equipped with an airbag was on the road in the early 80th.
3. The nitrogen gas passes a filter before inflating the airbag.
4. Once an airbag is inflated it stays inflated all the time.
5. The airbag is deployed within 0,03 seconds.
6. The airbag is a part of the accident research.
7. Use of airbags has saved thousands of lives.
8. "Interior safety zone" includes the airbag and restraint seatbelts.
9. The passenger cell is safer through impact-protection measures.
10. The discharged gas passes outlet openings which are facing the occupants.
11. The gas from the deflating airbag is discharged into the atmosphere.

Vocabulary Unit 13

accident research	Unfallforschung
adjusting screw	Einstellschraube
asymmetric	asymmetrisch, ungleichförmig
to be dazzled	geblendet sein
bird's eye view	Vogelperspektive
board system	Bordnetz
break light	Bremslicht
clearance lamp	Begrenzungsleuchte
comfort system	Komfortsystem
complex	komplex, kompliziert
component	Komponente, Bestandteil
cone of light	Lichtkegel
consumption	Verbrauch
contour	Kontur, Umriss
cover cap	Abdeckkappe
crash sensor	Unfallsensor
dashboard	Armaturenbrett
density	Dichte
dimension	Dimension, Abmessung
dipped beam	Abblendlicht
distribution	Verteilung
dual-wire	*hier:* Bilux-Lampe
during operation	während des Betriebes
electrical connection	elektrische Verbindung
electrical consumers	elektrische Verbraucher
electrical spark	elektrischer Funke
electronic control unit (ECU)	elektronisches Steuergerät
era	Epoche
to establish	einrichten
feature	Merkmal
fitting	Ausstattung
fog light	Nebellicht
fuel system	Kraftstoffsystem
gas generator	Gasgenerator
halogen lamps	Halogenlampen
hazard warning light	Warnblinkanlage
heater	Heizung
horn	Hupe (Signalhorn)
to ignite	entzünden
to illuminate	beleuchten
impact protection	Aufprallschutz
inclination	Neigungswinkel
to increase	zunehmen
to indicate	anzeigen
indicator light	Blinklicht
inevitable	unvermeidlich
to inflat	aufblasen
injury	Verletzung
to install	installieren
intention	Absicht
interior light	Innenbeleuchtung
light system	Lichtanlage
main beam	Fernlicht
manoeuvre	Manöver
motor vehicle	Motorfahrzeug
nitrogen	Stickstoff
oil pressure	Öldruck
on-board computer	Bordcomputer
oncoming traffic	Gegenverkehr
parking light	Parklicht
passenger cell	Fahrgastzelle
pedestrian	Fußgänger
permissible	zufällig
power supply	Energieversorgung
to prevent	verhindern
previous	vorherig, vorausgegangen
purpose	Zweck
quartz glass	Quarzglas
to recharge	wiederbeladen
reflector	Reflektor
restraint system	Rückhaltesystem
reverse lamp	Rückfahrscheinwerfer
safety system	Sicherheitssystem
safety zone	Sicherheitszone
security system	Sicherheitssystem, *hier:* Diebstahlschutz
short distance	*hier:* Kurzstrecke
sodium azide	Natriumazid
source	Quelle
spring	Feder
starter motor	Starter (Anlasser)
steering column	Lenksäule
steering wheel	Lenkrad
surface	Oberfläche
switch statuse	Schalterstellung
term	hier: Ausdruck
trigger	Abzug
via	via/per
volute	hier: spiralförmig
window defroster	Scheibenheizung
windscreen wiper	Scheibenwischer

Unit 13

Dictionary English – German

a lot of	viele
abbreviation	Abkürzung
ability	Fähigkeit
above	oberhalb
to absorb	aufsaugen
to accelerate	beschleunigen
acceleration	Beschleunigung
accelerator pedal	Gaspedal
access	Zugang/Zugriff
accident	Unfall
accident research	Unfallforschung
accommodation	Unterkunft
according to	entsprechend/nach/gemäß
accuracy	Genauigkeit
accurate	genau
to achieve	erreichen
acid	Säure
acid rain	sauerer Regen
acronym	Abkürzung
to activate	aktivieren/auslösen
actually	genau genommen/ eigentlich
acute	spitzwinklig
to adapt	anpassen
to add	hinzufügen
additional	zusätzlich
address bus	Adressbus
adhesive bandage	Wundheftpflaster
adhesive tape	Heftpflaster
to adjust	einstellen
adjustable	einstellbar
adjusting screw	Einstellschraube
adjustment	Einstellung
administrator	Verwalter/Administrator
admittance	Zulassung/Zutritt
advanced	fortgeschritten/modern
advantage	Vorteil
advice	Rat
aerospace	Luftfahrt
to affect	beeinträchtigen/(ein)- wirken/beeinflussen/ sich auswirken
to afford	sich etwas leisten
affordable	leistbar
agenda	Tagesordnung
agricultural vehicle	landwirtschaftliches Fahrzeug
agriculture	Landwirtschaft
ahead	voraus
to aim	zielen
air filter	Luftfilter
air pollution	Luftverschmutzung
air-conditioned	klimatisiert
aircraft	Flugzeug
air-fuel mixture	Luft-Kraftstoff-Gemisch
airship	Luftschiff
to align	fluchten/ausrichten
all of a sudden	ganz plötzlich
Allen key	Innensechskantschlüssel
to allow	erlauben
almost	beinahe/fast
alternately	abwechselnd
alternator	Generator
although	obwohl
ammeter	Amperemeter

among	unter/bei/inmitten
amount	Menge
amp/ampere	Ampere
ancient	alt
angle	Winkel
annual	jährlich
apart from	außer
appliance	Gerät/Vorrichtung
application	Anwendung
application software	Anwenderprogramm
to apply	anwenden
to apply to	anlegen (einen Verband)
appointment	Verabredung
apprentice	Auszubildender/Lehrling
apprenticeship	Ausbildung/Lehre
to approach	annähern
appropriate	angemessen/passend
approximately	annähernd/ungefähr
apron	Schürze
area	Gebiet/Region
to arise	sich ergeben (Situation)
arithmetic logic unit	Rechenwerk
arrow	Pfeil
articulated lorry	Sattelzug
to assign	zuweisen/zuordnen
to assist	unterstützen
assisting equipment	Hilfseinrichtungen
asymmetric	asymetrisch/ ungleichförmig
asynchronous	asynchron
at least	wenigstens
at the bottom	unten
at the top	oben
atmosphere	Atmosphäre
to attach	beiheften/an~
attached	angehängt
attack	Angriff
attempt	Versuch
to attend	besuchen/teilnehmen
attention	Beachtung/ Aufmerksamkeit
attractive	anziehend
auto range	automatische Bereichswahl
available	verfügbar
average	durchschnittlich/ Durchschnitt
to avoid	vermeiden
axis	Achse
axle	Achse (Mot.)
background	Hintergrund
bacteria (pl)	Bakterien
balance	Waage
bar	Stab/Stange
bare hand	bloße Hand
barrier	Sperre/Schranke
base	Basis/Sockel
bath tub	Badewanne
to be able	können/in der Lage sein
to be aware	einer Sache bewußt sein
to be based on	sich stützen auf/ basieren auf
to be dazzled	geblendet sein
to be electrocuted	einen elektrischen Schlag bekommen
to be familiar with	vertraut sein mit

Dictionary English – German

English	German
to be interested in	interessiert sein an
to be situated	liegen (Ort)
to be located	liegen (Stadt)
to be trapped	festsitzen
to be twinned with	Partnerschaft haben mit
beam	Strahl
bearing	Lager
to become	werden
behaviour	Verhalten
belt-sander	Bandschleifer
bench	(Sitz-) Bank
bench grinder	Schleifbock
to bend	biegen
bi-directional	bidirektional/in zwei Richtungen gehend
bill	Rechnung
bimetallic thermometer	Bimetallthermometer
biomass	Biomasse
bird's eye view	Vogelperspektive
blade	Flügel/Blatt
to blow	auslösen
blower fan	Gebläse
blue temper	blaue Anlauffarbe
board system	Bordnetz
to boil	kochen
boiler	Dampfkessel
boiling point	Siedepunkt
bolt	Bolzen, Schraube
bonnet	Motorhaube
to boost up	hochtransformieren/ verstärken
boot	Kofferraum
border	Grenze
boring	langweilig
both ... and	sowohl ... als auch
bottle	Flasche
bottom dead centre	unterer Totpunkt
boundary	Grenzlinie
bracket	Klammer
brain	Gehirn
brake	Bremse
brake calliper	Bremssattel
brake disc	Bremsscheibe
brake drum	Bremstrommel
brake fading	Bremsfading
brake fluid	Bremsflüssigkeit
brake hose	Bremsschlauch
brake light	Bremslicht
brake lining	Bremsbelag
brake pad	Bremsklotz
brake pedal	Bremspedal
brake pipe	Bremsleitung
brake servo	Bremskraftverstärker
brake shoes	Bremsbacken
brake system	Bremsanlage
branch	Ast/Zweig
to break down	versagen
to break the circuit	den Stromkreis unter-brechen
breakage	Bruch
to bridge a fuse	Sicherung überbrücken
briefly	kurz/knapp
bright light	helles Licht
brittle	spröde
to broaden	erweitern
bubble	Luftblase
bumper	Stoßfänger
burr	Grat
bus width	Busbreite
by heart	auswendig
by means of	mit Hilfe von
cable	Kabel
CAD (computer aided design)	computergestütztes Zeichnen
cage	Käfig
CAM (computer aided manufacture)	computergestützte Herstellung
camshaft	Nockenwelle
cancer	Krebs
canteen	Kantine
capacitance	Kapazität (elektr.)
capacitor motor	Kondensatormotor
capillary tube	Kapillargefäß
car engine	Motor
car lift	Hebebühne
car pool	Fahrgemeinschaft
carbon	Kohlenstoff
carbon dioxide	Kohlendioxyd
carbon monoxide	Kohlenmonoxid
carburettor	Vergaser
cardboard	Pappe
careless	nachlässig
carpenter	Zimmermann
carriage	Kutsche/Wagen/Schlitten
to carry out	ausführen
carving	Schnitzwerk/Bildhauer-arbeit
case	Fall
casing	Gehäuse
casualty	Unfallopfer
catalyst	Katalysator (chem.)
catalytic converter	Katalysator (techn.)
cathedral	Dom, Kathedrale
to cause	verursachen
cause	Grund/Ursache
caution	Vorsicht
cell	Zelle
central processing unit	Zentraleinheit
centre line	Mittellinie
century	Jahrhundert
certain(ly)	gewiss/sicherlich
chain	Kette
chain reaction	Kettenreaktion
chamfer	Führungsfase
to change gears	einen Gang umschalten
characteristic	Merkmal/Eigenschaft
chassis	Chassis/Montagerahmen
to check	überprüfen
chemical	chemisch
chip	Span
chipboard	Spanplatte
chisel	Meißel
chisel edge	Querschneide
chlorofluorocarbons	Fluor-Chlor-Kohlenwasser-stoffe
to choose	auswählen/wählen
chuck	Futter (Spann~)
chuck key	Futterschlüssel
circle	Kreis
circuit	Kreis (Strom~)

Dictionary English – German

circuit board	Leiterplatte
circuit diagram	Schaltplan
circuitry	Schaltkreise, Schaltung
circular	kreisförmig
circular saw	Kreissäge
circumference	Umfang
clamp	Klemme
to clamp	einspannen, klemmen
clamp ammeter	Stromzange
clamp screw	Feststellschraube
classification	Klassifizierung
to classify	einteilen/ordnen
clearance	Spiel
clearance lamp	Begrenzungsleuchte
clearance surface	Freifläche
climate	Klima
clock	Uhr
clockwise	im Uhrzeigersinn
clutch	Kupplung
CNC (computer numeric control)	computergestützte Maschinensteuerung
coach	Überlandbus (Reisebus)
cold pack	Kühlbeutel
colleague	Kollege
to collect	einsammeln/sammeln
collection	Sammlung (An~)
colour	Farbe
column	Säule/Spalte
combination pliers	Kombizange
to combine	kombinieren, verbinden
combustible	entflammbar/brennbar
combustion	Verbrennung
combustion camber	Verbrennungsraum/ Brennkammer
to come lost	verloren gehen
comfort system	Komfortsystem
command	Befehl
command line	Befehlszeile
commercial vehicle	Nutzfahrzeug
common	gebräuchlich/üblich/ gewöhnlich
commonly	allgemein
communication software	Datenübertragungs-software
to compare	vergleichen
comparison	Vergleich
competence	Kompetenz
competition	Wettbewerb
complete	vollständig
complex	komplex/kompliziert
component	Komponente/Bestandteil
compound	Verbindung
comprehensive	umfassend
to compress	verdichten/zusammen-drücken
compression	Kompression/ Verdichtung
compression stroke	Verdichtungstakt
compressor	Kompressor
concave	konkav
conclusion	Schlussfolgerung
concrete	Beton
condense	kondensieren
condenser	Kondensator
condition	Bedingung

to conduct	leiten (elektr.)
conductive	leitend
conductor	elektrischer Leiter
conductor line	Leiterbahn
cone	Kegel
cone of light	Lichtkegel
conical	kegelförmig
to connect	anschließen/verbinden
to connect in parallel	parallel schalten
to connect in series	in Reihe schalten
connecting rod	Pleuelstange
connecting socket	Anschlussbuchse
connector	Steckverbindung
consequence	Folge/Konsequenz
to consider (as)	ansehen/betrachten (als)
considerably	beträchtlich
to consist of	bestehen aus
consistently	folgerichtig
constant-current source	Konstantstromquelle
constituent	Bestandteil
to construct	bauen
construction site	Bauplatz/Baustelle
to consume	verbrauchen
consumer	Verbraucher
consumption	Verbrauch
to contain	enthalten/beinhalten
container	Behälter/Behältnis
contest	Wettbewerb
continuation	Fortsetzung
to continue	fortsetzen
contour	Kontur/Umriss
to contract	zusammenziehen
to contribute	beisteuern
to control	steuern
control bus	Steuerbus
control circuit	Steuerstromkreis
control rod	Regelstab
control unit	Steuereinheit
controller	Steuerbaustein
convenient	bequem
conventional	herkömmlich
to convert	umformen/umwandeln
converter	Wandler (Um~)
convex	konvex
to convince	überzeugen
cooling fan	Ventilator
cooling system	Kühlsystem
cooling tower	Kühlturm
to coordinate	koordinieren
copper	Kupfer
cord	Kabel
cordless	kabellos
core	Kern
corner	Ecke
cotton wool wad	Baumwoll-Knäuel
county	Grafschaft
a couple of	einige
cover	Abdeckung
to cover	bedecken
cover cap	Abdeckkappe
cover plate	Abdeckplatte
crack	Spalte/Riss
crank case	Kurbelgehäuse
crank mechanism	Kurbeltrieb
crankshaft	Kurbelwelle

Dictionary English – German

crash sensor	Unfallsensor
to create	erstellen/erschaffen/ schaffen
cross section	Querschnitt
cross slide	Werkzeugschlitten
crosscutting	Schnitt quer zur Faser
crosswise	quer
crowded	überfüllt
cube	Würfel
cubical	würfelförmig
current	Strom
curved	gekrümmt
cutting force	Schnittkraft
cutting edge	Schneidkante/Schnittkante
cutting motion	Schnittbewegung
cutting speed	Schnittgeschwindigkeit
cycle	Zyklus/Kreislauf
cylinder	Zylinder
cylinder head	Zylinderkopf
cylindrical	zylindrisch
daily routine	Tagesablauf
to damage	beschädigen
damage	Schaden
danger	Gefahr
darkness	Dunkelheit
dashboard	Armaturenbrett
data	Daten
data protection	Datenschutz
day release class	Teilzeitklasse
dead centre	Querschneide (mittig)
to deal with	handeln von/behandeln
decade	Jahrzehnt
to decide	entscheiden
decision	Entscheidung
to declare	erklären
to decrease	verringern/senken/ abnehmen
defective	defekt
defence	Schutz
to define	bestimmen
definite	bestimmt/definitiv
degree	Grad
to deliver	liefern
delivery truck	Lieferwagen
demand	Nachfrage
density	Dichte
department	Abteilung
departure	Abreise
to depend on	abhängen von
to deploy	einsetzen
deposition	Ablagerung
depth	Tiefe
depth bar	Tiefenmessgerät
depth setting	*hier:* Zustellung
to derive from	ableiten von
to describe	beschreiben
description	Beschreibung
to design	konstruieren/entwerfen/ gestalten
design	Konstruktion/Bauform/ Ausführung
to destroy	zerstören
destruction	Zerstörung
to determine	bestimmen
to develop	entwickeln

developing country	Entwicklungsland
development	Entwicklung
device	Vorrichtung/Gerät
diagnostic centre	Diagnosezentrum
diagonal	diagonal/schräg
to dial	wählen (Telefonnummer)
diameter	Durchmesser
difference	Unterschied
different	verschieden/ unterschiedlich
differential	Differential
difficult	schwierig
dimension	Dimension/Abmessung
dipped beam	Abblendlicht
direction	Richtung
disadvantage	Nachteil
to discharge	entladen
to disconnect	trennen
discontinuous	unterbrochen
to displace	verschieben
to dissolve	auflösen
distance	Entfernung
distinction	Unterscheidung
to distinguish	unterscheiden
distribution	Verteilung
to disturb	stören
to divide	(auf-)teilen
donator	Spender
dot-matrix display	Punktmatrix Anzeige
doubt	Zweifel
downward	nach unten
downwards	abwärts
to drag along	mitschleppen
to drain	ableiten/ablaufen lassen
to draw	zeichnen
drawing	Zeichnung
to drill	bohren
drill bit	Bohrer
drill-point angle	Spitzenwinkel
to drip	tropfen
drive	Laufwerk
drive shaft	Antriebswelle
drive slot	Laufwerksschacht
drive train	Antriebstrakt
driver	Treiber
to drop	fallen
to drop in	vorbeikommen
drought	Dürre
to drown	ertrinken
dual system	duales System
dual-wire	Bilux-Lampe
dump truck	Kipper (Baustellenfahr- zeug)
during operation	während des Betriebes
dust	Staub
dust mask	Staubmaske
ear plugs	Ohrenstöpsel
to earth	erden
earth-free bonding	erdfreier Potential- ausgleich
earthquake	Erdbeben
economically	wirtschaftlich
eddy currents	Wirbelströme
edge	Kante/Rand
editor	Redakteur

Dictionary English – German

effect	Wirksamkeit/Folge
efficiency	Wirkungsgrad
efficient	wirkungsvoll
electric current	elektrischer Strom
electric drill	elektrische Bohrmaschine
electric plane	Elektrohobel
electric shock	elektrischer Schlag
electrical connection	elektrische Verbindung
electrical consumers	elektrische Verbraucher
electrical equipment	elektrische Ausrüstung
electrical separation	Schutztrennung
electrical spark	elektrischer Funke
electronic system	elektronisches System
electrolysis	Elektrolyse
electrolyte	Elektrolyt
electrolytic capacitor	Elektrolytkondensator
electronic component	elektronisches Bauteil
electronic control unit (ECU)	elektronisches Steuergerät
electronic part	elektronisches Bauteil
electronically controlled	elektronisch gesteuert
emergency exit	Notausgang
emergency switch	Notausschalter
emission	Ausstoß, Emission/Abgas
to emit	ausstoßen/emitieren
to emphasize	betonen
employee	Angestellte(r)
employer	Arbeitgeber(in)
to enable	befähigen/ermöglichen
to enclose	einschließen/beilegen/ beifügen
to encounter	jmd. begegnen
encyclopaedia	Lexikon/Enzyklopädie
to endanger	gefährden
energy losses	Energieverluste
energy meter	kWh-Zähler
energy source	Energiequelle
to engage	einstellen/anstellen
engine	Motor
engine block	Motorblock
engine frame	Maschinengestell
engineer	Ingenieur/in
to enhance	verbessern
to enjoy	genießen
enough	genug
to ensure	sicherstellen/gewährleisten
enthusiastic	begeistert
entire	ganz/vollständig
envelope	Umschlag
environment	Umgebung/Umwelt
environmentalist	Umweltschützer
environmental protection	Umweltschutz
environmental technician	Umwelttechniker/in
equal	gleich
to equalize	ausgleichen
equation	Gleichung (math.)
to equip	ausstatten
equipment	Ausrüstung/Ausstattung
equivalent to	soviel wie
era	Epoche
error	Irrtum/Fehler
to escape	entkommen
especially	besonders
essential	wesentlich
to establish	einrichten
estuary	Mündung (von Fluss)
ethane	Ethangas
exactly	genau
to exceed	überschreiten
excerpt	Auszug
excessive	ausgedehnt
to exchange	austauschen
exchange partner	Austauschpartner(in)
exchange programme	Austauschprogramm
exchange student	Austauschschüler(in)
exhaust/exhaust fume	Abgase
exhaust pipe	Auspuff
exhaust stroke	Ausstoßtakt
exhaust system	Auspuffsystem
exit	Ausgang
to expand	ausdehnen
expansion slot	Steckplatz für Steckkarte
to expect	erwarten
experienced	erfahren
to expire	ab-, auslaufen/verfallen
expiry date	Verfalldatum
to explain	erklären
explanation	Erklärung
exposed	offen
expression	Ausdruck
extension cord	Verlängerungskabel
extensive	umfangreich
external diameter	Außendurchmesser
to extinguish	löschen
to extract	herausziehen/extrahieren/ gewinnen
eye pad	Augenklappe
façade	Fassade
to face	gegenüberstehen/ vor etwas stehen
face	Gesicht/Stirnfläche
face milling	Stirnfräsen
facility	Einrichtung/Leichtigkeit
to fade away	verschwinden
familiar	gewohnt/vertraut
famous	berühmt
fan	Lüfter
fan belt	Keilriemen
to fasten	befestigen
fault	Fehler/Defekt
feature	Kennzeichen/Merkmal
feed	Vorschub
feed direction	Vorschubrichtung
feed gear levers	Vorschubgetriebehebel
feed shaft	Zugspindel
to feed	zuführen
feeler gauge	Fühlerlehre
female thread	Innengewinde
file	Feile/Datei
finally	endlich/schließlich
to finance	finanzieren
fingertip bandage	Fingerkuppenverband
to finish	beenden
fire extinguisher	Feuerlöscher
firmly	fest
first aid container	Erste Hilfe Behälter
first aid course	Erste Hilfe Kurs
first aid guide	Erste Hilfe Broschüre
first name	Vorname

Dictionary English – German

to fit	anbringen/montieren/ anpassen
fitting	Ausstattung
to fix	befestigen
fixed jaw	fester Messschenkel
to flake away	ausbröckeln
flammable	entzündbar/brennbar
flange	Flansch
flashlight	Taschenlampe
flat	leer/entladen
flat point	flache Spitze
flight controllers	Fluglotsen
flour	Mehl
to flow	fließen
to flush	spülen
flute	Spannut/Nut
flute width	Spannutbreite
fog light	Nebellicht
folding rule	Gliedermaßstab
foot	Fuß (30,38 cm)
for instance	zum Beispiel
force	Kraft
foreign language	Fremdsprache
forklift truck	Gabelstabler
format	Format
formation	Bildung
former	frühere(r)
fossil fuel	fossiler Brennstoff
to found	gründen
four-stroke engine	Viertaktmotor
four-wheel drive	Allradantrieb
fraction	Bruch (~zahl)
freezer	Gefrierschrank
freezing point	Gefrierpunkt
frequency counter	Frequenzzähler
frequently	häufig/oft
friction	Reibung
front	vordere(r)
fuel	Treibstoff
fuel cell	Brennstoffzelle
fuel gauge	Tankuhr
fuel system	Kraftstoffsystem
to fulfil	erfüllen
to function	funktionieren
function key	Funktionstaste
further	weiter/mehr
further reaction	weitere Reaktion
furthermore	darüber hinaus
fuse	Sicherung
garage manual	Werkstatt Handbuch
garage owner	Werkstattbesitzer
garden shed	Gartenhäuschen
gas generator	Gasgenerator
gaseous	gasförmig
gauge	Lehre
gauze bandage	Mullverband
gear	Getriebe/Gang/Übersetzung
gearbox	Getriebe(gehäuse)
gear stick	Schalthebel
gear wheel	Zahnrad
general	allgemein
to generate	erzeugen
generous	großzügig
geometric triangle	Geodreieck
geometrically defined	geometrisch bestimmt
geothermal energy	Energie aus Erdwärme
to get rid of	loswerden
giant	riesig
to glide	gleiten
global	weltweit/global
glory	Glanz
goods	Güter, Waren
gorge	Schlucht
gradual	allmählich
grain	Getreide
graphic card	Graphikkarte
graphical user interface	graphische Benutzer-oberfläche
gravitational pull	Anziehungskraft
gravity	Schwerkraft
green product	umweltschonendes Produkt
greenhouse effect	Treibhauseffekt
to grind	mahlen/schleifen
grinder	Schleifmaschine
groove	Nut
ground	Masse
ground water	Grundwasser
to guess	vermuten
guest	Gast
guideline	Anrisslinie
guidelines	Richtlinien
habit	Gewohnheit
halogen lamp	Halogenlampe
hand wheel	Handrad
handbrake	Handbremse
to handle	handhaben/umgehen mit
handle	Handgriff
hands-on training	Praktikum
hard metal tip	Hartmetallplättchen
hardcopy	(Papier-) Ausdruck
harm	Verletzung
to harm	schaden
harmful	schädlich
hazard	Gefahr/Risiko
hazard warning light	Warnblinkanlage
hazardous area	Gefahrenzone
head office	Hauptsitz
head stock	Spindelstock
headlight	Scheinwerfer
headphone	Kopfhörer
heat resistance	Hitzefestigkeit
heater	Heizung
heavy-duty	strapazierfähig
heavy-duty truck	Schwerlastkraftwagen
height	Höhe
helix angle	Drallsteigungswinkel
helmet	Helm
hexagonal	sechseckig
high tensile steel	Stahl mit großer Streck-grenze
high water mark	Hochwassermarke
highly visible	gut sichtbar
high-voltage pylon	Hochspannungsmast
history	Geschichte
hole	Loch
holster	Halfter/Tasche
home economics	Hauswirtschaft
honest	ehrlich
honey comb	Bienenwabe

hook	Haken
horn	Hupe
host	Gastgeber
hostile	feindlich
household	Haushalt
however	jedoch
humidity	Feuchtigkeit
hydraulic brake system	hydraulische Bremsanlage
hydro electric plant	Wasserkraftwerk
hydro energy	Wasserenergie
hydrocarbon	Kohlenwasserstoff
hydrogen	Wasserstoff
hygroscopic	wasserziehend
iceberg	Eisberg
icon	graphisches Symbol
to identify	identifizieren
to ignite	entzünden
ignition switch	Zündschloss
ignition system	Zündsystem
to illuminate	beleuchten
image	Bild
to imagine	sich etwas vorstellen
immediately	sofort/unmittelbar
impact	Auswirkung
impact protection	Aufprallschutz
imperial	imperial
importance	Wichtigkeit/Bedeutung
important	wichtig
to improve	verbessern
in addition	zusätzlich
in case of	im Falle, dass ...
in common	gemeinsam
in general	im Allgemeinen
in order to	um ... zu
in relation to	im Verhältnis zu
inaccurate	ungenau
incident	Vorfall/Zwischenfall
incineration plant	Verbrennungsanlage
inclination	Neigungswinkel
to include	einschließen
including/inclusive	einschließlich
incompressible	nicht komprimierbar
increase	Anstieg/Zunahme
to increase	erhöhen/vergrößern/(an)steigen
independence	Unabhängigkeit
indeployed	nicht eingesetzt
to indicate	anzeigen
indicator	Anzeiger, Blinker
indicator light	Blinklicht
individual	eigen/individuell
induction	Aufnahme/Induktion
industrial nation	Industrienation
inevitable	unvermeidlich
infeed	Zustellung
infinitely	stufenlos
inflammable	entzündbar/brennbar
to inflate	aufblasen
inhabitant	Einwohner
injection system	Einspritzsystem
injury	Verletzung
input	Eingabe
input impedance	Eingangswiderstand
to insert	einsetzen
inside	innerhalb
inside jaw	Messschenkel für Innenmessung
insight	Einblick
to inspect	überprüfen
to install	installieren
instruction	Anweisung
instruction manual	Bedienungshandbuch
instructor	Ausbilder
instrument circuit	Messstromkreis
to insulate	isolieren (elektr.)
intake manifold	Ansaugstutzen
intake stroke	Ansaugtakt
integrated circuit	integrierter Schaltkreis
to intend	beabsichtigen
intention	Absicht
interchange	Autobahnkreuz
interior light	Innenbeleuchtung
internal	innere(n)
internal combustion engine	Verbrennungsmotor
internal diameter	Innendurchmesser
to introduce	einführen/vorstellen
introduction	Bekanntmachung/Vorstellung
to invent	erfinden
invention	Erfindung
to invert	umkehren
to invite	einladen
to involve	beteiligen
iron	Eisen
item	Gegenstand
jack	Wagenheber
job card	Arbeitskarte
joiner's shop	Tischlerwerkstatt
jump leads	Starthilfekabel
jump-start	Starthilfe
junction	Anschlussstelle/Auffahrt/Ab~
keyhole saw	Stichsäge
kind	freundlich
kind of	Art/Sorte von
knowledge	Wissen
laboratory	Labor
labour	Arbeit
lack	Mangel
to lag behind	hinterherhinken
land	*hier:* Führungsfase
landfill gas	Gas aus Müll
landmark	Wahrzeichen
large	groß
lathe	Drehmaschine
to laugh	lachen
launched	hier: präsentiert
law	Gesetz
law of nature	Naturgesetz
lawn	Rasen
layer	Lage/Schicht
lead	Leiter (elektr.)
lead shaft	Leitspindel
leader	Führer
leak	Leck
left over crops	Erntereste
length	Länge
lengthwise	der Länge nach
less	weniger

less likely	wenig wahrscheinlich
lever	Hebel/Brechstange
lifesaving equipment	lebensrettende Ausrüstung
light system	Lichtanlage
light-duty truck	kleiner Lastkraftwagen
limestone	Kalkstein
linear motor	Linearmotor
to link	verbinden
lip clearance area	Freifläche
liquid	flüssig/Flüssigkeit
liquid thermometer	Flüssigkeitsthermometer
little (money)	wenig (Geld)
live wire	spannungsführende Leitung
lively	lebendig/quirlig
load	Last
location	Lage/Standort
longitudinal	Längs-
long-nose pliers	Schnabelzange
to loosen	lösen/lockern
lorry	Lastkraftwagen (LKW)
loud noise	laute Geräusche
low	niedrig
lubrication system	Schmiersystem
luggage	Gepäck
lumber	Bauholz
machine tool	Werkzeugmaschine
magnetic field	Magnetfeld
magnetic sheet steel	Elektroblech
main	Haupt-
main beam	Fernlicht
main part	Hauptteil
mainly	hauptsächlich
mains	(Strom)Netz
to maintain	warten/pflegen
maintenance-free	wartungsfrei
major	Haupt-
majority	Mehrheit
to make sure	sicherstellen
male thread	Außengewinde
mandatory	gesetzlich vorgeschrieben
mankind	Menschheit
manoeuvre	Manöver
manual	Handbuch
to manufacture	herstellen/fertigen
manufacturer	Hersteller
map	Landkarte
margin	Rand
mark	Markierung
to mark	kennzeichnen/markieren
mass	Masse
mass production	Massenproduktion
to match	zusammenbringen/ zusammengehören
means of transportation	Verkehrsmittel
meanwhile	inzwischen
to measure	messen
measure	Maßeinheit/Maßnahme
measurement	Messung
measurement technology	Messtechnik
measuring line	Messleitung
mechanical engineering	Maschinenbau
medical treatment	medizinische Behandlung
to melt	schmelzen
memory	Speicher
to mend	reparieren
to mention	erwähnen
menu bar	Menüleiste
mercury	Quecksilber
merger	Zusammenschluss
metal frame	Metallrahmen
metal work	Metallarbeiten
meter	Zähler
metric	metrisch
micrometer	Messschraube
microphone	Mikrofon
to minimize	minimieren
to mirror	spiegeln
mixture	Mischung
mixture formation	Gemischaufbereitung
modern-day	heutige/moderne
to modify	erneuern, abändern
molecule	Molekül
motherboard	Hauptplatine
motor vehicle	Kraftfahrzeug
motorway	Autobahn
to mount	montieren/errichten/ befestigen
mounting bracket	Befestigungsklammer
movable (also: moveable)	beweglich
movable jaw	beweglicher Messschenkel
movement	Bewegung
multimeter	Vielfachmessgerät
to multiply	mal nehmen/multiplizieren
multi-purpose vehicle	Mehrzweckfahrzeug
muscle cramp	Muskelkrampf
nail	Nagel
to nail	nageln/an~
to name	benennen
narrow	eng/schmal
National Vocational Qualification (NVQ)	staatlicher Berufsabschluss an einem College
natural gas	Erdgas
necessary	notwendig/erforderlich
negative pole	Minuspol
to neglect	vernachlässigen
to negotiate	verhandeln
neither ... nor	weder ... noch
to network	vernetzen
news	Nachrichten
next door	nebenan
nitric acid	Salpetersäure
nitrogen oxide	Stickoxid
nomenclature	Bezeichnungen
non-conducting location	nicht-leitender Raum
north of	nördlich von
notice	Notiz/Schild
nowadays	heutzutage
nozzle	Düse
nuclear fission	Kernspaltung
nuclear power	Atomkraft
nucleus	Atomkern
number plate	Nummernschild
numerous	zahlreich
nut	(Schrauben)Mutter
nutrition	Ernährung/Nahrung
obligation	Verpflichtung
to observe	beachten
obstacle	Hindernis
to obtain	erhalten

occasion	Gelegenheit
to occur	geschehen/auftreten/vorkommen
odourless	geruchlos
off-centre	außermittig
to offer	anbieten
offer	Angebot
oil pressure	Öldruck
oil sump	Ölwanne
on a large scale	im großen Rahmen
on top of	oben auf/über
on-board computer	Bordcomputer
oncoming traffic	Gegenverkehr
on-screen	auf dem Bildschirm
open-ended spanner	Maulschlüssel
opening	Inbetriebnahme
to operate	funktionieren
operating level	Betriebsspannung
operating system	Betriebssystem
operation	Funktionsweise
ordinary	gewöhnlich
organic	organisch
otherwise	anderenfalls
output	Ausgabe/(Produktions)-leistung
outside	außerhalb
outside jaw	Messschenkel für Außenmessung
over head line	Überlandleitung
overload protection	Überlastschutz
overvoltage	Überspannung
overview	Überblick
to oxidize	oxidieren
oxygen	Sauerstoff
ozone layer	Ozonschicht
pace	Schritt/Tempo
packaging	Verpackung
paint lacquer	Lackfarben
parking light	Parklicht
part	Teil
participant	Teilnehmer
pass	Durchgang
passenger cars	Personenwagen
passenger cell	Fahrgastzelle
pathway	Weg/Pfad
to pay attention to	beachten/aufpassen/Aufmerksamkeit schenken
pedal	Pedal
pedestrian	Fußgänger
pencil	Bleistift
penetration	Durchbruch
per cent	Prozent
to perform	durchführen/ausführen
peripheral device	Peripheriegerät/Anschlussgerät
peripheral speed	Umfangsgeschwingkeit
periphery	Rand
permanently	ständig
permissible	zulässig
to persuade	überreden
petrol	Benzin
Phillips screwdriver	Kreuzschlitzschraubendreher
pincers (a pair of)	Kneifzange
pipe	Rohr
piston	Kolben
to pivot	schwenken
place	Ort
plane	Flugzeug/Hobel
plant	Fabrikanlage/Anlage/Pflanze
platinum	Platin
to please	erfreuen
pleasure	Vergnügen
pliers (a pair of)	Zange
plug	Stecker
plumbing	Klempnern
plywood	Schichtholz
to point	zeigen
point angle	Spitzenwinkel
pointed	spitz
poison	Gift
to poison	vergiften
poisonous	giftig
pollutant	Schadstoff
polluter	Umweltsünder
pollution	Umweltverschmutzung/Schadstoffbelastung
popular	beliebt
porcelain	Porzellan
porous	porös
portable	tragbar
portal	Eingangsportal
positive pole	Pluspol
possibility	Möglichkeit
position display	Positionsanzeige
potential difference	Potentialdifferenz
pottery	Töpferwaren
povidon-iodine pad	Jodbausch
to power	antreiben
power cord	Elektrokabel
power flow	Kraftfluss
power plant	Kraftwerk
power source	Stromquelle
power stroke	Arbeitstakt
power supply	Energieversorgung
power supply cable	Verbindung für die Stromversorgung
power tool	angetriebenes Werkzeug
powerful	mächtig
practical	praktisch
practice	Verfahren/Methode
precaution	Sicherheitsmaßnahme/Vorsichtsmaßnahme
precious	wertvoll
precise	präzise/genau
precision	Genauigkeit
precision resistor	Präzisionswiderstand
to predict	vorhersagen
preferable	vorzugsweise
preparation	Vorbereitung
to prepare	vorbereiten
present	gegenwärtig
pressure	Druck
pressure gauge	Druckanzeiger
to prevent	verhindern
previous	vorherig; vorausgegangen
prickle	Kribbeln, Stechen
principal	Direktor(in)

priority	Vorrang
prize	Preis/Gewinn
probability	Wahrscheinlichkeit
probably	wahrscheinlich
probe	Sonde
probe tip	Messspitze
procedure	Vorgehensweise/Verfahren
process	Vorgang
to produce	herstellen
professional	fachmännisch
prohibition	Verbot
propeller shaft	Kardanwelle
properly	korrekt/richtig
proportion	Anteil/Verhältnis
to protect	schützen
protection	Schutz
protective conductor	Schutzleiter
protective equipment	Schutzausrüstung
protective goggles	Schutzbrille
proton	Proton
prototype	Muster/Prototyp
to prove	beweisen
to provide	liefern/bereitstellen
public transportation	öffentliche Verkehrsmittel
to publish	veröffentlichen
to purify	reinigen
purpose	Zweck
purpose of use	Einsatzzweck
to push	schieben
qualified	qualifiziert
quartz glass	Quarzglas
quite	ziemlich
radiator	Heizkörper
radio engineer	Rundfunktechniker
radiused	abgerundet
to raise	heben/erhöhen
random access memory	Speicher mit wahlfreiem Zugriff
range	Bereich/Mess~
range (a wide ~)	eine große Anzahl
range selector	Messbereichswähler
rapid	schnell/rasch/rapide
rare	selten
ratchet	Knarre/Ratsche
rate of expansion	Ausdehnungs-geschwindigkeit
ratio	Verhältnis
to realize	erkennen
rear	hintere(r)
rear-wheel drive	Heckantrieb
reasonable	vernünftig
to recall	sich erinnern
to receive	empfangen
recent	*hier:* neu
to recharge	(wieder)aufladen
rechargeable	wieder aufladbar
reciprocal movement	Hin- und Herbewegung
to recommend	empfehlen
to recover	sich erholen
recovery position	stabile Seitenlage
rectangle	Rechteck
rectangular	rechteckig
rectangular solid	Quader
reddish-brown	rotbraun
to reduce	reduzieren/verringern
to refer to	Bezug nehmen auf
to refill	auffüllen/nachfüllen
reflector	Reflektor
to refuel	auftanken
to refuse	verweigern
to regard	betrachten
region	Gebiet/Region
register	Register/Speicher/Verzeichnis
to register	registrieren
regular	regelmäßig
regulations	Vorschriften
regulator	Regler
re-ignition	Wiederentzündung
to reinsert	wieder einstecken
to reject	zurückweisen
relationship	Verhältnis
relative air humidity (R.H.)	relative Luftfeuchtigkeit
relative	Verwandte/r
relay	Relais
to release	freisetzen/freigeben
reliable	verlässlich
to remain	(übrig)bleiben
to remind of	erinnern an
to remove	entfernen
renewable	erneuerbar
renewal	Erneuerung
to replace	ersetzen
report	Bericht
to represent	darstellen
repulsive	abstoßend
to require	erfordern/brauchen
requirement	Anforderung/Bedarf
to rescue	retten
resealable plastic bag	wieder verschließbare Plastiktasche
resistance	Widerstand
resolution	Auflösung
resources	Hilfsmittel, Reserven
responsible for	verantwortlich für
restraint system	Rückhaltesystem
result	Ergebnis
to result in	führen zu
to reunite	wiedervereinigen
to reverse	umkehren
reverse gear	Rückwärtsgang
reverse lamp	Rückfahrscheinwerfer
revolution	Umdrehung/Drehung
rim	Felge
rim wrench	Radkreuz
ring pin	Sicherungsring
ring spanner	Ringschlüssel
rip guide slot	Nut für den Führungs-anschlag
ripping	Längsschnitt
ripsaw guide	Führungsanschlag
to rise	steigen/an~
risk	Risiko
road	Straße
robust	robust
rocker arm	Kipphebel
rocker cover	Ventildeckel
rocker shaft	Kipphebelwelle
rope	Seil

Dictionary English – German

to rotate	drehen
rotating movement	drehende Bewegung
rotation	Umdrehung/Rotation
rotation axis	Rotationsachse
rotor blade	Flügelblatt
rotor end ring	Kurzschlussring
rotor hub	Rotornabe
rotor lamination pack	Läuferblechpaket
round bracket	runde Klammer (math.)
roundabout	Kreisverkehr
to route	führen/weiterleiten
rubber	Gummi
rubber mallet	Gummihammer
rubbish	Abfall
rule	Regel
rust	Rost
safety	Sicherheit
safety cover	Schutzhaube
safety glasses	Schutzbrille
safety guard	Schutzeinrichtung
safety pins	Sicherheitsnadeln
safety shield	Schutzschild
safety shoes	Sicherheitsschuhe
safety sign	Sicherheitsschild
safety system	Sicherheitssystem
safety zone	Sicherheitszone
saloon	Limousine
sander	Schleifer (Schleifpapier)
sandstone	Sandstein
to save	sichern/sparen
saw	Säge
to saw	sägen
saw dust ejection	Späneauswurf
scaffolding	Gerüst
scale	Skala/Gradeinteilung
scene	Bildfläche
schematic diagram	Schaltplan
school magazine	Schülerzeitung
science	Wissenschaft
scientist	Wissenschaftler(in)
scissors	Schere
scrap yard	Schrottplatz
scrap	Abfall/Schrott
screen	Bildschirm
screw	Schraube
to screw	(an)schrauben
screw driver	Schraubendreher
to search	suchen
to seat	*hier:* einpassen
section	Abschnitt/Teilabschnitt
to secure	absichern
security	Sicherheit/Schutz
security system	Sicherheitssystem
to select	auswählen
selection	Auswahl
semi trailer (AE)	Sattelzug
semicircle	Halbkreis
semicircular	halbkreisförmig
semi-conducting material	Halbleitermaterial
sense	Sinn
sensor	Sensor
separate	getrennt
serious	ernst/schlimm
set buffet	kaltes Buffet
setting	Einstellung

several	einige
severe	schwer/ernsthaft
shaded-pole motor	Spaltpolmotor
shaft	Welle
shank	Schaft
shape	Form
to shape	Form geben
to sharpen	schärfen
sharpness	Schärfe
sheet	Blatt
shelf	Regal(-brett)
to ship	verfrachten
short circuit	Kurzschluss
to short circuit	kurzschließen
short distance	Kurzstrecke
shortage	Knappheit
to shut off	abstellen/abschalten
side cutter	Seitenschneider
sight seeing trip	Stadtrundfahrt
similar	ähnlich
simple	einfach
simultaneously	gleichzeitig
sited (to be ~)	aufgestellt sein/ errichtet sein
size	Größe
skill	Fähigkeit/Geschick
slackness	Spiel (techn.)
sleeve	Ärmel
to slide	gleiten/rutschen/schieben
slider	Schieber
slip	Schlupf
slip ring motor	Schleifringläufermotor
slip road	Autobahnzubringer
slot	Schlitz/Rille/Nut
smooth	glatt
to snap back	zurückschnappen
to snatch	einhaken
society	Gesellschaft
socket	Nuss (für Ratsche)/ Steckdose
socket set	Steckschlüsselsatz
socket wrench	Steckschlüssel
sodium azide	Natriumazid
soil	Erde/Boden
solar panel	Sonnenkollektor
to solder	löten
soldering iron	Lötkolben
solid	fest
solid wood	Vollholz
to solve	lösen
to sort	sortieren
SOS (save our souls)	internationaler Hilferuf
sound	Schall
source	Quelle
space blanket	Rettungsdecke
to span	überspannen
spare time	Freizeit
spark	Funke
spark plug wrench	Zündkerzenschlüssel
spark(ing) plug	Zündkerze
specifications	technische Daten
speed	Geschwindigkeit
speed of sound	Schallgeschwindigkeit
speedometer	Tachometer
to spend	verbringen

English	German
sphere	Kugel
spherical	kugelförmig
to spin	drehen
spiral	spiralförmig
splinter	Splitter
to split	spalten
to split up	aufspalten
sports car	Sportwagen
spring	Feder
spring balance	Federwaage
spring guard	Federabdeckung
sprocket	Kettenrad
square	Quadrat/quadratisch
square with	im rechten Winkel zu
squirrel cage motor	Käfigläufermotor
stable	stabil
stage	Stufe/Etappe
to stall	stehen bleiben (z. B. Motor)
stamp	Briefmarke
starter motor	Starter (Anlasser)
start-up	Start/Inbetriebnahme
state of repair	Zustand
statesman	Staatsmann
static electricity	statische Aufladung
stationary	stehend
stator lamination pack	Ständerblechpaket
stator winding	Ständerwicklung
status	Stellung/Rang
to stay	bleiben/wohnen
stay	Aufenthalt
steam	Dampf
steam bubbles	Dampfblasen
steam ship	Dampfschiff
steel	Stahl
steep	steil
steering	Lenkung
steering column	Lenksäule
steering wheel	Lenkrad
step	Schritt
stepping motor	Schrittmotor
sterile	steril/keimfrei
sterile gauze swab	Mulltupfer
still	noch
stock	Vorrat
stone-mason	Steinmetz
storage space	Speicherplatz
to store	speichern
to stow	verstauen
straight	gerade
straight on	geradeaus (fahren)
strap wrench	Bandschlüssel
strength	Kraft/Stärke
stretcher	Krankentrage
to strike	treffen (auf od. gegen)/ zuschlagen
stroke	Takt
to study	studieren/lernen
to subdivide	unterteilen
subject	Unterrichtsfach
substance	Stoff, Substanz
substation	Umspannwerk
suburb	Vorort
successful	erfolgreich
to suffer from	leiden an
sugar refining	Zuckerherstellung
to suggest	vorschlagen
suitable	geeignet
suitably	entsprechend
sulphur	Schwefel
sulphuric acid	Schwefelsäure
supersonic	Überschall-
supply	Versorgung
to support	unterstützen
support	Unterstützung
to suppose	annehmen/vermuten
sure	sicher
surface	Oberfläche
surname	Nachname
surprised	überrascht
suspension	Federung/Aufhängung
to swamp	überschwemmen
swarf tray	Spänewanne
switch	Schalter
to switch on/off	einschalten/aus~
switch statuse	Schalterstellung
synchronous milling	Gleichlauffräsen
synchronous motor	Synchronmotor
table	Tabelle
tailstock	Reitstock
to take place	stattfinden
tap	Wasserhahn
tax	Steuer
technical draftswoman	technische Zeichnerin
technology	Technologie/Technik
telephone line	Telefonleitung
temper	Härte
temporary	zeitweilig
to tend to	neigen zu
tendency	Neigung/Trend
term	Begriff/Ausdruck
theoretical training	theoretische Ausbildung
thermal power station	Wärmekraftwerk
thickness	Stärke/Dicke
to thin	ausspitzen/ausdünnen
thoroughly	sorgfältig
thread	Gewinde
three-dimensional	dreidimensional
three-jaw tool	Dreibackenwerkzeug
thus	so/auf diese Art
tidal range	Tidenhub
to tighten	festziehen/anziehen
tightly	fest/eng
times	mal (math.)
timing	Steuerung
timing control	Ventilsteuerung
tobacco processing	Tabakverarbeitung
tool	Werkzeug
tool clamp	Werkzeughalter
tool kit	Funktionen/ Hilfsprogramme
tool rest	Werkzeugauflage
tool trolley	Werkzeugwagen
toolmaker	Werkzeugmacher
top dead centre	oberer Totpunkt
top view	Draufsicht
topic	Thema
torque	Drehmoment
torque wrench	Drehmomentschlüssel
to touch	berühren

tough	zäh
towards	auf etwas zu
toxic	giftig
toxic liquid	giftige Flüssigkeit
track	Pfad/Weg
tractor (agricultural vehicle)	Traktor
trading centre	Handelszentrum
traffic	Verkehr
traffic jam	Stau
traffic light	Ampel
trainee	Auszubildende(r)
training	Ausbildung
to transfer	übertragen
transfer	Übertragung
to transform	umformen
transformer	Transformator
transistor gain	Transistorverstärkung
translation	Übersetzung
transmission	Übertragung/Getriebe
transmission box	Getriebegehäuse
transmission line	Hochspannungsleitung
transmission pole	Hochspannungsmast
to transmit	übertragen/senden
transparent	durchsichtig
transverse	Quer-
to treat	behandeln
triangle	Dreieck
triangular	dreieckig
triangular cloth	Dreieckstuch
trigger	Auslöseschalter/Abzug
trigger latch	Knopf zum Halten des Schalters
to trim	trimmen
trip	Reise
true circle	rund
turntable	Drehscheibe
tweezers	Pinzette
twice	zweimal
twin town	Partnerstadt
twist drill	Spiralbohrer
two-dimensional	zweidimensional
type	Art/Typ
tyre	Reifen
unconscious	bewusstlos
undersurface	Unterseite
undivided	ungeteilt
uni-directional	in eine Richtung gehend
unit	Einheit
to unload	entladen
unpleasant	unangenehm
to unplug	Stecker entfernen/heraus-ziehen
to unscrew	abschrauben/auf~
unsual	ungewöhnlich
up-cut milling	Gegenlauffräsen
to update	aktualisieren
upper body	Oberkörper
upwards	aufwärts
uranium	Uran
urgently	dringend
usually	gewöhnlich
to utilize	nutzen
vacant	frei
valley	Tal
value	Wert
valve	Ventil
valve gap	Ventilspiel
valve spring	Ventilfeder
van	Kleintransporter
vapour	Dunst/Dampf/Nebel
variety	Vielfalt
various	verschiedene
to vary	verändern
vehicle	Fahrzeug
ventricular fibrillation	Herzkammerflimmern
to verify	überprüfen
vernier	Nonius
vernier calliper (BE)	Messschieber
versus	gegen
via	via/per
vice	Schraubstock
victim	Opfer
vigorously	energisch/heftig
village	Dorf
vinyl gloves	Einmalhandschuhe
visible	sichtbar
to visit	besuchen
vocational school	Berufsschule
vocational training	Berufsausbildung
voltage	Spannung
voltage tester	Spannungsprüfer
volume	Volumen/Lautstärke
volute	spiralförmig
wall socket	Steckdose
warehouse	Lagerhalle/Lagerhaus
warning	Warnung
to waste	vergeuden/verschwenden
waste	Abfall
to water	gießen
water level	Wasserstandslinie
water treatment plant	Wasseraufbereitungs - anlage
to weaken	schwächen
wear and tear	Verschleiß
weather forecast	Wettervorhersage
web thinning	Ausspitzen
to wedge	festklemmen
wedge shaped	keilförmig
to weigh	wiegen
weight	Gewicht
to welcome	willkommen heißen
welding machine	Schweißgerät
wheel	Rad
wheel cylinder	Radbremszylinder
whereas	während/wohingegen
wherever	wo auch immer
whether	ob
whole	ganz
wide	breit
width	Weite/Breite
wildlife	Tierwelt
window defroster	Scheibenheizung
windscreen	Windschutzscheibe
windscreen wiper	Scheibenwischer
wing	Kotflügel
wing mirror	Seitenspiegel
wire	Draht/Leitung
with respect to	in Bezug auf
withdraw	zurückziehen

Dictionary English – German

without	ohne
to withstand	widerstehen
witness	Zeuge
wooden	aus Holz/hölzern
word processing	Textverarbeitung
workbench	Werkbank
worksheet	Arbeitsblatt
workshop	Werkstatt
workshop manager	Werkstattleiter
workstation	Arbeitsplatz am Computer
wound	Wunde
to wrap	einwickeln
wrench	Schraubenschlüssel
yaw system	Windrichtungsnachführung
zinc	Zink

Dictionary German – English

Abblendlicht	dipped headlight
Abdeckkappe	cover cap
Abdeckplatte	cover plate
Abdeckung	cover
Abfall	rubbish/ garbage/ waste
Abgas	emission/exhaust fume
abgesehen von	apart from/except for
abhängen von	to depend on
Abkürzung	abbreviation
Ablagerung	deposition
ablaufen lassen	to drain
ableiten	to derive from/to drain
Abmessung	dimension
Abreise	departure
abschalten	to shut off/to switch off
Abschnitt	section
abschrauben	to unscrew
absichern	to secure
Absicht	intention
abstellen, abschalten	to shut off
abstoßend	repulsive
Abteilung	department
abwärts	downwards
abwechselnd	alternately
Abzug	trigger
Achse	axle
Achse (Dreh~)	axis
Administrator	administrator
Adressbus	address bus
ähnlich	similar
aktivieren	to activate
aktualisieren	to update
allgemein	common/general
Allgemeinen (im ~)	in general
allmählich	gradual
Allradantrieb	four-wheel drive
alt	ancient
Ampel	traffic light
Ampre	ampere
Amperemeter	ammeter
anbieten	to offer
anbringen	to fix/to fit
anderenfalls	otherwise
Anforderung	requirement
Angebot	offer
angehängt	attached
angemessen	appropriate
angeordnet	located
Angestellter	employee
angetriebenes Werkzeug	power tool
Angriff	attack
anheften	to attach
Anlasser	starter motor
Anlauffarbe blau	blue temper
anlegen	to apply to
annageln	to nail
annähern	to approach
annähernd	approximately/roughly
anpassen	to adapt/to fit
Anrisslinie	guideline
Ansammlung	accumulation/collection
Ansaugstutzen	intake manifold
Ansaugtakt	intake stroke
anschließen	to connect
Anschlussbuchse	connecting socket
Anschlussgerät	*here* peripheral device
Anschlussstelle (z. B. Autobahn)	junction
anschrauben	to screw/to bolt
ansehen	to look at/ to take a look at
ansteigen	to increase/to rise
anstellen (jmd.)	to employ
Anstieg	increase/rise
Anteil	proportion
antreiben	to power
Antriebstrakt	drive train
Antriebswelle	drive shaft
Anweisung	instruction
anwenden	to apply
Anwenderprogramm	application software
Anwendung	application
anzeigen	to indicate
Anzeiger	indicator
anziehen (z. B. Schraube)	to tighten
anziehend	attractive
Anziehungskraft	gravitational pull
Arbeit	labour
Arbeitgeber(in)	employer
Arbeitsblatt	worksheet
Arbeitskarte	job card
Arbeitsplatz am Computer	workstation
Arbeitstakt	power stroke
Armaturenbrett	dashboard
Ärmel	sleeve
Art	kind of/sort of/type
Ast	branch
asymmetrisch	asymmetric
asynchron	asynchronous
Atmosphäre	atmosphere
Atomkern	nucleus

Dictionary German – English

Atomkraftwerk	nuclear power
auf dem Bildschirm	on-screen
auf etwas zu	towards
aufblasen	to inflate
Aufenthalt	stay
aufführen	to perform
auffüllen	to refill
aufgestellt sein	to be set up
Aufhängung (Auto)	suspension
Aufladung (statische ~)	static electricity
auflösen	to dissolve
Auflösung	resolution
Aufmerksamkeit	attention
aufpassen	to pay attention
Aufprallschutz	impact protection
aufsaugen	to absorb
aufschrauben	to unscrew
aufspalten	to split up
auftanken	to refuel
auftreten	to occur/to arise
aufwärts	upwards
Augenklappe	eye pad
aus Holz	wooden
Ausbilder	instructor
Ausbildung	apprenticeship/training
Ausbildung (theoretisch)	theoretical training
ausbröckeln	to flake away
ausdehnen	to expand
Ausdehnungsgeschwindigkeit	rate of expansion
Ausdruck	expression/hardcopy
ausdünnen	to reduce/to thin
ausführen	to carry out
Ausgabe	output
Ausgang	exit
ausgleichen	to equalize
auslösen	to activate/*here:* to blow
Auslöseschalter	trigger
Auspuff	exhaust pipe
Auspuffsystem	exhaust system
ausrichten	to align
Ausrüstung (elektr.)	electrical equipment
Ausrüstung, Ausstattung	equipment
ausschalten	to switch off
Außen~	external ~
Außendurchmesser	external diameter
Außengewinde	male thread
außerdem	besides
außerhalb	outside
außermittig	off-centre
ausspitzen	to thin
Ausspitzen	web thinning
ausstatten	to equip
Ausstattung	fitting/equipment
Ausstoß	emission
ausstoßen	to emit
Ausstoßtakt	exhaust stroke
Austauschpartner(in)	exchange partner
austauschen	to exchange
Austauschprogramm	exchange programme
Austauschschüler(in)	exchange student
Auswahl	selection
auswählen	to choose/to select
auswendig	by heart
Auswirkung	impact
Auszubildende(r)	apprentice/trainee
Auszug	excerpt
Autobahn	motorway
Autobahnkreuz	interchange
Autobahnzubringer	slip road
automatische Bereichswahl	auto range
Badewanne	bath tub
Bakterien	bacteria (pl)
Bandschleifer	belt-sander
Bandschlüssel	strap wrench
basieren auf	to be based on
Basis	base/ basis
bauen	to construct
Bauholz	lumber
Bauplatz	construction site
Bauteil (elektr.)	electronic component/ ~ part
beabsichtigen	to intend
beachten	to observe/to pay attention
Beachtung	attention
Bedarf	requirement/need
bedecken	to cover
Bedienungshandbuch	instruction manual
Bedingung	condition
beeinflussen	to affect
beeinträchtigen	to disturb
beenden	to finish
befähigen	to enable
Befehl	command
Befehlszeile	command line
befestigen	to fasten/to fix/ to mount
befestigt an	fixed to
Befestigungsklammer	mounting bracket
begegnen	to encounter
begeistert	enthusiastic
Begrenzungsleuchten	clearance lamp
Begriff	term
Behälter/ Behältnis	container
behandeln	to deal with/to treat
Behandlung (med.)	medical treatment
beibehalten	to maintain
beifügen	to enclose
beiheften	to attach
beilegen	to enclose
beinahe	almost/nearly
beinhalten	to contain
Beispiel (zum ~)	example/for example/ for instance
beisteuern	to contribute
Bekanntmachung	introduction
beleuchten	to illuminate
beliebt	popular
benennen	to name
Benutzeroberfläche (geografische ~)	graphical user interface
Benzin	petrol
bequem	convenient
Bereich	range
bereitstellen	to provide
Bericht	report
Berufsausbildung	vocational training
Berufsschule	vocational school

berühmt	famous
berühren	to touch
beschädigen	to damage
beschleunigen	to accelerate
Beschleunigung	acceleration
beschreiben	to describe
Beschreibung	description
besonders	especially
Bestandteil	component/constituent
bestehen aus	to consist of
bestimmen	to define/to determine
besuchen	to attend/to visit
beteiligt	to be involved
Beton	concrete
betonen	to emphasize
betrachten	to consider/to regard
beträchtlich	considerably
betreffen (jmd.)	to concern (sb.)
Betriebsspannung	operating level
Betriebssystem	operating system
beweglich	movable (also: moveable)
beweglicher Messschenkel	movable jaw
Bewegung	movement
beweisen	to prove
bewusst werden	to be aware of
bewusstlos	unconscious
Bezeichnungen	nomenclature
Bezug nehmen auf	to refer to
bidirektional	bi-directional
biegen	to bend
Bienenwabe	honey comb
Bildfläche	scene
Bildhauerarbeit	carving/sculpture
Bildschirm	screen
Bildung (techn.)	formation
Bimetallthermometer	bimetallic thermometer
Biomasse	biomass
Blatt	sheet
blenden	to dazzle
Blinklicht	indicator light
bloße Hand	bare hand
Boden	soil
bohren	to drill
Bohrer	drill bit
Bohrmaschine (elektr.)	electric drill
Bolzen	bolt
Bordcomputer	on-board computer
Bordnetz	board system
brauchen	to require
breit	wide
Breite	width
Bremsanlage (hydraulisch)	hydraulic brake system
Bremsbacken	brake shoes
Bremsbelag	brake lining
Bremse	brake
Bremsfading	brake fading
Bremsflüssigkeit	brake fluid
Bremsklotz	brake pad
Bremskraftverstärker	brake servo
Bremsleitung	brake pipe
Bremslicht	brake light
Bremspedal	brake pedal
Bremssattel	brake calliper
Bremsscheibe	brake disc
Bremsschlauch	brake hose
Bremstrommel	brake drum
brennbar	combustible/ (in)flammable
Brennkammer	combustion chamber
Brennstoffzelle	fuel cell
Bruch	breakage/fraction
Buffet (kaltes ~)	set buffet
Bus	bus
Busbreite (comp.)	bus width
Chassis	chassis
chemisch	chemical
computergestützte Herstellung	CAM (computer aided manufacture)
computergestützte Maschinensteuerung	CNC (computer numeric control)
computergestütztes Zeichnen	CAD (computer aided design)
Dampf	steam/ vapour
Dampfblasen	steam bubbles
Dampfkessel	boiler
Dampfschiff	steam ship
darauf achten	to pay attention to
darstellen (etwas)	to represent
darüber hinaus	furthermore
Datei	file
Daten	data
Daten (tech.)	specifications
Datenschutz	data protection
Datenübertragungs-software	communication software
defekt	defective
Defekt	fault
definitiv	definite
Diagnosezentrum	diagnostic centre
diagonal/schräg	diagonal
Dichte	density
Dicke	thickness
Differential	differential
Dimension	dimension
Direktor(in)	principal
dividieren	to divide
Dom	cathedral
Dorf	village
Draht	wire
Drallsteigungswinkel	helix angle
Draufsicht	top view
drehen	to rotate/to spin
drehende Bewegung	rotating movement
Drehmaschine	lathe
Drehmoment	torque
Drehmomentschlüssel	torque wrench
Drehscheibe	turntable
Drehung	revolution
Dreibackenwerkzeug	three-jaw tool
dreidimensional	three-dimensional
Dreieck	triangle
dreieckig	triangular
Dreieckstuch	triangular cloth
dringend	urgently
Druck	pressure
Druckanzeiger	pressure gauge
duales System	dual system
Dunkelheit	darkness
Dunst	mist/haze
Durchbruch	penetration

durchführen (von z. B. Experiment)	to perform
Durchgang	pass
Durchmesser	diameter
Durchschnitt	average
durchschnittlich	average
durchsichtig	transparent
Dürre	drought
Düse	nozzle
Ecke	corner
editieren (Zeichnungselemente ändern)	to edit
effizient	efficient
ehrlich	honest
Eigenschaft	quality
Einblick	insight
einfach	simple
einführen	to introduce
Eingabe	input
Eingangsportal	portal
Eingangswiderstand	input impedance
einhaken	to snatch
Einheit	unit
einige	a couple of/several
einladen	to invite
Einmalhandschuhe	vinyl gloves
einpassen	to seat
einrichten	to establish
Einrichtung	facility
einsammeln	to collect
Einsatzzweck	purpose of use
einschließen	to enclose/to include
einschließlich	including/inclusive
einsetzen	to insert
einspannen (Werkstück)	to clamp
Einspritzsystem	injection system
einstecken (wieder ~)	to reinsert
einstellbar	adjustable
einstellen	to adjust/to engage
Einstellschraube	adjusting screw
Einstellung	adjustment/ setting
einteilen	to classify
einwickeln	to wrap
Einwohner	inhabitant
Eisberg	iceberg
Eisen	iron
elektrischer Strom	electric current
Elektroblech	magnetic sheet steel
Elektrohobel	electric plane
Elektrokabel	power cord
Elektrolyse	electrolysis
Elektrolyt	electrolyte
Elektrolytkondensator	electrolytic capacitor
elektronisches System	electronic system
elektrostatisch	electrostatic
Emission	emission
emitieren	to emit
empfangen	to receive
empfehlen	to recommend
enden	to expire
endlich	finally/at last
Energiequelle	energy source
Energieverluste	energy losses
Energieversorgung	power supply
energisch	vigorously
eng, schmal	narrow/tight
entfernen	to remove
Entfernung	distance
entflammbar	inflammable/combustible
enthalten	to contain/to enclose/ to include
entkommen	to escape
entladen	to discharge/to unload
entladen	flat/discharged
entscheiden	to decide
Entscheidung	decision
entsprechend	according to/ corresponding/suitably
entwerfen	to design
entwickeln	to develop
Entwicklung	development
Entwicklungsland	developing country
entzündbar	inflammable
entzünden	to ignite
entzündet	flamed/ignited
Enzyklopädie	encyclopaedia
Epoche	era
Erdbeben	earthquake
Erde (Erdreich)	soil
erden	to earth
Erdgas	natural gas
Erdwärme (Energie aus ~)	geothermal energy
erfahren sein	to be experienced
erfinden	to invent
Erfindung	invention
erfolgreich	successful
erforderlich	necessary
erfordern	to require
erfüllen	to fulfil
Ergebnis	result
erhalten	to obtain
erhöhen	to increase/to raise
erholen (sich ~)	recover
erinnern	to remind
erinnern (jdn ~ an)	to remind sb of
erkennen	to realize
erklären	to explain
Erklärung	explanation
erlauben	to allow
ermöglichen	to enable
Ernährung	feeding/nutrition
erneuerbar	renewable
erneuern	to modify
Erneuerung	renewal
ernst/ernsthaft	serious
Erntereste	left over crops
erreichen	to achieve
errichten	to mount
erschaffen	to create
erschwinglich	affordable
ersetzen	to replace
Erste Hilfe Behälter	first aid container
Erste Hilfe Broschüre	first aid guide
Erste Hilfe Kurs	first aid course
erstellen	to create
ertrinken	to drown
erwähnen	to mention
erwarten	to expect
erweitern	to broaden

Dictionary German – English

erzeugen	to generate
Elektrizität erzeugen	generating electricity
Ethangas	ethane
exakt	exactly
extrahieren	to extract
Fabrikanlage	(manufacturing) plant
fachmännisch	professional
Fähigkeit	ability/ skill
Fahrgastzelle	passenger cell
Fahrgemeinschaft	car pool
Fahrzeug	vehicle
Fall	case
fallen	to drop
Farbe	colour paint
Fassade	façade
fast	almost/nearly
Feder	spring
Federabdeckung	spring guard
Federung	suspension
Federwaage	spring balance
Fehler	error/fault
Feile	file
feindlich	hostile
Felge	rim
Fernlicht	main beam
fertigen	to manufacture
fest	firmly/fixed/solid/tight
festklemmen	to wedge
festsitzen	to be trapped
Feststellschraube	clamp screw
festziehen	to tighten
Feuchtigkeit	humidity
Feuerlöscher	fire extinguisher
finanzieren	to finance
Fingerkuppenverband	fingertip bandage
flache Spitze	flat point
Flansch	flange
Flasche	bottle
fließen	to flow
fluchten	to aligne
Flügel (Ventilator~)	wing/blade
Flügelblatt	rotor blade
Fluglotsen	flight controllers
Flugzeug	aircraft/plane
flüssig, Flüssigkeit	liquid
Flüssigkeitsthermometer	liquid thermometer
Folge	consequence/effect
folgerichtig	consequently
Form	shape
Form geben	to shape
Format	format
fortsetzen	to continue
Fortsetzung	continuation
fossiler Brennstoff	fossil fuel
frei	vacant
Freifläche	clearance surface
freisetzen	to release
Freizeit	spare time
Fremdsprache	foreign language
Frequenzzähler	frequency counter
freundlich	kind
frühere(r)	former
Fühlerlehre	feeler gauge
führen zu	to result in
Führer	leader
Führungsanschlag	ripsaw guide
Führungsfase	land
Funke (elektr.)	electrical spark
Funktionen, Hilfsprogramme	tool kit
funktionieren	to function/to operate
Funktionstaste	function key
Funktionsweise	operation
Fuß (30,38 cm)	foot
Fußgänger	pedestrian
Futterschlüssel	chuck key
Gabelstabler	forklift truck
Gang	gear
ganz	entire/whole
Gartenhäuschen	garden shed
Gase aus Müll	landfill gas
gasförmig	gaseous
Gasgenerator	gas generator
Gaspedal	accelerator pedal
Gast	guest
Gastgeber	host
Gebiet	area/region
Gebläse	blower fan
geblendet sein	to be dazzled
gebräuchlich	common/usual
geeignet	proper/suitable
Gefahr	danger/hazard
gefährden	to endanger
Gefahrenzone	hazardous area
gefaltet	folded
Gefrierpunkt	freezing point
Gefrierschrank	freezer
gegen	against/versus
Gegenlauffräsen	up-cut milling
Gegenstand	item
gegenüberstehen	to face
Gegenverkehr	oncoming traffic
gegenwärtig	present
Gehäuse	casing
Gehirn	brain
gelegen sein (Ort)	to be situated
Gelegenheit	occasion
Gelenkbus	city bus
gemäß	in accordance with
gemeinsam	in common
Gemischaufbereitung	mixture formation
genau	exactly/accurate
genau genommen	strictly speaking
Genauigkeit	accuracy/precision
Generator	alternator
genießen	enjoy
genug	enough
Geodreieck	geometric triangle
geometrisch bestimmt	geometrically defined
Gepäck	luggage
gerade	straight
geradeaus	straight on
Gerät	appliance/gadget
Geräusche (laute ~)	noises (loud ~)
geruchlos	odourless
Gerüst	scaffolding
geschehen	to occur/to happen
Geschichte	history
Geschick	skill/expertise
Geschwindigkeit	speed

German	English
Gesellschaft	society
Gesetz	law
gesetzlich vorgeschrieben	mandatory
gestalten	to design
gesteuert (elektr.)	electronic controlled
geteilt (math.)	over
Getreide	grain
getrennt	separate
Getriebe	gear/transmission
Getriebegehäuse	transmission box/ gear box
gewährleisten	to ensure/to garantee
Gewicht	weight
Gewinde	thread
gewinnen	to extract
gewiss	certain
Gewohnheit	habit
gewöhnlich	usual/common/ordinary
gewohnte(r)	familiar
gewünscht	desired
gießen	to water
Gift	poison
giftig	poisonous/toxic
giftige Flüssigkeit	toxic liquid
Glanz	glory
glatt	smooth
gleich	equal
Gleichlauffräsen	synchronous milling
Gleichung (math.)	equation
gleichzeitig	simultaneously
gleiten	to glide
Gliedermaßstab	folding rule
global	global/worldwide
Grad	degree
Gradeinteilung	scale/calibration
Grafschaft	county
Graphikkarte	graphic card
graphische Benutzer-oberfläche	graphical user interface
graphisches Symbol	icon
Grat	burr
Grenze	border
Grenzlinie	boundary
Gripzange	vice-grip pliers
groß	large
Größe	size
großzügig	generous
Grund	cause
gründen	to found
Grundlage	basis
Grundwasser	ground water
Gummi	rubber
Gummihammer	rubber mallet
Güter	goods
Haken	hook
Halbkreis	semicircle
halbkreisförmig	semicircular
Halbleitermaterial	semi-conducting material
Halfter	holster/halter
Halogenlampe	halogen lamp
Handbremse	handbrake
Handbuch	manual
handeln von	to deal with
Handelszentrum	trading centre
Handgriff	handle
handhaben	to handle
Handrad	hand wheel
Härte (Metall)	temper
Hartmetallplättchen	hard metal tip
häufig	frequently/often
Haupt~	major
Hauptplatine	motherboard
hauptsächlich	mainly
Hauptsitz	head office
Hauptteile	main parts
Haushalt	household
Hauswirtschaft	home economics
Hebebühne	car lift
Hebel	lever
heben	to raise/to lift
Heckantrieb	rear-wheel drive
heftig	violent/intense
Heftpflaster	adhesive tape
Heizung	heater
Heizkörper	radiator
helles Licht	bright light
Helm	helmet
herausziehen	to extract
herkömmlich	conventional
herstellen	to manufacture/ to produce
Hersteller	manufacturer/producer
Herzkammerflimmern	ventricular fibrillation
heutige(r/s)	modern-day/nowadays
Hilferuf	SOS (save our souls)
Hilfseinrichtungen	assisting equipment
Hilfsprogramme	tool kit/ relief programme
Hin- und Herbewegung	reciprocal movement
Hindernis	obstacle
Hintergrund	background
hinterherhinken	to lag behind
hinzufügen	to add
Hitzefestigkeit	heat resistance
Hobel	plane
Hochspannungsleitung	transmission line
Hochspannungsmast	high-voltage pole/ transmission pole
hochtransformieren	to boost up
Hochwassermarke	high water mark
Höhe	height
hölzern	wooden
Hupe	horn
hydraulische Bremsanlage	hydraulic brake system
identifizieren	to identify
Impuls	momentary contact
in Bezug auf	with respect to
in der Lage sein	to be able to
in Reihe schalten	to connect in series
Inbetriebnahme	start-up/opening
individuell	individual
Induktion	induction
Industrienation	industrial nation
Ingenieur(in)	engineer
Innenbeleuchtung	interior light
Innendurchmesser	internal diameter
Innengewinde	female thread
Innensechskantschlüssel	Allen key
innere(n)	internal
innerhalb	inside

Dictionary German – English

installieren	to install
integrierter Schaltkreis	integrated circuit
interessiert sein an	be interested in
involvieren	to involve
inzwischen	meanwhile
Irrtum	error
isolieren (elektr.)	to insulate
isoliert	insulated
Jahrhundert	century
jährlich	annual
Jahrzehnt	decade
jedoch	however
Jodbausch	povidon-iodine pad
Kabel	cable/cord
kabellos	cordless
Käfig	cage
Käfigläufermotor	squirrel cage motor
Kalkstein	limestone
Kante	edge
Kantine	canteen
Kapazität	capacitance
Kapillargefäß	capillary tube
Kardanwelle	propeller shaft
Katalysator (chem.)	catalyst
Katalysator (techn.)	catalytic converter
Kathedrale	cathedral
Kegel	cone
kegelförmig	conical
keilförmig	wedge shaped
Keilriemen	fan belt
keimfrei	sterile/sterilized
Kennzeichen	feature
kennzeichnen	to mark
Kern	core
Kernspaltung	nuclear fission
Kette	chain
Kettenrad	sprocket
Kettenreaktion	chain reaction
Kipper (Baustellenfahrzeug)	dump truck
Kipphebel	rocker arm
Kipphebelwelle	rocker shaft
Klammer	bracket
klassifizieren	to classify
Klassifizierung	classification
Kleintransporter	van
Klemme	clamp
Klempner	plumber
Klima	climate
klimatisiert	air-conditioned
Knappheit	shortage
Knarre	ratchet
Knäuel aus Baumwolle	cotton wool wad
Kneifzange	pincers (a pair of)
Knopf zum Halten des Schalters	trigger latch
kochen	to boil
Kofferraum	boot
Kohlendioxyd	carbon dioxide
Kohlenmonoxid	carbon monoxide
Kohlenstoff	carbon
Kohlenwasserstoff	hydrocarbon
Kolben	piston
Kollege	colleague
Kombi	estate car
kombinieren	to combine
Kombizange	combination pliers
Komfortsystem	comfort system
Kompetenz	competence
komplex	complex
kompliziert	complicated
Komponente	component
Kompression	compression
Kompressor	compressor
Kondensator	condenser (techn.)/ capacitor (elektr.)
Kondensatormotor	capacitor motor
kondensieren	condense
konkav	concave
Konsequenz	consequence
Konstantstromquelle	constant-current source
konstruieren	to design
Konstruktion	design
Kontur	contour
konvex	convex
koordinieren	to coordinate
Kopfhörer	headphone
korrekt	correct
Kotflügel	wing
Kraft	force/strength/power
Kraftfahrzeug	motor vehicle
Kraftfluss	power flow
Kraftstoffsystem	fuel system
Kraftwerk	power plant
Krankentrage	stretcher
Krebs	cancer
Kreis	circle
kreisförmig	circular
Kreislauf	circulation/cycle
Kreissäge	circular saw
Kreisverkehr	roundabout
Kreuzschlitzschraubendreher	Phillips screwdriver
Kribbeln	prickle/itching
Kugel	sphere
kugelförmig	spherical
Kühlbeutel	cold pack
Kühlsystem	cooling system
Kühlturm	cooling tower
Kupfer	copper
Kupplung	clutch
Kurbelgehäuse	crank case
Kurbeltrieb	crank mechanism
Kurbelwelle	crankshaft
kurz (zeitlich)	brief
kurzschließen	to short circuit
Kurzschluss	short circuit
Kurzschlussring	rotor end ring
Kurzstrecke	short distance
Kutsche	carriage
kWh-Zähler	energy meter
Labor	laboratory
lachen	to laugh
Lackfarben	paint lacquer
Lage	location/situation
Lage (Schicht)	layer
Lager	bearings
Lagerhalle/Lagerhaus	warehouse
Landkarte	map

landwirtschafliches Fahrzeug	agricultural vehicle
Landwirtschaft	agriculture
Länge	length
längs	alongside/lengthwise
Längsschnitt	ripping
langweilig	boring
Last	load
Lastkraftwagen (LKW)	lorry
Lastkraftwagen (Schwer~)	heavy-duty truck
Läuferblechpaket	rotor lamination pack
Laufwerk	drive (noun)
Laufwerksschacht	drive slot
laute Geräusche	loud noises
lebendig	lively
lebensrettende Ausrüstung	lifesaving equipment
Leck	leak
Lehre	apprenticeship/gauge
leicht	easy/lightly
Leichtigkeit	facility
leiden an	to suffer from
leiten	to conduct
Leiter (elektr.)	conductor
Leiterbahn	conductor line
Leiterplatte	circuit board
Leitspindel	lead shaft
Leitung (elek.)	cable/wire/lead
Leitung (spannungsführende ~)	live wire
Lenkrad	steering wheel
Lenksäule	steering column
Lenkung	steering
lernen	to learn/to study
Lexikon	encyclopaedia
Lichtanlage	light system
Lichtkegel	cone of light
liefern	to deliver/to provide
Lieferwagen	delivery truck
Limousine	saloon
Linearmotor	linear motor
Loch	hole
löschen	to extinguish
lösen (z.B. Problem)	to solve
lösen (z.B. Schraube)	to loosen
loswerden	to get rid of
löten	to solder
Lötkolben	soldering iron
Luftblase	bubble
Lüfter	fan
Luftfahrt	aerospace
Luftfeuchtigkeit (relative ~)	relative air humidity (R.H.)
Luftfilter	air filter
Luft-Kraftstoff-Gemisch	air-fuel mixture
Luftschiff	airship
Luftverschmutzung	air pollution
mächtig	powerful
Magnetfeld	magnetic field
mahlen	to grind
mal (math.)	times
mal nehmen	to multiply
Mangel	lack
Manöver	manoeuvre
markieren	to mark
Markierung	mark

Maschinenbau	engineering/mechanical engineering
Maschinengestell	engine frame
Maß	measure
Masse	ground (elektr.)/mass
Maßeinheit	unit of measurement/ measure
Massenproduktion	mass production
Maßnahme	measure
Maulschlüssel	open-ended spanner
medizinische Behandlung	medical treatment
Mehl	flour
Mehrheit	majority
Mehrzweckfahrzeug	multi-purpose vehicle
Meißel	chisel
Menge	amount
Menschheit	mankind
Menüleiste	menu bar
Merkmal	feature/characteristic
Messbereich	range
Messbereichswähler	range selector
messen	to measure
Messleitung	measuring line
Messschenkel (beweglich)	movable jaw
Messschenkel fest	fixed jaw
Messschenkel für Außenmessung	outside jaw
Messschenkel für Innenmessung	inside jaw
Messschieber	vernier calliper (BE)
Messschraube	micrometer
Messspitze	probe tip
Messstromkreis	measuring circuit
Messtechnik	measurement technology
Messung	measurement
Metallarbeiten	metal work
Metallrahmen	metal frame
metrisch	metric
Mikrofon	microphone
minimieren	to minimize
Minuspol	negative pole
Mischung	mixture
mit Hilfe von	by means of
mitschleppen	to drag along
Mittel	means
Mittellinie	centre line
modern	modern
Möglichkeit	possibility
Molekül	molecule
Montagerahmen	chassis
montieren	to fit/to mount
montiert	mounted
Motor	car engine/engine
Motorblock	engine block
Motorhaube	bonnet
müde	tired
Mulltupfer	sterile gauze swab
Mullverband	gauze bandage
multiplizieren	to multiply
Mündung (Fluss~)	estuary
Muskelkrampf	muscle cramp
Muster	sample/prototype
Mutter (Schrauben~)	nut
nach unten	downward
nachfüllen	to refill

Dictionary German – English

Nachfrage	demand
nachlässig	careless
Nachname	surname
Nachrichten	news
Nachteil	disadvantage
Nagel	nail
Nahrung	food/nutrition
Natriumazid	sodium azide
Naturgesetz	law of nature
Nebel	fog/mist
Nebellicht	fog light
neigen	to tend
Neigung	tendency
Neigungswinkel	inclination
nicht eingesetzt	indeployed
nicht komprimierbar	incompressible
nicht-leitender Raum	non-conducting location
niedrig	low
noch	still
Nockenwelle	camshaft
Nonius	vernier
nördlich von	north of
Notausgang	emergency exit
Notausschalter	emergency switch
notwendig	necessary
Nummernschild	number plate
Nuss (Steck~)	nut (socket)
Nut	groove
Nut für den Führungsanschlag	rip guide slot
nutzen	to utilize
Nutzfahrzeug	commercial vehicle
oberer Totpunkt	top dead centre
Oberfläche	surface
oberhalb	above
Oberkörper	upper body
obwohl	although
offen (freigelegt)	exposed
öffentliche Verkehrsmittel	public transportation
Ohrenstöpsel	ear plugs
Öldruck	oil pressure
Ölwanne	oil sump
Opfer	victim
ordnen	to arrange
organisch	organic
Ort	place
oxidieren	to oxidize
Ozonschicht	ozone layer
Pappe	cardboard
parallel schalten	to connect in parallel
Parklicht	parking light
Partnerschaft haben mit	to be twinned with
Partnerstadt	twin town
Pedal	pedal
per	pro
Peripheriegerät	peripheral device
Personenwagen	passenger cars
Pfad	path
Pfeil	arrow
Pflanze	plant
Phasen	phases
Pinzette	tweezers
Plastiktasche (wieder verschließbare ~)	resealable plastic bag
Platin	platinum
Pleuelstange	connecting rod
Pluspol	positive pole
porös	porous
Porzellan	porcelain
Positionsanzeige	position display
Potentialausgleich erdfrei	earth-free bonding
Potentialdifferenz	potential difference
Praktikum	hands-on training
praktisch	practical
präzise	precise
Präzisionswiderstand	precision resistor
Preis (Gewinnprämie)	prize
Produktionsleistung	output
Proton	proton
Prototyp	prototype
Prozent	per cent
Punktmatrix-Anzeige	dot-matrix display
Quader	rectangular solid
Quadrat/quadratisch	square
qualifiziert	qualified
Quarzglas	quartz glass
Quecksilber	mercury
Quelle	source
quer	crosswise
Quer-	transverse/diagonally
Querschneide	chisel edge/dead centre
Querschnitt	cross section
Rad	wheel
Radbremszylinder	wheel cylinder
Radkreuz	rim wrench
Rand	edge/margin/periphery
Rang	status
rasch	quick/rapid
Rasen	lawn
Rat	advice
Reaktion	reaction
Rechenwerk	arithmetic logic unit
Rechnung	bill
Rechteck	rectangle
rechteckig	rectangular
Redakteur	editor
reduzieren	to reduce
Reflektor	reflector
Regal	shelf
Regel	rule
regelmäßig	regular
Regelstab	control rod
Region	region
Register	register
registrieren	to register
Regler	regulator
Reibung	friction
Reifen	tyre
reinigen	to purify
Reise	trip
Reitstock	tailstock
Relais	relay
relative Luftfeuchtigkeit	relative air humidity (R.H.)
reparieren	to mend/to repair
retten	to rescue
Rettungsdecke	space blanket
Richtlinien	guidelines
Richtung	direction
riesig	giant

Rille	slot
Ringschlüssel	ring spanner
Risiko	risk
robust	robust
Rohr	pipe
Rost	rust
Rotation	rotation
Rotationsachse	rotation axis
rotbraun	reddish-brown
Rotornabe	rotor hub
Rückfahrscheinwerfer	reverse lamp
Rückhaltesystem	restraint system
Rückwärtsgang	reverse gear
rund	true circle/round
Rundfunktechniker	radio engineer
rutschen	to slip/to slide
Säge	saw
sägen	to saw
Salpetersäure	nitric acid
sammeln	to collect
Sammlung	collection
Sandstein	sandstone
Sattelzug	articulated lorry and trailer (BE)/ semi trailer (AE)
Sauerstoff	oxygen
Säule	column
Säure	acid
saurer Regen	acid rain
Schaden	damage
schaden	to harm
Schadstoff	pollutant
Schadstoffbelastung	pollution
schädlich	harmful
Schaft	shank
Schall	sound
Schallgeschwindigkeit	speed of sound
schalten (ein/aus)	to switch (on/off)
Schalter	switch
Schalterstellung	switch statuse
Schalthebel	gear lever
Schaltkreise	circuitry
Schaltplan	circuit diagram/ schematic diagram
Schaltung	circuitry
Schärfe	sharpness
schärfen	to sharpen
Scheibenheizung	window defroster
Scheibenwischer	windscreen wiper
Scheinwerfer	headlight
Schere	scissors
Schicht	layer
Schichtholz	plywood
schieben	to push/to slide
Schieber	slider
Schild	sign/notice
Schlag (elektrisch)	electric shock
Schleifbock	bench grinder
schleifen	to grind/to sharpen
Schleifer (Sandpapier)	sander
Schleifmaschine	grinder
Schleifringläufermotor	slip ring motor
schließlich	finally
schlimm	serious/dreadful/severe
Schlitten	carriage

Schlitz	slot
Schlucht	gorge
Schlupf	slip
Schlussfolgerung	conclusion
schmelzen	to melt
Schmiersystem	lubrication system
Schnabelzange	long-nose pliers
Schneidkante	cutting lip
schnell	fast/rapid/prompt
Schnitt quer zur Faser	crosscutting
Schnittbewegung	cutting motion
Schnittgeschwindigkeit	cutting speed
Schnittkraft	cutting force
Schnitzarbeit	carving
Schranke	barrier
Schraube	screw/bolt
Schraubendreher	screw driver
Schraubenschlüssel	wrench/spanner
Schraubstock	vice
Schritt	pace/step
Schrittmotor	stepping motor
Schrott	scrap
Schrottplatz	scrap yard
Schülerzeitung	school magazine
Schürze	apron
Schutz	defence/protection
Schutzausrüstung	protective equipment
Schutzbrille	protective goggles/ safety glasses
Schutzeinrichtung	safety guard
schützen	to protect
Schutzhaube	safety cover
Schutzleiter	protective conductor
Schutzschild	safety shield
Schutztrennung	electrical separation
schwächen	to weaken
Schwefel	sulphur
Schwefelsäure	sulphuric acid
Schweißgerät	welding machine
schwenken	to pivot
Schwerkraft	gravitation/gravity
schwierig	difficult
sechseckig	hexagonal
Seil	rope
Seitenlage (stabile ~)	recovery position
Seitenschneider	side cutter
Seitenspiegel	wing mirror
senken	to decrease
Sensor	sensor
sich auswirken	to affect
sich ergeben (Situation)	to arise
sich erholen	to recover
sich erinnern	to recall/to remember
sich etwas leisten	to afford
sich etwas vorstellen	to imagine
sich stützen auf	to be based on
sicher	secure
sicher (~ sein)	sure (to be ~)
sicher stellen	to ensure
Sicherheit	safety
Sicherheitsschild	safety sign
Sicherheitsmaßnahme	precaution
Sicherheitsnadeln	safety pins
Sicherheitsschuhe	safety shoes

Sicherheitssystem	safety system/ security system
Sicherheitszone	safety zone
sicherlich	surely
sichern	to protect/to secure
sicherstellen	to make sure
Sicherung	fuse
Sicherung überbrücken	to bridge a fuse
Sicherungsring	ring pin
sichtbar	visible
sichtbar (gut ~)	highly visible
Siedepunkt	boiling point
Silizium	silicon
Sinn	sense
Skala	scale
sofort	immediately/at once
Sonde	probe
Sonnenkollektor	solar panel
sorgfältig	thoroughly
Sorte	kind/variety
sortieren	to sort
soviel … wie	equivalent to
sowohl … als auch	both … and/ … as well as …
Spalte	column/crack
spalten	to split
Spaltpolmotor	shaded-pole motor
Span	chip
Späneauswurf	saw dust ejection
Spänewanne	swarf tray
spannen (ein-, Werkstück)	to clamp
Spannung	voltage
spannungsführende Leitung	live wire
Spannungsprüfer	voltage tester
Spannut	chip flute
Spannutbreite	flute width
Spanplatte	chipboard
sparen	to save
Speicher	memory/store/register
Speicher mit wahlfreiem Zugriff	random access memory
speichern	to store
Speicherplatz	storage space
Spender	donator
Sperre	barrier/barricade
Spiegeln	mirroring
Spiel (tech.)	slackness/clearance
Spindelstock	head stock
Spiralbohrer	twist drill
spiralförmig	spiral/volute
spitz	pointed
Spitzenwinkel	drill-point angle
spitzwinklig	acute
Splitter	splinter
Sportwagen	sports car
spröde	brittle
spülen	to flush
Staatsmann	statesman
Stab	rod/bar
stabil	stable
stabile Seitenlage	recovery position
Stadtrundfahrt	sight seeing trip
Stahl	steel

Stahl mit großer Streckgrenze	high tensile steel
Ständerblechpaket	stator lamination pack
Ständerwicklung	stator winding
ständig	permanently
Standort	location/position
Stange	rod/bar/pole
Stärke	strength/thickness/power
Start	start-up
Starter (Anlasser)	starter motor
Starthilfe	jump-start
Starthilfekabel	jump lead
statische Aufladung	static electricity
stattfinden	to take place
Stau	traffic jam
Staub	dust
Staubmaske	dust mask
Stechen	prickle/stitch
Steckdose	socket/wall socket
Stecker	plug
Stecker entfernen/ Stecker herausziehen	to unplug
Steckplatz für Steckkarte	expansion slot
Steckschlüssel	socket wrench
Steckschlüsseleinsatz	socket/bit
Steckschlüsselsatz	socket set
Steckverbindung	connector
stehen bleiben (z. B. Motor)	to stall
stehend	stationary
steigen	to rise
steil	steep
Steinmetz	stone-mason
Stellung	status
steril	sterile
Steuer	tax
Steuerbaustein	controller
Steuerbus	control bus
Steuereinheit	control unit
Steuergerät (elektr.)	electronic control unit (ECU)
steuern	to control
Steuerstromkreis	control circuit
Steuerung	timing
Stichsäge	keyhole saw
Stickoxid	nitrogen oxide
Stillstand (zum ~ bringen)	to stall
Stirnfläche	face
Stirnfräsen	face milling
Stoff (chem.)	substance
stören	to disturb
Stoßfänger	bumper
Strahl (z. B. Licht~)	beam (e.g. beam of light)
strapazierfähig	heavy-duty
Straße	road
Streckgrenze (Stahl mit großer ~)	high tensile steel
Strom	current
Stromkreis (elektr.)	circuit
Stromkreis unterbrechen	to break the circuit
Stromnetz	mains/power supply system

Stromquelle	power source
Stromzange	clamp ammeter
studieren	to study
Stufe	stage
stufenlos	infinitely/variable
Substanz	substance
suchen	to search/to look for
Symbol (graphisch)	icon
Synchronmotor	synchronous motor
Tabakverarbeitung	tobacco processing
Tabelle	table/chart
Tachometer	speedometer
Tagesablauf	daily routine
Tagesordnung	agenda
Takt	stroke
Tal	valley
Tankuhr	fuel gauge
Taschenlampe	flashlight
tatsächlich	actual/real
Technik	technology
technische Daten	specifications
technische Zeichnerin	technical draftswoman
Technologie	technology
Teil	part
Teilabschnitt	section
teilen	to divide
Teilnehmer	participant
Teilzeitklasse	day release class
Telefonleitung	telephone line
Textverarbeitung	word processing
Thema	topic
theoretische Ausbildung	theoretical training
Tidenhub	tidal range
Tiefe	depth
Tiefenmessgerät	depth bar
Tierwelt	wildlife
Tischlerwerkstatt	joiner's shop
Töpferwaren	pottery
tragbar	portable
Trägheit	inertia
Traktor	tractor (agricultural vehicle)
Transformator	transformer
Transistorverstärkung	transistor gain
treffen (auf od. gegen)	to strike
Treiber	driver
Treibhauseffekt	greenhouse effect
Treibstoff	fuel
trennen	to disconnect
trimmen	to trim
tropfen	to drip
Typ	type
Überblick	overview
überfüllt	crowded
Überlandleitung	over head line
Überlastschutz	overload protection
überprüfen	to check/to verify/ to inspect
überrascht	surprised
überreden	to persuade
Überschall	supersonic
überschreiten	to exceed
überschwemmen	to swamp
Übersetzung	transmision/gear/ratio/ translation
überspannen	to span
Überspannung	overvoltage
übertragen	to transfer/to transmit
Übertragung	transfer/transmission
überzeugen	to convince
üblich	usual
übliches Verfahren	practice
übrig bleiben	to remain/to be left
Uhr	clock
Uhrzeigersinn, im ~	clockwise
um … zu	in order to
Umdrehung	rotation/revolution
Umfang	circumference
umfangreich	extensive
Umfangsgeschwindigkeit	peripheral speed
umfassend	comprehensive
umformen	to convert/to transform
Umgebung	environment
umgehen mit	to handle with/to treat
umkehren	to invert/to reverse
Umriss	contour/outline
Umschlag	envelope
Umspannwerk	substation
umwandeln	to convert
Umwelt	environment
umweltschonendes Produkt	green product
Umweltschutz	environmental protection
Umweltschützer	environmentalist
Umweltsünder	polluter
Umwelttechniker(in)	environmental technician
Umweltverschmutzung	pollution
Unabhängigkeit	independence
unangenehm	unpleasant
Unfall	accident
Unfallforschung	accident research
Unfallopfer	casualty
Unfallsensor	crash sensor
ungefähr	approximately/roughly
ungenau	inaccurate
ungewöhnlich	unusual
ungleich	unequal/different
unmittelbar	immediately/direct
unten	at the bottom
unter	among
unterbrochen	discontinuous
unterer Totpunkt	bottom dead centre
Unterkunft	accommodation
Unterrichtsfach	subject
unterscheiden	to distinguish
Unterscheidung	distinction
Unterschied	difference
unterschiedlich	different
Unterseite	undersurface
unterstützen	to assist/to support
Unterstützung	support
unterteilen	to subdivide
unvermeidlich	inevitable
Uran	uranium
Ursache	reason/cause
Ventil	valve
Ventilator	cooling fan
Ventildeckel	rocker cover
Ventilfeder	valve spring
Ventilspiel	valve gap

Dictionary German – English

Ventilsteuerung	timing control
Verabredung	appointment
verändern	to vary
verantwortlich (für)	responsible (for)
verbessern	to enhance/to improve
verbinden	to combine/to connect/ to join/to link
Verbindung	compound
Verbindung (elektr.)	electrical connection
Verbindung für die Stromversorgung	power supply cable
Verbot	prohibition
Verbrauch	consumption
verbrauchen	to consume
Verbraucher	consumer
Verbraucher (elektr.)	electrical consumers
Verbrennung	combustion
Verbrennungen	burns
Verbrennungsanlage	incineration plant
Verbrennungsmotor	internal combustion engine
Verbrennungsraum	combustion camber
verbringen	to spend
verdichten	to compress
Verdichtung	compression
Verdichtungstakt	compression stroke
Verfahren	process
Verfalldatum	expiry date
verfrachten	to ship
verfügbar	available
Vergaser	carburettor
vergeuden	to waste
vergiften	to poison
Vergleich	comparison
vergleichen	to compare
Vergnügen	pleasure
vergrößern	increase/to magnify
Verhalten	behaviour
Verhältnis	ratio/relationship
verhandeln	to negotiate
verhindern	to prevent
Verkehr	traffic
Verkehrsampel	traffic-lights
Verkehrsmittel	means of transportation
Verlängerungskabel	extension cord
verlässlich	reliable
Verletzung	harm/injury
verloren gehen	to come lost
vermeiden	to avoid
vermuten	to guess/to suppose
vernachlässigen	to neglect
vernetzen	to network
vernünftig	reasonable
veröffentlichen	to publish
Verpackung	packaging
Verpflichtung	obligation
verringern	to decrease/to reduce
versagen	to break down
verschieben	to displace
verschieden	different/various
Verschleiß	wear and tear
verschwenden	to waste
verschwinden	to fade away
Versorgung	supply
verstauen	to stow
Versuch	attempt
Verteilung	distribution
vertraut sein mit	to be familiar with
vertraut werden	familiarised
verursachen	to cause
Verwalter(in)	administrator/manager
Verwandte(r)	relative/s
verweigern	to refuse
Verzeichnis	register
Vielfachmessgerät	multimeter
Vielfalt	variety
Viertaktmotor	four-stroke engine
Vogelperspektieve	bird's eye view
Vollholz	solid wood
vollständig	complete/entire
Volumen	volume
vor etwas stehen	to face
voraus	ahead
vorbeikommen	to drop in
vorbereiten	to prepare
Vorbereitung	preparation
vordere(r)	front
Vorfall	incident/occurrence
Vorgang	process
Vorgehensweise	procedure
vorherig/ vorausgegangen	previous
vorhersagen	to predict
vorkommen	to be found/to happen/ to occur
Vorname	first name
Vorort	suburb
Vorrang	priority
Vorrat	stock
Vorrichtung	device/gadget
Vorrichtung/Gerät	device
vorschlagen	to suggest
Vorschriften	regulations
Vorschub	feed
Vorschubgetriebehebel	feed gear levers
Vorschubrichtung	feed direction
Vorsicht	caution
Vorsichtsmaßnahmen	precautions
vorstellen	to introduce
Vorstellung	introduction
Vorteil	advantage
vorzugsweise	preferable
Waage	balance
Wagen	carriage/car/coach
Wagenheber	jack
wählen	to choose
wählen (Telefonnummer)	to dial
während	during/whereas
wahrscheinlich	probably
Wahrscheinlichkeit	probability
Wahrzeichen	landmark
Wandler	converter
Waren	goods
Wärmekraftwerk	thermal power station
Warnblinkanlage	hazard warning light
Warnung	warning
wartungsfrei	maintenance-free
Wasseraufbereitungs-anlage	water treatment plant
Wasserenergie	hydro energy
Wasserhahn	tap

Dictionary German – English

Wasserkraftwerk	hydro electric plant
Wasserstandslinie	water level
Wasserstoff	hydrogen
wasserziehend	hygroscopic
weder ... noch	neither ... nor
Weg	pathway/track
wegzeigen von	facing away
Weite	width
weiter	further
weiterleiten	to pass on/to route
Welle	shaft
weltweit	global/worldwide
wenigstens	at least
Werkbank	bench/workbench
Werkstatt	workshop
Werkstatt Handbuch	garage manual
Werkstattbesitzer	garage owner
Werkstattleiter	workshop manager
Werkzeug	tool
Werkzeug (angetrieben)	power tool
Werkzeugauflage	tool rest
Werkzeughalter	tool post
Werkzeugmacher	toolmaker
Werkzeugmaschine	machine tool
Werkzeugschlitten	cross slide
Werkzeugwagen	tool trolley
Wert	value
wertvoll	precious
wesentlich	essential
Wettbewerb	competition/contest
Wettervorhersage	weather forecast
wichtig	important
Wichtigkeit	importance
Widerstand (phys.)	resistance
Widerstand (Bauteil)	resistor
widerstehen	to withstand
wieder aufladbar	rechargeable
wieder neu laden	to recharge
wiederholt	repeated
wiedervereinigen	to reunite
wiegen	to weigh
willkommen heißen	to welcome
Windrichtungs-nachführung	yaw system
Windschutzscheibe	windscreen
Winkel	angle
Wirbelströme	eddy currents
Wirksamkeit	effect
Wirkungsgrad	efficiency
wirkungsvoll	efficient
wirtschaftlich	economically
Wissen	knowledge
Wissenschaft	science
Wissenschaftler	scientist
Wunde	wound
Wundheftpflaster	adhesive bandage
Würfel	cube
würfelförmig	cubical
zäh	tough
Zähler	meter
zahlreich	numerous
Zahnrad	gear wheel (gear)
Zange	pliers (a pair of)
zeichnen	to draw
Zeichnung	drawing
zeigen (auf)	to point (at)
zeitweilig	temporary
Zelle	cell
Zentraleinheit	central processing unit
zerstören	to destroy
Zerstörung	destruction
Zeuge	witness
zielen	to aim
ziemlich	quite
Zimmermann	carpenter
Zink	zinc
Zuckerherstellung	sugar refining
zuführen	to feed/to supply
Zugang	access
Zugriff	access
Zugspindel	feed shaft
Zulassung	admittance
Zunahme	increase
Zündkerze	spark(ing) plug
Zündkerzenschlüssel	spark plug wrench
Zündschloss	ignition switch
Zündsystem	ignition system
zuordnen	to assign
zurückschnappen	to snap back
zurückweisen	to reject
zurückziehen	to withdraw
zusammenbringen	to match
zusammendrücken	to compress
zusammenpassen	to match
Zusammenschluss	merger
zusammenziehen	to contract
zusätzlich	additional/in addition
Zustand	state of repair
Zustellung	depth setting/infeed
zuweisen	to assign/to allocate
Zweck	purpose
zweidimensional	two-dimensional
Zweifel	doubt
Zweig	branch
Zwischenfall	incident/accident
Zyklus	cycle
Zylinder	cylinder
Zylinderkopf	cylinder head
zylindrisch	cylindrical

Bildquellenverzeichnis

Die Autoren und der Verlag danken folgenden Firmen und Institutionen, die sie bei der Bearbeitung einzelner Themen durch Beratung, Druckschriften und Bilder unterstützt haben:

ABB, Mannheim;
BMW-Group, München;
Bristol City Council, GB;
Chauvin-Amoux, Kehl am Rhein;
Conrad Elektronic, Hirschau;
Daimler Chrysler AG, Stuttgart
Dombauhütte Regensburg;
FP Werbung, F. Flade, München;
Gedore Werkzeug Fabrik, Remscheid;
GLORIA GmbH, Wadersloh
Kettering University Archives, Flint, Michigan;
Metabowerke GmbH, Nürtingen;
Motoren Ventilatoren Landshut GmbH;
Reiner Schmidt, Gillersheim;
Saab Deutschland, Bad Homburg;
Severin GmbH, Sundern;
Siemens AG Photoservice, München;
Transrapid International
W. Söhngen GmbH, Taunusstein